My Life In Music,

and Other Pastimes

(*Dramma giocoso*)

ALMOST THE UNVARNISHED TRUTH

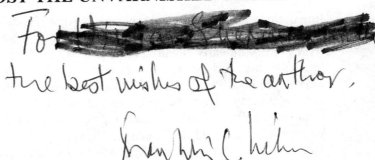

FRANKLIN S. MILLER

i

Published in the U.S.A. by
Lifestyles Press
P.O. Box 493
Greensboro, NC 27402

Illustrations on the collage cover are as follows: the musical examples are, at the top, an excerpt from *Wie schön leuchet der Morgenstern* (BWV 739), an early organ chorale prelude by Johann Sebastian Bach, probably the earliest known example of his handwriting. (Berlin, Staatsbibliothek Preussischer Kulturbesitz, Mus.ms.Bach P488); at the bottom, a portion from the fourth movement of the string quartet no.5 by Béla Bartók, from "Musical Autographs," Vol.II, plate 189, ed. Emanuel Winternitz, published by Princeton University Press, 1955, reissued in 1965 by Dover Publications, Inc., Minneola, New York, original in the Library of Congress. Used with permission. The organ case is that of the 1735 Christian Müller instrument in the Grote Kerk, Haarlem, Holland. The photo of the author and his wife was taken in 1994 at the University of Wisconsin-Eau Claire Viennese ball.

TABLE OF CONTENTS

ERRATA ET ADDENDA

The author deeply regrets the presence of an inordinate number of typographical errors and grammatical infelicities which have infected the text of this narrative. He apologizes for their appearance, and trusts that the reader will be charitable in ascribing them to haste in editing the text. There are a number of additional errors not listed below which the reader will continue to discover as well, and it is the author's plan to issue a revised and corrected edition of the book within a year or two.

TEXT

p. 15, instead of "Omnia Gallia est divisi in partis tres", read "Gallia omnia in partes tres divisa est".

p. 38, instead of "One morning in August", read "The morning of July 20".

p. 42, instead of "Heifitz'", read "Heifetz".

p. 68, instead of "he put me to put to work", read "he put me to work".

p. 79, instead of "Dmitri Mitropolis", read "Dimitri Mitropoulus".

p. 84, instead of "a young Jewish girl", read "a young woman".

p. 87, instead of "*Claiverübung*". read "*Clavierübung*".

p. 91, instead of "Eifel", read "Eiffel".

p. 135, instead of "Cornell University", read "Syracuse University".

p. 148, paragraph 2, line 8, instead of "literautre" read "literature".

p. 161, instead of "(BVW)" read "(BWV)".

p. 171, picture caption, read (1 to r) "Claudia , Gisela (I think), Gudrun, Karin (I think), Martin and Doris."

p. 196, instead of "Uta and Eckahard" read "Ute and Eckehard".

p. 197, instead of "...where Silbermann had built..." read "where Johann Andreas Silbermann, his son, had built...".

p. 198, instead of "Strassburg" read "Strasbourg".

p. 225, line 3, instead of "apoIntment" read "appointment".

p. 233, instead of "Tuesday, August 24,...", read "Tuesday, August 25...".

p. 238, paragraph 2, instead of "One of this best..." read "One of his best...".

p. 244, instead of "Ludwig Herrmann, was by now teaching in a German 'Gymnasium'" read "Ludwig Herrmann, was by now Dean of religious studies in the schools of Konstanz and surrounding areas".

p. 246, instead of "Pekarsky" read "Peckarsky".

p. 255, instead of "Pazzullo" read "Puzzullo".

p. 261, instead of "Milwaukeens", read "Milwaukeans".

p. 268, picture caption, instead of "July 5, 1985" read "July 6, 1985"; instead of "Connie" read "Colleen".

p. 273, picture caption, instead of "Heidelburg" read "Heidelberg"

p. 275, instead of "Pietro Petrobelli" read "Pierluigi Petrobelli".

p. 276, picture caption, instead of "Heidelburg University" read "Heidelberg University"; instead of "Ludwing" read "Ludwig".

p. 281, instead of "Chancllor" read "Chancellor"; bottom line, read "only that [they] be as patient...".

p. 283, instead of "James Fennimore Cooper" read "James Fenimore Cooper".

p. 314, instead of "in the fall of 1988" read "in the fall of 1998".

p. 326, instead of "my cousin Mary Eloise, an Episcopal clergy", read "my cousin Mary Eloise, a member of the Episcopal clergy".

p. 328, instead of "Hildegard Schmitt" read "Hildegard Schmid".

p. 331, second line from bottom: instead of "...which had built from...", read "...which had been built from..."

p. 340, instead of "Ferrucio Busoni" read "Ferruccio Busoni".

INDEX

ACRONYMS AND ABBREVIATIONS

There are a small number of acronyms and abbreviations which I have employed during the course of this book that require a brief explanation.

AMS is the acronym for "American Musicological Society," of which I had been a member since the early 1950s. In 1982 I was elected president of the Midwest chapter for a two-year term.

A.R.C.O. is the acronym for "Associate, Royal College of Organists".

BWV following a citation for music by Bach, is the abbreviation for "Bach Werke Verzeichnis," or "Bach Works Catalog," the standard listing tool for the complete works of the composer. The numbering carries almost no chronological implication or any special place in the compositional order of Bach's music.

CMC is the acronym for "Chicago Musical College," where I earned my bachelor and master of music degrees.

F.A.G.O. is the acronym for "Fellow, American Guild of Organists."

IMS is the acronym for "International Musicological Society."

K. following a citation of music by Mozart stands for "Köchel," the man who first provided a large-scale numbering of Mozart's music. Ludwig von Köchel was an Austrian mineralogist, taxonomist and lover of the composer's music. The catalog is arranged in a roughly chronological order, and ranges from K. 1, written when the composer was six years old, to K. 626, his unfinished *Requiem*.

MGG is the acronym for "Die Musik in Geschichte und Gegenwart" ("Music in History and the Present"), the comprehensive, 17-volume German music encyclopedia which began appearing in 1949, and was finally completed in 1986. It has already been supplanted by a new edition, at this time (2000) still in the process of publication.

UWM is the acronym for "University of Wisconsin-Milwaukee", where I spent the last 23 years of my career.

INTRODUCTION

In the summer of 1999, following the death of my aunt Elinor, at the ripe young age of 96 the previous October, our family made a decision to hold a large family reunion, as a kind of memorial celebration of her life. Because Aunt Elinor had an especially warm spot in her heart for the Black Hills of South Dakota, our family decided to get together in Spearfish, at the northern edge of the "Hills," as we called them.

It was the first time that almost all my family members were present, in addition to many relatives from my mother's side of the family. As a result of this family reunion, the thought began to germinate in my mind of providing a record of my life for my family and friends.

Additionally, I had the opportunity to read a wonderful book by my dear friend Robert Noehren, the highly-esteemed, world-renowned retired organist of the University of Michigan, whom I have known for over forty years. Bob has recently assembled a compilation of his writings over the past fifty years, republishing them in a volume called *An Organist's Reader*, which appeared under the Harmonie House Press aegis in 1999. The chapter entitled "Autobiographical Sketches" particularly caught my eye. In it, Noehren chronicled his start in music and reminisced about growing up in Buffalo, New York. His reflections stimulated me to think about my own life in music, and to consider doing something similar.

Another source of inspiration was the thoroughly enjoyable book by another friend and colleague. *The Odyssey of an American Composer* by the late Otto Luening, a native Milwaukee composer, is one of the most delightful recountings of a life in music that I have ever read. Luening was one of the first composers to experiment with electronic sound sources.

Literally hundreds of autobiographies have been written by musicians and artists. I think of Artur Rubinstein's *My Young Years* and *My Many Years* as two of the best recent ones, but there have been many others over the past century. I am not aware that musicologists or scholars in other academic fields have written accounts of their lives, though I am certain many do exist. Those of us in the academic community are most often commemorated within the pages of ubiquitous *Festschriften*, but because I don't merit such recognition, this narrative must serve as the closest I will ever come to such a publication.

I suppose it is rather presumptuous of me to assume that my life can ever be as exciting, interesting or successful as writers' or musicians'; however, the reader may enjoy some of my reflections and the retelling of oftentimes hilarious, at other times, serious events. Most important, I wish to recognize or commemorate here those individuals to whom I owe an eternal debt of gratitude for their guidance, support, faith and love throughout my life. I have also reflected, if only briefly, on some of my own musical philosophy. Finally, it is my hope that my children and grandchildren may derive pleasure and satisfaction from reading about their father and "Opa" here.

Looking over the nearly completed manuscript, I became

aware of some red threads which continually recur, in the manner of an *idée fixe*. One of these is my lifelong fascination and interest in the pipe organ, its design, construction and literature. Another is my consuming passion for the teaching profession, and the joy of introducing students to the body of great music and the contributions of fine scholars and musicians in assisting us to understand and deepen our appreciation of it. Finally, my interest in knowing and understanding other human beings, my family, other dear, close friends and professional colleagues for whom I have the profoundest admiration, has given me untold joy and satisfaction. To all of these people, students, as well as colleagues, I am indebted in so many ways that I cannot begin to thank them all.

I consider myself basically a cultural historian. It is important, however, to remember that history is not merely chronology: history is more than dates; it is more than the "when" or the "what." History includes questions of "why," and thereby implies judgment, a conscious choice between preserving certain events and the exclusion of others not deemed of particular relevance. What any civilization or culture deems important for preservation is what is recorded for future generations. Contemporary culture, with its often commendable trait of collecting and preserving every scrap of information about a multitude of events and persons, is probably the first in history to do so.

Numerous events in my life are not recorded here; the reader can imagine what they might be. Hence, the subtitle of this autobiography: *Almost the Unvarnished Truth*. (I am indebted to my colleague and friend Marshall Dermer, professor of psychology at the University of Wisconsin-Milwaukee, for suggesting this most apropos *caveat lector*.) In some instances I have refrained from identifying someone, but because the incident which involved them is either so important, or so humorous, I simply could not omit telling about them in these pages. I trust the reader will understand and accept my circumspection at these points. I might also have disguised identities, as the late Gerard Flynn, professor of Spanish at the University of Wisconsin-Milwaukee has so admirably done in his autobiography *The Bronx Boy*, though I have neither the imagination nor the literary skills to do this successfully.

I have benefited from the advice and counsel of several people, whom I wish to acknowledge here. My children, especially Claudia and Doris, and my granddaughter Leah, have read parts of the manuscript. My cousin Mary Eloise Husby and her husband, E. Milton Husby, have corrected factual errors in Chapter 1. My close friend Henry Ratenski read parts of Chapter 2 and suggested some corrections there. I am particularly grateful to my publisher, Steven Mundahl, and his wife Sandy, who have encouraged and given me confidence every step of the way in writing this autobiography, and to Henri Forget, my excellent editor. To all three I owe a debt of gratitude which can never be fully repaid.

Most of all, I am indebted to Gudrun, my dear wife of forty-seven years, who patiently read every word of this often fra-c-tur-ed, missspeled, perhaps even a bit *EXAGGERATED* and *embellished* account of events in my life, correcting typographical errors and suggesting improvements to the general style of the narrative. In the process, she may also have learned some things about her husband that she did not know before! She has also beautifully executed the musical examples. I dedicate this autobiography to her, with love and thanks.

Ars longa, vita brevis
--Hippocrates

June 13, 2000
Milwaukee, Wisconsin

banno tenuto m'banno coff

CHAPTER 1

CHILDHOOD; "BUS"; THE REED ORGAN; A FAIR MAIDEN'S HONOR; YOUTH AND TEENAGE YEARS: THE "GOLDEN WEDDING OVERTURE" (1926-1944)

I was born on January 17, 1926, in Sioux Falls Hospital, Sioux Falls, South Dakota, located at 19th Street and Minnesota Avenue. We lived in a small house at 711 W. 16th Street with a white picket fence in the rear. My earliest memories, at approximately three and a half years of age, include riding my tricycle in front of the house, our dog "Boots," and watching the streetcars go by on Summit Avenue, a half a block east of our house.

My father, E. S. Miller (he never used his first name "Edward" and was known only by his middle name, "Sherwood") came to Sioux Falls in 1919, working initially as a city salesman for Jewitt Brothers wholesale grocery company. On July 1, 1920, he was hired to be the secretary-manager of the newly formed Associated Retailers, a position he held for over forty years, until his retirement in 1961. He married my mother, Doris Albina Brown, a native of the city, on June 17, 1922.

My sister Martha was born in 1928, and in 1930 we moved to the house at 110 E. 23rd Street where I grew up and retain the strongest memories of my childhood and youth. Although this period coincides with the beginning of the Great Depression following the stock market crash of 1929, I was never aware of how it may have affected my family. I remember my childhood as basically a happy time. Elizabeth, my younger sister, was born in 1932. That year father found it necessary, because of his growing family, to add a large second-floor porch, stretching the entire width of the front of the house.

My father had a small collection of phonograph records which he occasionally played on a mammoth wind-up phonograph in the front room of the house, a room which also contained a radio, a music box, and, later, a beautiful secretary desk which my mother inherited from a distant aunt in Minneapolis. We were to understand that this room was basically my father's, where he would sit and listen to the radio, read the newspaper, smoke cigarettes and, on occasion, play cribbage with my mother. I have only the vaguest memory of what music my father listened to, but I do remember such works as Grieg's *Peer Gynt Suite no. 2*, and operetta music by Léhar and Johann Strauss, Jr., as well as songs such as "Ah, Sweet Mystery of Life" and "Vienna, City of my Dreams", music which, many years later, I would come to love as well, though, by the time I was a teenager and had started to know the "classical" repertoire, I thought was superficial, and unimportant.

When I was eight years old, I began taking piano lessons with a woman who lived just four houses from us down the street on First Avenue, which dead ended into 23rd Street in front of our house. Mrs. Goodman was a local piano teacher with a fairly large number of young students whom she presented in recital each spring. I remember sitting in her dining room on those occasions, waiting my turn to perform on the big Steinway in the living room, as the proud parents listened. I do not remember anything I played, except for the "Berceuse" from the opera *Jocelyn*, by Benjamin Godard. My little piano stood in father's front room, and was called a "Minipiano," proudly displaying an advertisement stating that then Princess Elizabeth of England owned one. It was missing the top four or five keys, which was presumably the reason it was named "Minipiano." Mrs. Goodman was a demanding teacher, although I was a somewhat indifferent student, preferring to ride my tricycle around the block pretending to be a bus driver. I became so enamoured with driving my "bus" that my father began to call me "Bus," a name I retained for many years, even after I became a teenager.

I had my first experience attending a YMCA camp for boys in the summer of 1936, and went by bus to the campgrounds, located on an island in the middle of a lake about four miles north of Big Stone City, in northeastern South Dakota, just across the state line from Ortonville, Minnesota. It was the first time I had been away from home for an extended length of time, and my fears were exacerbated when I discovered that only oil or kerosene lamps were available to provide light. I could hardly wait to return to civilization again after two weeks! I remembered with terror an

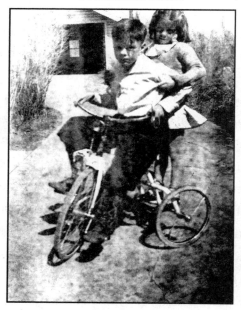

The "bus" is seen here picking up a "passenger."
The "passenger" is my sister, Martha.

earlier experience when I was seven and visiting the farm of one of our maids, Sylvia Diebedahl, who lived near Baltic, South Dakota. Upon arriving at the farm with my parents, who had arranged for me to visit for several days during the summer, I discovered, to my horror, that there was no electricity, and adamantly refused to remain, insisting upon returning to Sioux Falls as soon as possible!

When I was ten years old, I began to become more interested in music, making it a point to listen to the radio broadcasts of the Metropolitan Opera and the New York Philharmonic Orchestra. In that same year of 1936 I remember making a significant entry in a diary which I kept at the time: "Listen to last concert by Arturo Toscanini with the New York Philharmonic before he returns to Italy." (He did, in fact come back the following year to become

4

conductor of the newly formed NBC Symphony.) I must have listened to the concert, though I have no memory of what was performed.

An interesting and significant event took place in 1936 when my church, Calvary Episcopal Cathedral, embarked on the purchase of a new pipe organ. My father was a member of the parish vestry at the time, and also a member of the organ committee. The old organ, a two-manual tracker instrument by Johnson and Son, was installed in a large chamber at the front of the church, in the chancel, between the nave and the altar. The choir (altos and tenors on the left, sopranos and basses on the right in front of the organ chamber) sat in that area.

The parish chose Pilcher and Sons, of Louisville, Kentucky, to build a two-manual, sixteen rank instrument for the cathedral, with both Great and Swell divisions enclosed, and a detached console on the other side of the sanctuary. As a boy of ten, I remember clearly seeing the large 16' Pedal Bourdon pipes lying in the center aisle of the church, waiting to be installed in the new organ. At the same time, a thorough renovation of the church was undertaken, and included new furniture, painting of the interior and removal of a rood screen which had been erected between the nave and chancel.

The organist of the cathedral was Bernice Halverson, a lovely and conscientious, though somewhat nervous spinster. She studied with Rupert Sircom, the organist of St. Mark's Cathedral in Minneapolis, Minnesota. A well-known recitalist, he was chosen to play the dedicatory recital on the new Pilcher in 1937. I had the honor of turning pages for him on the occasion. By then I had

5

become very interested in the organ, and often begged Miss Halverson to let me play the new organ in the cathedral. (Mrs. Goodman, my piano teacher, was also the director of the junior choir at the cathedral, and I was a member of the group.)

About this time I became determined to have my own organ, and my father spoke to his friend and fellow Rotarian Arthur Godfrey (not THE Arthur Godfrey of radio and television fame) about the possibility of procuring a reed organ for me. Mr. Godfrey was the manager of Williams Piano Company, the largest music store in Sioux Falls, a place I often visited. He was a somewhat brusque, rather short man who, it seemed to me, was always chomping on a cigar, and I felt would have made an excellent used-car salesman. My fondest wish was finally fulfilled when the reed organ was delivered to the house. However, we had no place for it inside, so it ended up in our garage, where I would play it every evening when the weather was nice, to the delight of our neighbors. It also provided me with the first introduction to such things as touch and registration on the organ. This idyllic state of affairs lasted several years, until a boy friend of mine, determined to help me clean the instrument, decided one day to spray it with a garden hose.

When I was twelve, I was asked to play for Sunday School services in the undercroft of the cathedral at 9:30 a.m. each Sunday morning at the same time as Morning Prayer was being conducted upstairs. I played a little Estey reed organ, and on more than one occasion I also had the great thrill of being called away suddenly from my duties to rush upstairs and fill in on the new Pilcher when Miss Halverson was unavoidably detained. My parents also promised me that, if I would master it, I could perform the hymn "God of our Fathers", complete with the opening fanfares on the trumpet stop, on the large organ.

In addition to my interest in music, I started a small newspaper, called the *Southside Weekly*, printed on the mimeograph machine in the Credit Bureau office, my father kindly assisting me by allowing one of the secretaries in the office to type stencils for us. Richard Wirzbach was the assistant editor, my good friend John Brooks was the sports editor, and Barbara Blecher was the movie critic. Our greatest scoop involved an interview conducted in the city jail with a thief and prostitute. The headline in the next issue of the *Southside Weekly* read: "Olivia Leach Talks!"

Dick Wirzbach and I would peddle the paper downtown each week, until we had gathered enough money from our sales to go over to Clifford's and indulge ourselves in one of their famous malted milks, which cost fifteen cents at the time. I believe our venture lasted about six months, but we were featured in a newspaper story by Walter Simmons, a reporter for the *Argus Leader*, which, in itself, is an interesting tale.

Simmons had married a woman who, at one time, had also been enamoured of my father. They were later divorced, though "Aunt Sally," as we came to call her, would occasionally come to town to visit our family. She was a real character and we children would always talk about her. (She was somewhat obese, and, in the words of my sister Martha, "oozed out all over.") On one occasion, Aunt Sally took the train to Sioux Falls to visit us. Her entire luggage consisted of a large paper bag which contained, in addition to personal items, a light bulb. When questioned as to the purpose of the light bulb, she responded that this was in case the lights on the train went out! (Sally Simmons later moved to New York City, where she became a good friend of the composer Ned Rorem. She wrote me once in the mid-1960s.)

Many years later Walter Simmons became a managing editor for the *Chicago Tribune*. In 1959 I submitted an amusing story, dealing with the birth of our first child, to the paper for publication in a column titled "The Day my Baby was Born". The story happened to catch Simmons' eye, who, remembering my name, not only published the story, but wrote me a personal note reminding me of my youth in Sioux Falls some twenty-four years earlier!

As a boy I had the misfortune to develop a severe overbite between my upper and lower teeth, and it became necessary to fit me with braces. (My condition was so severe that my father, who was a rather large man, tall and big boned, could slip his thumb between my upper and lower teeth.) In those days the specialty of orthodontia was quite new, and, as there was no dentist in Sioux Falls who could perform the work, I began to make trips with my parents to Minneapolis, Minnesota every six weeks or so starting in 1936 and continuing until 1942. I was seen by one of the first orthodontists in the Midwest, Dr. Bernard DeVries. These trips, which usually began on Friday morning, were always a highlight of my young life, affording me an opportunity to visit a large city, with all its interesting attractions. (I was also excused from school on those Fridays.)

A picture, taken about 1935, in front of the house on East 23rd Street, when I would have been nine years old. A close examination of my mouth will reveal the unmistakable signs of my overbite, which necessitated the orthodontia treatment in Minneapolis. To my left is my sister Martha, and the little fellow is Tom Brown, my first cousin. Next to him is my sister, Elizabeth.

The appointment was on Saturday morning, and we would stay over that night, returning to Sioux Falls on Sunday. Some of my most delightful experiences during these visits involved riding the Oak-Harriet streetcar line from one end of the city to the other. (By this time Sioux Falls no longer had any streetcars.)

On a few visits to Minneapolis, we stayed at the home of a distant aunt and uncle who owned a large three-storied mansion on Waverly Place overlooking the downtown area. I thought this was the grandest house I had ever been in. It certainly was the only one I'd seen with its own elevator! It also had an ingenious internal communication system similar to a ship's: when one blew into a small metal device in the wall, it was heard in the kitchen, where the maid could then speak into a receiver, and one could clearly hear the person on the other end. (In May of 1987 my wife and I spent a weekend in Minneapolis, and drove by the location: Alas, the beautiful Victorian mansion had been demolished and replaced by an ultramodern building.) My aunt Cecile was an interesting old lady, whose husband, Uncle Jay, was totally bedridden.

My developing interest in the organ led me to undertake visits to the various churches in Minneapolis to examine the organs. I was also curious about the new electronic instruments, especially one called the "Orgatron.". It was apparently developed as an answer to the very popular Hammond electric. Each time I was in Minneapolis I would stop in at a music store downtown and play the Orgatron. I was sure that such an instrument might be the wave of the future, though I did enjoy trying out the various pipe organs I found in Minneapolis, and developed a knack for discovering where the organist had hidden the key to the console. (In those days most churches remained unlocked during the day.)

I often spent time at my maternal grandmother's house on south Phillips Avenue. Grandmother was a stately woman whom I always enjoyed visiting. I particularly appreciated her support when my mother would scold me or fret about my behavior. "Oh, Doris, leave the boy alone, he'll be all right," she often admonished her. Because of my interest in music she showed me, at one time, a one key flute she possessed which had been played by one of my relatives during the Civil War. Although my grandfather was stone deaf, we could communicate with him by writing in a small book or on a piece of paper. He could speak perfectly well. (Many years later I had cause to remember this when I studied some of the extremely valuable so-called "conversation books" of the deaf Beethoven, which have been preserved.)

When I was thirteen a friend of my grandmother's presented me with a volume of the thirty-two Beethoven sonatas. I was very proud to own the volume, and began to learn the Opus 27, no. 2 ("Moonlight") although I hadn't the slightest idea what the rest of the music was like. Only much later, after I had become a musicologist, I did some research on the volume, and, aided by Professor William Newman of the University of North Carolina, learned that the edition was a very rare one, in all probability edited by Franz Liszt.

In 1939, on one trip to the Twin Cities, I experienced what was to be a significant event in my musical development. My parents took me to a new kind of movie theater for a performance of a musical movie called "Fantasia," which had just been released by Walt Disney. It was explained that the theater had been renovated in order to provide for a number of loudspeakers to be placed throughout the room, producing a stereo effect. I was totally entranced by the music, and by the man who appeared at the beginning of the movie and conducted the *Toccata and Fugue in D minor* by Bach with the Philadelphia Orchestra. (The conductor was, of course, Leopold Stokowski, and I later often thought that it must have been quite the day when, as a child, he had first discovered his hands!) I also went down to Williams Piano Co,

11

and purchased the Busoni piano transcription of the Bach *Toccata and Fugue in D minor*, attempting to learn it, but with little success.

A few years later, trying to recall the music I had heard in the movie and knowing that one of the pieces which had so impressed me was a story about the creation of the world, complete with dinosaurs and exploding volcanos, I assumed that the music was that of Haydn's *The Creation*! (I knew nothing of music history, nor did I know anything of musical style.) A few years later I learned some works of Igor Stravinsky, and discovered that the music in *Fantasia* which accompanied the cartoon was that of the *Rite of Spring*, a picture of pagan Russia, hardly the creation of the world!

In addition to music and newspaper work, I was also attracted to radio broadcasting and often spent time at the studios of KSOO, Sioux Falls' first radio station, which was then located on the sixth floor of the Carpenter Hotel. The station operated only during the daylight hours and one evening, as I stood in the studio waiting for the station to go off the air for the night, I was invited in to the control booth by the announcer, Verl Thompson, a handsome man with a deep, resonant voice, who looked like Clark Gable. He allowed me to assist him in signing the station off for the night by saying "good night" to the listeners. Ironically, I did, in fact, become a radio announcer for a time many years later, and was even issued a third-class broadcasting license; the episode forms part of Chapter 5.

About the time I reached my twelfth birthday, I began to take an increasing interest in the fair sex, and experienced my first kiss!

Nancy Hyde and I were standing outside, on a cold winter day, near the ice cream stand in McKennen Park. I suggested that we run around the stand in opposite directions, and when we ran into each other, the great event would then naturally take place. I recall that it was a rather hit-and-miss affair, and we were so embarrassed and awkward that we both ran off, in opposite directions, toward our respective houses! Another young lady in whom I was interested was Avis Storey. This led, however, to a nasty altercation with Henry Carlson who, it turned out, also had an interest in her. He was bigger than I, and one afternoon after school, he accosted me on East 21st Street. After he had taken a few swings at me, I turned tail and ran all the way home. That evening my father attempted to instruct his son in the "manly art of self-defense," to little avail. I guess I am basically pacifistic in nature, and abhor violence, even if it involved defending a fair maiden's honor!

***

In January of 1940 I entered Washington High School to continue my education. My courses included the study of Latin, algebra, English and science. I was a poor math student, and failed the first semester of freshman algebra twice before finally passing it during summer school on the campus of Sioux Falls College. I also failed second-semester algebra, and needed to take it a second time. My parents, concerned about my poor scholastic showing, had engaged a private tutor to assist me in my mathematics studies while I was still in the eighth grade. My first year Latin teacher was Irene Cummings, a tiny, hunch-backed woman of indeterminate age, whom I came to love dearly.

In addition to music, newspaper work and radio announcing, I also became interested in flying. The first airport in Sioux Falls, "Soo Skyways," was on the far southwest edge of town, actually in the country, and in 1934 I experienced my first airplane ride, in a Ford Trimotor (called affectionately a "Tin Goose"), which landed on a dirt runway in a field bordered by Western Avenue on the east, and the Sioux River on the west, south of 41st Street. In 1939 an airport was built on the far north side of town, and I would occasionally ride my bicycle, having by then graduated from the tricycle of earlier years, out to the new field, where I enjoyed talking to private pilots such as Knapp Brown, who would often take me along with them as they practiced takeoffs and landings. I was also interested in meteorology, and took a serious interest in weather forecasting. At one time I had a device to measure direction and speed of the wind in the back yard.

My father was of the opinion that I should avail myself of the opportunity to participate in sports, football, baseball and other athletic pursuits, citing young Billy Grigsby as someone I should emulate. I know my father often despaired of my interest in esoteric subjects such as philosophy, the arts and especially my musical studies. In addition to these pursuits, I also had another strike against me, at least as far as my father was concerned: I was left-handed. I sensed that he considered anyone who was left-handed just a bit suspect. (After all, in Latin the word for the left hand is "manu sinistra," the "sinister hand"!) I imagine that my father often complained to my mother: "Doris, where have we gone wrong? Not only is he left-handed, he also wants to become a musician!"

Though my father had only a high school education, I always considered him well educated and literate. I suspect that, at a time when few men and women went on to a college education, a good high school education was probably quite respectable. He had an excellent command of English grammar and syntax, and would often quiz us children regarding language errors in publications which he received. His knowledge of the classics of literature was impressive: He could recite the entire opening of Caesar's "Gallic Wars" in Latin beginning with: "Omnia Gallia est divisi in partis tres...," and he knew several of Shakespeare's sonnets from memory. In addition, he had a basic command of German, and could converse with Rabbi Karl Richter, from Mannheim, Germany, whose family had escaped the Holocaust, and lived around the corner from our house on 23rd Street.

By the time I entered high school I had decided that I didn't wish to continue my piano studies with Mrs. Goodman, deciding instead to become a funeral director. My friend Dick Wirzbach passed his free time at the Miller Funeral Home (no relation) at 11th and Main, which had been built in 1924 by L.D. Miller, in art deco style. I always thought it rather ironic that, next to the funeral home was Moe Hospital, across the street was my church, and to complete the picture: at the next corner was a monument works! It was also pointed out to me by Ken Krieger and Orin Bowen, two of the funeral home employees, that I could easily combine my interest in becoming a funeral director with my love of playing the organ, as the organ was always needed for music duing funeral services.

Shortly before I began my second year of high school, World War II began. On Monday, December 8, 1941, the principal of Washington High School, Lyman Fort, convened a special school assembly in the auditorium so that we could all listen, on a large floor model radio which had been hooked into the PA system of the auditorium, as President Roosevelt, addressing Congress, dramatically announced: "Yesterday, December 7, 1941, a date which will live in infamy, the United States of America was suddenly and deliberately attacked by naval and air forces of the Empire of Japan...." I have little recollection, however, that this event and those which followed, had any marked effect on my day-to-day existence, at least for the first year or two, and I continued on with my life, still enjoying and learning music. I do recall that occasionally, in the years following the start of World War II, we had a few air raid drills in Sioux Falls, when all the streetlights were turned off and sirens wailed. However, it was never clear to me why we did this, as I couldn't understand how Japan (or Germany, one of the other Axis countries) could ever reach as far inland as the plains of South Dakota.

As was typical of many young boys, I considered becoming either a fire fighter, or a police detective. At the police station, I was befriended by Lt. Joe Wilcox, who was the radio operator, desk sergeant and general factotum, and Chief of Detectives Rex Gullick, who, my mother often reminded me, was a fellow student of hers during grade school days. By the time I was sixteen I had become thoroughly engrossed in the fictional exploits of the great

Sherlock Holmes, and had studied the "art of deduction." I often sat in my room imagining myself to be the great detective, even to taking one of my father's pipes and pretending to smoke it as I read such stories as "The Sign of Four" or "The Hound of the Baskervilles."

In the spring of 1942, a series of mysterious robberies of neighborhood grocery stores caught my interest, and I began a private investigation of the circumstances surrounding the crimes. The robberies were referred to in the press as the "Silk Stocking Robberies" because of the fact that the robber always wore a silk stocking over his face as a disguise. After several months of digging, I actually came across some evidence which seemed to point to a likely suspect, but just as I was presenting my findings to the police, it was discovered that the man in question had fled the city, and disappeared without a clue. Of course, I always assumed that the suspect sensed I was closing in on him and decided to skip town! I do not recall whether the police eventually caught up with the perpetrator or not, or if my "deductions" had even been accurate.

In the fall of 1942 a large air force base opened at the Sioux Falls Municipal Airport. As many as 20,000 air force officers and men were stationed in dozens of makeshift quonset huts stretching south of the airport. The base was a training school for radio operators and electronic technicians. Among those stationed at the base were a number of prominent professional musicians who had entered the service. The organist of National Cathedral in Washington, D.C., Paul Callaway, was stationed at the base, and I often was able to sneak into Calvary Cathedral while he practiced.

I had never heard such fine playing, and even though I never met him, I knew he must have been a superb musician, who had studied with Leo Sowerby in Chicago and Marcel Dupré in Paris. Soon, a number of soldiers began to become a part of our extended family, including Millard Shea, a fine tenor, whom I accompanied on occasion in arias from Handel's "Messiah." Other servicemen stationed at the base who visited us included Larry Summergrade and "Bud" Hand.

The year 1942 also marked for me a pivotal and important turning point in my intellectual and musical development, and represented a return to the field of music after a hiatus of almost two years. Several factors were responsible for this, but the most important was the discovery, on the campus of Augustana College, of the so-called "Carnegie Record Library". The Carnegie Corporation had placed record libraries in a number of colleges throughout the country, consisting of a carefully selected collection of over 500 individual titles, a cross-indexed catalog, and an excellent Magnavox record player.

I paid my first visit to the "Carnegie Room" in the summer of 1942, in the company of my friend Laurie Vallier, a double bass player and music lover, who had already visited the facility a number of times. From this moment on, my love of music and my knowledge of the literature began to grow incrementally! My ability to absorb an enormous amount of new music, and my curiosity about all kinds of music, orchestral, keyboard, choral and chamber music from all eras, was stimulated by opportunities to spend time at this facility.

Soon I was well on my way toward building a small record collection. I still recall that the first four works of the symphonic repertoire with which I became intimately familiar were the Brahms Symphony no. 1, the Beethoven Symphony no. 5, the Franck D minor Symphony, and the Mozart G minor Symphony (K. 550), followed in rapid succession by other staples of the literature: the 2nd and 5th *Brandenburg Concertos* of Bach, Mussorgsky's *Pictures at an Exhibition* (in the Lucien Caillet orchestration), harpsichord sonatas by Scarlatti performed by Ralph Kirkpatrick, keyboard Partitas of Bach in the recordings of Walter Gieseking and Harold Samuel, the second Handel Concerto Grosso, the 2nd Symphony of Sibelius, Vaughn-William's music to Aristophanes *The Wasps*, an excerpt from his 1929 opera, *Sir John in Love*, which later became famous as the "Fantasie on Greensleeves," as well as lesser known works such as the "Toccata" from the 5th organ symphony by Widor, Milhaud's *La Creation du Monde*, and the *Preludio a Cristóbal Colón*, for soprano with five instruments in fractional tones by the Mexican microtonal composer Julian Carrillo.

About this time I also began to work at my first place of employment, not counting the newspaper route I had for a few months, when I started in as a shoe salesman at Fusfield's woman's store on Phillips Ave. Fusfield's was just across the alley from Williams Piano Co., and as soon as I received my first paycheck, I immediately ran over to Williams to buy some records. Our family doctor, who delivered me, by the way, was Dr. Paul Billingsly. Dr. Billingsly was also a fine amateur violinist, and had a large record collection. Knowing of my interest in music and recordings, he gave me a small record player which brought me great satisfaction, as I added to my record collection. The influence of two other men, more than anyone else, gave me the impetus toward acquiring knowledge of music. Often, our intellectual and musical development may be traced to the strong influence of a specific person or persons, and these two men were, for me, my strongest influences.

Dean Arlton was an Augustana College music major, and worked as an attendant in the Carnegie Room. He was an excellent pianist, a modest, retiring person, and quite knowledgeable about music. In addition, he had absolute pitch, and was capable of reproducing portions of the repertoire on the piano from having simply heard the work. Dean had evidently received excellent piano instruction, and his repertoire, all memorized, included portions of Book I of the Well Tempered Keyboard of Bach, several Scarlatti sonatas, the Mozart F major sonata (K. 332), and the G minor Rhapsody of Brahms.

For the next two years, until I entered the navy, I spent many hours talking with Dean about music. He had come to Augustana College from Mitchell, South Dakota, where his father was a professor of biology at Dakota Wesleyan University there. Eventually, I met his two equally talented brothers, Stan and Roland. Roland was the oldest, and Stan the youngest. There was also a fourth brother, Paul, somewhat younger, whom I never met. All three of the Arlton brothers were geniuses, reportedly with I.Q.'s in excess of 150, and all three had absolute pitch. I shall have more to say about them later.

The other person who had a most profound effect on my musical development, and one of the strongest musical influences of my life was J. Earl Lee, a professor of piano at Augustana College. Lee was probably the finest musician I had ever known, and it soon became clear to me that I wanted to resume piano study with him. My grandmother paid for the lessons until I was graduated from high school. My piano lessons were on Thursday afternoon after school, and after six months, Lee began to teach me music theory without charging me anything. The theory lessons were on Saturday afternoons. We would also often listen to the Metropolitan Opera or, on Sundays, the concerts of the New York Philharmonic.

Earl Lee was probably the most cultivated, well-read person I had met until then. In addition to music, he was equally at home discussing art, literature or history. In his studio, which was on the top floor of "Old Main" at Augustana College, the bookshelves were stuffed with hundreds of scores of the standard repertoire: Mozart, Haydn, Beethoven symphonies, chamber music and keyboard works, Bach cantatas, operas and other vocal and choral works. I'm afraid I was only an average student in piano. I seemed to have an interest in so much music of all genres and media, that I never concentrated on becoming a really fine pianist, nor was I certain that I had either the temperament or patience to become a concert artist.

Years later I came to the realization that, to become a first-rate performer required an enormous amount of time spent practicing, usually a rather narrow repertoire of music, the ability to discipline oneself, and the physical stamina to become focused closely on mastering the instrument. I finally became convinced that learning to play a musical instrument is somewhat akin to learning how to be an Olympic champion figure skater, an extremely swift typist or a top hitter on a professional baseball team. The constant repetition, and the training of muscles, nerves and other physical and mental faculties would result in a high level of achievement. To this, of course, must be added a specific trait supposedly found in musicians: that certain, undefinable quality which some call "talent."

I began to do a little composing at this time, as well as improvising at the piano. Although I had begun to learn a bit about common practice harmony and musical structure, I was still naive and unaware of the totality of the art of music. In August of 1942, my maternal grandparents celebrated their fiftieth wedding anniversary, and I decided to write a "Golden Wedding Overture" for the occasion. The piece amounted to a mishmash of rhythms and motives from the opening three shorts and a long of Beethoven's Fifth Symphony, with an attempt at imitative counterpoint. My long-suffering family, good naturedly, endured my performance on the occasion. My deaf grandfather enjoyed it thoroughly.

I continued to practice the organ, and often found myself on the third floor of the Masonic temple on West 10th Street, where a fine little Johnson and Son two manual tracker instrument was located. On this instrument I attempted to learn the "Toccata" from the 5th organ symphony of Widor, with only limited success.

August, 1942. The one and only performance of the Golden Wedding Overture, on my grandparents 50th wedding anniversary. (l to r) My sister, Martha, standing; Aunt Esther, Uncle Jim Thatcher, Rebecca Thatcher, Grandmother, sitting; My first cousin Mary Eloise, standing; Grandfather, my sister Elizabeth, sitting on the floor; my father, E. Sherwood Miller, the composer, at the piano; my mother Doris Miller, uncle Ashley Brown, standing; Aunt Elinor Funk, Warren Funk, seated; cousin Tom Brown.

It was not that the music was so difficult; it was simply that my hands got tired playing the endless arpeggios in the work on a tracker instrument! My grandfather held some type of administrative post at the Masonic lodge and allowed me to play the instrument to my heart's content. He had been Grand Master of the South Dakota lodge, as had his father, and as was to be his son, Roger. (This is apparently the only instance in the history of

Free Masonry in the United States where three generations in one family have become Grand Masters.)

About this time I also began to develop a great interest in philosophy, psychology and history. For a time I was interested in the writings of the Russian philosopher P.D. Ouspensky, whose most important book *Tertium Organum*, published in 1926, contained a "new model of the universe," in which the author purported to describe a so-called "fourth dimension." I am also chagrined to admit that, for a few weeks I was quite taken by the pseudo science of phrenology, studying the bumps on one's head to determine personality and/or intelligence. At this stage in my life I was absorbing so much knowledge and information that there were bound to be a few dead-ends.

My visits to the Carnegie Room at Augustana College increased, and I even found myself skipping church on Sunday mornings in order to sneak into the room and listen to the B minor Mass of Bach. I considered that, by so doing, I was somehow fulfilling my Sunday obligation to attend church. My knowledge of the repertoire continued to grow, and I became well acquainted with Stravinsky's three Russian period ballets (*The Firebird, Petrushka* and *Le Sacre du Printemps*), as well as Bach cantatas such as "Christ lag in Todesbanden" (BWV 4) and "Wachet Auf" (BWV 140), which Earl Lee had generously allowed me to borrow from his collection. Other works with which I became familiar during this time included additional Mozart symphonies, concertos and chamber music (D minor quartet, K. 421 and G minor quintet, K. 516), the Beethoven G major piano concerto, Opus 58, the

Brahms violin concerto and the first and fifth symphonies of Shostakovitch.

In the early winter of 1943, I heard the fascinating sounds of the harpsichord (actually a Neupert spinet) and the recorder for the first time, when the Trapp Family Singers performed a program at Augustana College. My interest in these instruments was stimulated as never before by this wonderful concert, which included trio sonatas by Loeillet, and Bach chorale harmonizations, and I became determined to some day purchase my own harpsichord. I even had the opportunity to meet some of the members of the Trapp Family Singers on the day after the concert, when I happened to be eating in the Carpenter Hotel, where they were staying. I immediately fell in love with one of the beautiful girls in the family choir, with her typically clear European complexion and blond, braided hair.

I also became infatuated with the young violin virtuoso Patricia Travers, who was at that time beginning to make quite a splash on the concert stage. I enlisted the aid of Earl Lee to assist me in writing her a "fan" letter, although I'd never even heard her play, and sent it to her. I recall that I received an autographed photo of the young lady, who was just a year my junior.

When I was about sixteen, I began to date Noreen Woodard. We would occasionally go to the movies, or, if I could get the car, I would take her to the nearest church, where I would make her sit, in the darkened sanctuary, while I played the organ. I'm sure she often wondered at this strange idea of a date! We did, however, have one memorable experience. I had asked Noreen to go to the junior prom with me, and a contest was being held for the most

25

original method of transportation in order to get to the dance, in view of wartime gasoline rationing.

My father, who could be quite creative, called his good friend Glenn Minor, the manager of Miller Funeral Home, and proposed that my date and I arrive at the prom via the funeral home ambulance. Mr. Minor thought this a capital idea, and as the funeral home was just around the corner from the ballroom where the prom was being held, he gave us the go-ahead. With red lights and siren running, the ambulance, Ken Krieger and Orin Bowen in charge, pulled up in front of the Arkota Ballroom, and the ambulance cot, with the recumbent Noreen on it, was rolled onto the ballroom floor! Our arrival produced a sensation, and we won the prize: two gallons of gasoline, which I presented to the funeral home the next day.

***

I began to attend orchestra rehearsals of the Augustana Symphony, which were held in the basement of the old boys' dorm, and was directed by Richard Guderyahn, who was a professor of strings at the college. Guderyahn was a good violinist and cellist, and conducted the small orchestra of students, faculty and town people in regular concerts. Before long, he asked me to become a member of the orchestra, and I served as the tympanist for a year or so. This proved to be good training for me, as I had a rather poor rhythmic sense. I don't recall the repertoire we played, except for a concert given in the auditorium of Washington High School, sometime in 1943, during which we played the music from Grieg's "Sigurd Jorsalfar." At the climax of the overture, which included an important tympani roll, my youthful spirits got the best of me, and the head of one of my tympani sticks flew off, landing in the bell of a trombone in front of me. Quite a conclusion to the work!

In high school, I sang in the school chorus, directed by Boyd Bohlke. On one occasion we were to sing a rather flamboyant choral work with a patriotic theme. I was asked to play the *secondo* part of the four-hand accompaniment with Claire van Ausdahl, probably the best pianist in school. Claire was my hero, and I recall a beautiful, sensitive performance by him of the Variations in F minor by Haydn which deeply impressed me. In addition to Claire, there was a remarkably gifted girl in Sioux Falls by the name of Dorothy Ann Wheeler, whom I thought was destined for greatness as a concert pianist, though I never did hear anything about her, and I have never come across her name in the professional music fraternity. Claire van Ausdahl went on to a successful career as artists and repertoire director for Mercury Records in New York after teaching theory at the Eastman School of Music for a few years. His mother had served for many years as organist of the First Methodist Church in Sioux Falls, and was herself a successful local musician and piano teacher.

In 1943 I invited a group of eight or ten string players to begin meeting at our house to read through baroque chamber music. Among the players were violinists Roger and Dean Bowden, Audrey Walsted and Kathryn Piaggi, violists Dean Arlton and "Beegee" Bubbers, double bass player Laurie Vallier, and Claire van Ausdahl, who was also an excellent cellist. (Laurie appeared one evening for a rehearsal, having transported his double bass on

27

his bicycle!) Most of these people also played in the Augustana Symphony, and Mr. Guderyahn also came over and played cello. I would pull the piano out into the middle of the room, and attempt to play *basso continuo* parts on it.

Now, as 1943 drew to a close, and my graduation from high school became imminent, I was faced with the decision to report for duty in the armed forces. My father, who had served in both the army and navy, recommended that I join the navy, because, as he explained it, I would always have a place to sleep in the navy, rather then be consigned to a foxhole on a battlefield somewhere. The naval reserve had established a plan, which would allow a man who was nearing high school graduation to enlist in the navy, with the stipulation that as soon as he had graduated, he would then report to an assignment center to be shipped off to basic training somewhere. On January 6, 1944, after going through two days of physical and psychological tests and being issued a complete set of navy clothing, I was sworn into the United States naval reserve in Omaha, Nebraska, placed on inactive duty, and returned to finish my high school education. After graduation, I returned once more to Omaha, entering active duty on January 31, 1944.

CHAPTER 2

THE U. S. NAVY
A HOSPITAL CORPSMAN AND A CHANCE
TO MEET ELEANOR ROOSEVELT

It was a frightened, apprehensive eighteen-year-old who arrived at the railroad station in Omaha, Nebraska, and boarded a train bound for boot camp in faraway Farragut, Idaho, that cold morning of February 1, 1944. I had never been away from home for any length of time, nor had I seen any other cities or states except for my trips to Minneapolis as a young boy and a YMCA camp experience in Colorado in 1939. The thought of joining hundreds of other men in an unknown adventure was daunting, to say the least. For the majority of the time I spent on the train, I stood forlornly on the rear platform, not wanting those in the coaches to see my bitter tears, listening to the *clickety-click* of the rails, and gazing out at the tracks and the barren Nebraska prairies receding into the early twilight of a cold winter day. What had I gotten myself into? Where was I going? What lay ahead?

We arrived at Coeur d'Alene, Idaho, on a cold, clear, windless morning in early February. A vast compound, ringed by a dozen barracks and other buildings, was to be my home for the next six weeks. The two-storied barracks contained sleeping quarters for approximately three hundred men. Each man had been issued a duffel bag into which his entire worldly possessions, or at least those he was allowed to have, were stuffed unceremoniously. (I had picked up the January 1944 issue of *The Musical Quarterly* in an Omaha music store before leaving: It was my sole piece of musical literature for many months. I still have it.)

Our daily schedule started with breakfast at approximately 5:30 a.m., a time I had never known even existed, with breakfast, and continued all day with classroom lectures on aircraft recognition, detailed descriptions of various fighting ships of the navy, knot tying, firearms instruction, gas mask exercises, parade drill, inspections, guard duty and calisthenics.

There was little that was pleasant about much of what I experienced in the navy, and I often felt painfully lonely and terribly sensitive in the strange environment I now found myself. Yet, upon reflection, I would never have exchanged the time I spent in the service for any other life experiences. This time served not only to make me aware of the vastness of this country, and even other countries thousands of miles away, but also helped me to become tolerant of divergent opinions, differing lifestyles and customs, and the infinite variety of the human race, with all its strengths, its occasional ugliness and its moments of individual and collective greatness.

In the evening we were given the opportunity to visit the recreational facility on the base, where I found a piano, a small library and some records. One evening, as I sat at the piano, a young man approached and introduced himself as the base chaplain's assistant. He said he was a pianist, so I let him sit down and he began to play. It was immediately apparent that he was a superb pianist. He said he had studied in New York and Philadelphia before entering the service, and had already played some recitals there. He played several works for my great enjoyment and pleasure, including excerpts from Brahms' second piano concerto, an extremely difficult work. As we became better acquainted, I decided to inquire about his duties as a chaplain's assistant. He indicated that he played the organ for the various church services held on the base, acting also as secretary and office clerk for the chaplains. I became interested in the possibility of this type of assignment, and he said he would try to see what he could do. Unfortunately, an assignment as a chaplain's assistant was not possible; however, I was grateful to have had the opportunity to meet the young pianist. His name: William Kapell, who later went on to become one of the shining stars among the young pianists of the post-war period, until his tragic death at the age of thirty-one in 1953, in a plane crash outside San Francisco, while returning from a successful Australian tour.

As the end of my period of boot camp approached, it became necessary to make some kind of choice from among the various schools which offered specialized training to the navy seaman: signalman's school, radio operator's school, yeoman school (for those interested in becoming a ship's clerk), gunnery school, and hospital corps school. Because of an interest in medicine, I decided to opt for training as a hospital corpsman, or male nurse. There was another aspect of being a hospital corpsman which appealed to me as well: By the terms of the Geneva Convention, hospital corpsmen were exempt from carrying or operating firearms, and, as I was a pacifist, this appealed to me.

Shortly before graduation from Navy boot camp at Farragut, Idado. The uniform is "Dress Blues," and the stripes on the sleeve indicate my rank as Seaman, Second Class.

When I completed boot camp at the end of March I received a twenty-day leave before reporting back to Farragut for shipment to hospital corps school in San Diego, California. Returning once more to Farragut Naval Training Station at the conclusion of my leave, I promptly violated the cardinal rule of all whom serve in the armed forces: Never, NEVER volunteer for anything! As I checked into the facility again, an announcement was made: "Is there anyone here who can type?" In my naiveté, I raised my hand

and was immediately ushered into an office, where I spent the next few hours typing the names, serial numbers and other information of hundreds of incoming seamen reporting back to Farragut. It was a bitter lesson to learn.

Following a long, tiring two-day trip down the coast of Washington, Oregon and California, I finally arrived in San Diego on a warm spring evening to begin hospital corps school. I had never been in this part of the world, and was totally enthralled with such things as palm trees and warm weather after the cold and snow of Idaho. Balboa Park, a large and lush location containing a grand outdoor amphitheater and buildings constructed for the Panama-California Exposition of 1915-1916, had been taken over by the navy at the start of the war to be used as a hospital corps school. Adjacent to the San Diego Naval Hospital, this location would be my home for the next six weeks.

As I stood with my gear waiting to be assigned to quarters on the grounds of the park, I had a most singular and exciting experience. Suddenly I heard the unmistakable strains of the "Toccata" from the fifth organ symphony of Widor emanating from the stage of the large amphitheater. Totally enraptured, I began to walk toward the amphitheater, without bothering even to report to the officer in charge where I was going. I was dumbfounded to see a fine organist performing on a large, four-manual Austin pipe organ. But what really struck me as unique, was that the entire instrument stood out in the open. It was the famous outdoor pipe organ of seventy-two ranks in the Spreckels Organ Pavilion, the only one of its kind in the world. As things eventually developed, I was later to become a featured performer on this very instrument, though at the time I would never have imagined such a possibility in my wildest dreams!

Upon graduation from hospital corps school in June, I was promoted to the rank of "Hospital Corpsman 2nd Class," transferred to the naval hospital and assigned to ward duty, in order to acquire practical experience in nursing. The work of tending to the needs of severely injured navy and marine corps personnel made a deep impression on me. I was on duty early each day in wards where I took dozens of TPR's (Temperature, Pulse and Respiration), assisted patients in casts with their bodily functions, and had the opportunity to observe complex operations from the comfort of windowed amphitheaters.

We were allowed fairly liberal opportunities to go into downtown San Diego, and one day I ventured into a music store downtown and saw an announcement of a piano recital. I attended the recital, and heard a number of young pianists, a few of whom were rather gifted. The teacher who presented the young artists was a man by the name of Arthur Fraser, a short, slight, rather elegantly attired man with a wispy moustache whom I judged to be about sixty years old. After the recital, I introduced myself and inquired as to whether he might take me as a student. He was happy to accept me, but only with the understanding that the lessons were to be free of charge. It was, he explained, his way of supporting the war effort and in appreciation of the work of our armed forces. Later I discovered that he and my teacher in Sioux Falls, J. Earl Lee, both had studied in Chicago with Phillip Manual and Gavin Williamson, two highly respected piano, organ and harpsichord teachers.

Mr. Fraser was a most gracious teacher, soon allowing me to have a key to his studio so that I might have a private place to practice in the evening. Up to this time, I had had to use pianos at the various USO clubs in town, where I was constantly interrupted in my practice by servicemen asking me to play pop tunes, jazz, old classical chestnuts, and other pieces I considered "beneath me." I was a bit of a snob! On the inside front cover of my copy of the Haydn D major piano concerto, which I was studying with Fraser, I printed the following notice to those who interrupted my practicing: "I DO NOT KNOW HOW TO PLAY SWING, JASS [sic!], BOOGIE-WOOGIE, STRAUSS WALTZES, SEMI-CLASSICS, THE C# MINOR PRELUDE OR RUSTLES OF SPRING. I'M HERE TO PRACTICE, NOT ENTERTAIN, *SO PLEASE LEAVE ME ALONE.*"

Another person who provided me with many hours of delightful musical experiences was Gordon Stafford. He and his wife had one of the largest record collections I'd ever seen, and often invited service personnel to their home to listen to chamber music, symphonies and the concerto literature on a really high-quality audio system. They lived halfway down a mountainside at the very end of the streetcar line, in a delightful home which looked out on a lush valley. I became a regular visitor to their home, where I heard the middle and late Beethoven quartets for the first time. Becoming acquainted with this literature made an enormous impression on me, and I found my interest in chamber music growing.

I first had the opportunity to play the Spreckels Organ in Balboa Park toward the end of June. In the middle of July the chaplain's assistant of the hospital was shipped out to overseas duty, and I was approached about the possibility of transferring to the office to replace him. So now, having been unable to achieve an assignment as a chaplain's assistant during boot camp, I now found myself assigned to the very office I had so hoped to occupy. But the best was yet to come: One of the weekly duties of the chaplain's assistant was to perform a Sunday afternoon recital on the outdoor organ in Balboa Park! I was delirious with joy and excitement, and could hardly believe my good fortune.

Shortly after my inaugural recital on the great four-manual Austin, I was a guest in the home of Gordon Stafford, where we were having a delightful evening of music and good conversation. Among those present was a sprightly, middle-aged woman by the name of Constance Herreshoff, who was introduced to me as the music critic of the *San Diego Union*. Upon hearing of my recent "debut" at the Spreckels Organ Pavilion, she became interested in doing a feature story on this eighteen-year-old lad who was playing recitals on the organ. I was asked to come down to the newspaper where my photo was taken and I was interviewed by Miss Herreshoff. On Sunday, July 23, 1944, the headline of the lead story on the music page of the *San Diego Union* proclaimed: "Navy Man Gives Sunday Recitals on Park Organ." This was followed by a long feature article and my photograph.

On the same day on which this article appeared, there was to be a concert of the LaJolla Musical Arts Society. Featuring the celebrated American harpsichordist Ralph Kirkpatrick, who was to

PAGE TWO—C   San Diego Union   THE

Navy Man Gives Sunday Recitals on Park Organ

By CONSTANCE HERRESHOFF

Franklin S. Miller, h.a. 2c, offered his services to the U. S. navy when he finished high school last January. Two days after he received his diploma he left his home in Sioux Falls, S. D., for a boot camp. He is now posted in the chaplain's office in the Naval hospital. Part of his new duty will be to play a concert at the Balboa park organ Sunday afternoons at 2 o'clock. He began his series last Sunday and is all set for another concert today. These concerts are given for members of the service and their guests.

Miller is 18. He plays organ, piano, and tympani. When not serving as assistant organist in the Episcopal church at home he sang tenor in the choir. He studied piano and harmony, while attending high school, at Augustana college in Sioux Falls, and played tympani in the college orchestra.

GOING TO BUY INSTRUMENT

After the war, Miller is going to buy a harpsichordist. He has a picture of the harpsichord he is going to buy for $400 from John Challis, the Stradivarius of American harpsichord makers. Challis has his workshop in Ypsilanti, Mich. He is a pupil of Arnold Dolmetsch, player and maker of instruments of old types.

Miller has picked out the smallest one-manual harpsichord C h a l l i s makes. Later Miller plans to have one of the $2700 Challis models with two manuals and eight pedals. Miller already has a nice collection of harpsichord music and records. He is eagerly looking forward to hearing Kirkpatrick play the harpsichord in the Musical Arts concert this afternoon. Miller admires Kirkpatrick's recordings and says he "wouldn't miss his concert for anything."

PARTIAL TO BACH

When Miller gets his own harpsichord he is going to specialize in the music of Bach, D. Scarlatti, Purcell, Couperin and Rameau. He considers Bach "the high point in all music," and Mozart a close second. Miller became interested in the harpsichord and its literature through his piano teacher, J. Earl Lee, who is a friend of Challis.

At home, Miller was very active in a chamber music group composed of high school and college students. They were happy for hours at a time playing quartets of music for larger groups, such as Corelli's "Christmas Concerto." The conductor of the local symphony liked playing with this group so much that he has reorganized it as the Sioux Falls Chamber Music society.

When Miller was 10, his father gave him a little reed organ which he was allowed to play to his heart's content in the family garage. There is quite an art to reed organ playing, he says. You must forget your feet while using your hands and, above all, keep your shoulders still while pumping with your feet.

Music is Miller's big interest, but he also likes medicine, philosophy, psychology and newspaper work. When very young he was the business manager of the South Side

FRANKLIN S. MILLER.
. . . wants to be harpsichordist.

Feature story from the San Diego Union, Sunday, July 23, 1944. Notice the typographical error: "After the war, Miller is going to buy a harpsichordist...." (Who: Kirkpatrick, Landowska, Pessl, Ehlers??)

Feature story from the San Diego Union, Sunday, July 23, 1944. Notice the typographical error: "After the war, Miller is going to buy a harpsichordist..." (Who: Kirkpatrick, Landowska, Pessl, Ehlers??)

play the Haydn D major concerto, and some Mozart violin sonatas with Alexander Schneider, who had recently resigned as second violinist of the Budapest String Quartet to begin a performing partnership with Kirkpatrick. The program was to conclude with the Beethoven Quartet in F major, Opus 59. no. 1, the first of the so-called "Rasumovsky" quartets dedicated by the composer to the Russian ambassador in Vienna. Even to this day, any time I hear that lovely opening cello line, I conjure up memories of my time in San Diego and of the concert where I first heard the work:

I attended the concert, and with my photo appearing in the paper that day, was recognized by many of the concert goers, who asked whether I might like to meet the two artists. After the concert, I was ushered to the backstage area and introduced to both men, who were most gracious, though I'm sure they must have felt a little miffed to have been upstaged by a mere eighteen-year-old navy hospital corps-man as the lead story in the music section of the local paper that day!

One morning in August, as I worked in the chaplain's office, an urgent phone call was received from the commandant's office to the effect that there would be a world famous visitor arriving at the naval hospital in just two hours. This person was to address the assembled patients, doctors, corpsmen and other service personnel at the outdoor amphitheater in Balboa Park. Her name: Eleanor Roosevelt, the First Lady!

As her imminent arrival was completely unexpected, and no advance publicity had been prepared, it now became my task to get over to the great organ in the amphitheater and begin playing appropriate selections, in the hopes of drumming up an audience for Mrs. Roosevelt. I arrived at the Spreckels Organ Pavilion, had the great iron curtain covering the pipes rolled up by the custodian, and started to perform. My playing began to attract a crowd, and within thirty minutes a rather sizable audience had gathered, having been, in the meantime, informed that the First Lady was on her way.

Presently, an entourage of limousines containing secret service personnel and the top brass of the naval hospital appeared. Mrs. Roosevelt was introduced and spoke glowingly of the great work, sacrifices and dedication of the men and women of the armed forces. At the conclusion of her short speech, the audience was invited to sing the national anthem, and I accompanied the stirring rendition with as much enthusiasm as possible. At the conclusion of the singing, and as she was preparing to leave the stage, Eleanor Roosevelt stepped to the organ console, leaned over and, with her characteristic toothy smile, exclaimed: "You played very well, young man!" I was tremendously honored and thrilled, though I could have recommended an excellent orthodontist to her for that severe overbite!

Other enormously gratifying musical experiences are a part of my memories of my stay at the San Diego Naval Hospital. I had learned that there was a symphony orchestra in the city whose members were all in the armed forces. It should be remembered that, in addition to the naval hospital, there was a Marine Corps base and an army base within twenty miles of San Diego. Altogether there may have been as many as 25,000 armed services personnel in the area. A young, highly gifted and extremely energetic conductor had conceived the idea of forming a "Servicemen's Symphony Orchestra" consisting of professional musicians who were now in the service and stationed in the area.

The conductor's name was Frederick Fennell. Fennell later went on to a brilliant conducting career, as the founder of the Eastman Wind Ensemble, a popular clinician and guest conductor of major American orchestras. Fennell was, without question, the most charismatic conductor I had ever seen. His stick technique was superb, and his knowledge of the scores infallible. I regularly attended the rehearsals of the Servicemen's Symphony Orchestra, which took place in a large auditorium which had been converted into sleeping quarters for servicemen on leave, to enable them to stay off base until required to report back. Sitting on the empty bunks, I thoroughly enjoyed the excellent playing of such people as the DeTullio brothers, violinist and cellist, who had been members of the Los Angeles Philharmonic, or of the principal violist of the Pittsburgh Symphony. I well remember the wonderful concerts the orchestra gave, during which I became acquainted with ever more literature: Elgar's "Enigma Variations," the Handel Concerto Grosso, Opus 6, no. 10, Deems Taylor's Suite "Through the Looking Glass," and Paul White's "Five Miniatures" (originally piano pieces). I particularly remember a memorable performance of the orchestra at the Naval Hospital. They played outdoors, in a kind of courtyard, surrounded by three stories of wards of severely injured servicemen. The patients, many in body casts or with crutches, listened intently to the concert. At the end of each selection, instead of applause, I heard the eerie sound of crutches being rattled between the metal slats of the gratings surrounding the courtyard!

I regret to report, however, that the delightful and exciting days of studying piano with Arthur Fraser, listening to the Servicemen's Symphony Orchestra directed by Frederick Fennell, serving as chaplain's assistant at the naval hospital, and playing organ recitals on the outdoor organ in Balboa Park, were soon to come to an untimely and abrupt end.

The armed forces have always had rather strict regulations regarding the appearance of its members: clean shaven, shined shoes, hair cut short, trousers freshly pressed and clothes immaculately clean. To ensure that this tradition continued, weekly examinations, called "Captain's Inspection," were regularly held. I had apparently not taken too much notice of the length of my hair. After all, was I not a "long-haired musician"? One day I appeared for a Captain's Inspection, which took place, I later ruefully recalled, in the amphitheater right in front of the stage where I played the organ recitals. Though at the time I didn't give it much thought, it seemed as though the captain conducting the inspection took an inordinate amount of time examining my hair. The yeoman accompanying him then instructed me to get my hair cut as soon as possible. I took care of the order and thought nothing more of the incident.

About ten days later, standing in line waiting to enter the mess hall for a noon meal, one of my fellow barracks mates pointed to a list posted on a bulletin board and called out to me: "Hey, Miller,

41

looks like you're being shipped out!" Incredulous, I read the notice carefully. Yes, it was true, I had been transferred to combat duty, and was to report to Terminal Island, San Pedro, California, for assignment to the USS BUTTE, APA68 (Auxiliary Personnel Assault), a troop transport! My entire world came crashing down upon me as I realized that my idyllic existence in the chaplain's office at the naval hospital was about to end. In spite of attempts by the head chaplain on the base, a friendly Irish priest, to rescind the order, my fate had been sealed. It was because my hair was too long, I later learned.

As the USS BUTTE was still in the process of being built by Consolidated Steel in the shipyards at Wilmington, California, I was temporarily assigned to duty on the base as a typist. I spent each day stamping out dog tags on a large machine with a typewriter keyboard. The work was not too demanding, and shore leave was relatively generous. I often caught the PE (Pacific Electric), an interurban streetcar which ran from Long Beach into downtown Los Angeles, and availed myself of a number of excellent musical opportunities. My somewhat boorish fellow Navy comrades would sometimes ask what I was going to do on liberty. "Hey, Miller, you gonna find some broad and get laid?", they would inquire. "Why, no," I would answer, "Heifitz is doing the Beethoven concerto with the Los Angeles Philharmonic and I'm going to the concert." Such retorts always provoked a puzzled look.

Without question, one of the most impressive events I attended was a performance of the Bach B Minor Mass at the First Congregational Church. I had only heard the work on records, and the effect of a live performance on me was so intense and overwhelming that I wept through the entire opening "Kyrie."

Another musical experience, however, was not nearly as pleasant, though just as unforgettable. Artur Rubinstein was slated to play the Brahms 2nd Piano Concerto with the Los Angeles Philharmonic, Alfred Wallenstein conducting. Apparently, I had had something to eat at dinner, which was not agreeing with me at all, and as the concerto progressed, I felt myself becoming sicker and sicker. At the end of the slow, lyrical third movement, during an exquisitely soft passage in the solo cello and with delicate arpeggios in the piano part, I could no longer restrain myself, and committed the ultimate indiscretion: I began to vomit violently all over the aisle in the balcony where I was sitting! I hastened to the men's toilet where I continued to throw up. I never did hear the last movement, quickly returning to the base, where I ended up in sickbay for two days with an acute case of ptomaine poisoning.

Some five years later, as a student in Chicago, I took a job as an usher at Orchestra Hall. One evening Rubinstein played a solo recital at the hall. The entrance to the stage door in the basement was just across from the ushers' dressing room, and the pianist came past this door on his way out, with a woman on one arm and a cigar in his mouth. He stopped for a minute to greet the guard and a couple of ushers. I stepped up, shook his hand, congratulated him on his recital that night, and asked: "Sir, do you remember, about five years ago, when you performed the 2nd Brahms Concerto with Wallenstein and the Los Angeles Philharmonic?" He recalled the occasion, and I asked, "Do you remember what happened at the end of the slow movement?" He eyed me suspiciously and then exploded in laughter. In his slight, mellifluous Polish/German accent he snorted, "Vas dat you, jung man?" I could only nod yes; he turned on his heel and walked out. I didn't even have the opportunity to apologize for spoiling those last few measures of the third movement of the Brahms concerto!

One final musical experience in the Los Angeles area remains one of my fondest memories. I had the immense thrill of seeing a ballet performance in the Hollywood Bowl of Stravinsky's "Petrushka," with the composer conducting! All these wonderful experiences, I reminded myself repeatedly, would never have been possible, had it not been for my service in the navy, with the opportunity to travel to distant places and experience all kinds of music for the first time.

This was soon to end, as I settled down to a life of shipboard routine, a lengthy period of intense combat duty, emotional and physical hardship as a hospital corpsman and times of over-whelming fear and dread. For the next year I was to be involved in some of the most harrowing experiences I had ever known.

Shortly before I was to report to the USS BUTTE, I was attending a welcoming party on the base for the crew of the ship, in which we had an opportunity to become acquainted with other men with whom we were to share close quarters for over a year. As I stood around munching *hors d'oeuvres* and sipping a soft drink, I clearly heard someone whistling a theme from the second movement of Shostakovich's Fifth Symphony:

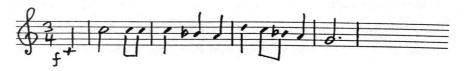

Who, I asked myself, could possibly know that piece of music here, in this crowd of sailors? I answered the first half of the tune, by whistling its conclusion:

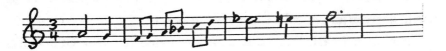

A young sailor walked up to me and smiling, said, "Did you just whistle the Shostakovich Fifth?" I answered in the affirmative, and we immediately began to discuss music together. Mozart, Bach, Beethoven, Brahms, Schubert and other composers names tumbled forth as we animatedly compared notes on our favorites. David Buckley was from Chicago, and was a fellow crewmember assigned to the USS BUTTE. He was in the signalman group, whose station was high up on the topside of the ship. There the men used flags and lights to communicate with other ships nearby. David, or as I soon came to call him, "Buck," was a constant friend during our many months on the Pacific Ocean, and we often spent time listening to the few records I had managed to bring aboard ship. For the better part of six months I had exactly four albums of music to my name: the first volume of the Brandenburg Concertos (1, 2, and 3) and the G minor unaccompanied violin sonata of Bach (BWV 1001), the *Grosse Fuge* (Opus 133), and C# minor string quartet (Opus 131) of Beethoven. In addition I had some keyboard music, including the complete *Art of the Fugue* of Bach, sections of which I occasionally played for Buckley on a small, portable reed organ which was stored in the "Brig" (prison). There was also an upright piano in the officers' mess, just in front of the ship sickbay on which I was able to practice a few times. (I learned the opening *Praeambulum* from the Bach Partita no. 5 [BWV 829] there in a couple of practice sessions, but had little chance to do much more practicing, particularly after we entered combat zones.)

The U.S.S. BUTTE was commissioned on November 22, 1944, and we went aboard her for "shakedown" cruises in the Pacific Ocean off of San Pedro and Long Beach. The skipper of our ship, Commander J.A. Gillis, was a grizzled, no-nonsense former merchant marine captain, about sixty-five years old, tall, gaunt, and thin as a rail. I considered him to be highly competent, with nerves of steel. His young executive officer, a lieutenant commander, was a regular navy officer, straight as a string and quite personable. The well-worn phrase "it's a small world" became particularly apropos when I discovered that the navigation officer of the ship, a lieutenant, junior grade, was none other than my former physical education teacher at Washington High School! He was the only person I ever met in the navy who also came from Sioux Falls, and we served together for the entire time I was aboard ship.

The ship's medical personnel consisted of two doctors, a dentist and fifteen hospital corpsmen, the normal complement for a troop transport of our size, and included a registered pharmacist and lab technician, as well other corpsmen with specialties such as the operating room, anesthesia and X-ray. At this time I also took the exam for promotion to Hospital Corpsman, First Class. Most of the corpsmen shared quarters in a room approximately eight feet by twelve feet, with four high bunk beds, and lockers at the end of the room for our possessions. The chief medical officer was a highly competent, older doctor in his mid-fifties with the rank of commander, and the second physician, a young, newly commissioned lieutenant junior grade, was a recent medical school graduate of Italian parentage, dark and handsome, a bit hot-headed, but concientious and a fine physician and surgeon.

On January 5, 1945, the USS BUTTE departed San Diego, having picked up a large contingent of marines, bound for Hawaii. Because of my typing abilities, I again found myself handling most

U.S.S. BUTTE (APA 68)
For some unknown reason, the designation here is given as "PA".
At the rear can be seen two twin forty-millimeter gun emplace-
ments. The ship looks like it could use a good paint job.

47

of the clerical duties for the "H" division, including the ubiquitous "morning report," which I dutifully delivered each day to the ship's office and the captain. We arrived in Honolulu on approximately January 15, where the marine troops disembarked. Many remains of the destruction inflicted by the Japanese attack on Pearl Harbor on December 7, 1941, were still in evidence.

One day, while the ship was tied up in Hawaii, we were surprised to learn that we were about to take on an additional eighteen hospital corpsmen and seven additional doctors. We wondered why it was necessary to provide us with all the additional medical personnel, until it was explained that the BUTTE had been designated an "auxiliary hospital ship" and, in addition to its duties as a troop transport, we would remove injured personnel to base hospitals. (The specialty of one of our newly assigned physicians was obstetrics, which seemed to us a bit far afield for our needs!) We also took on another contingent of troops in Hawaii.

On my nineteenth birthday, January 17, 1945, we departed from Hawaii, stopping en route at Eniwetok, in the Marshall Islands, on our way to the Marianas and certain combat duty with invasion forces. The United States was now steadily beating back the Japanese all across the central Pacific Ocean, having already secured the Marshall and Caroline Islands, as well as Saipan. On Saipan, airfields were being constructed to allow B-29s to launch attacks on Japan, and as we sat at anchor in the harbor there, we would often observe dozens of the planes departing for bombing runs on the Japanese mainland. However, because these bases were so distant many of the bombers were unable to return safely, and a closer location was urgently sought.

One thousand miles to the north lay the island of Iwo Jima, a tiny, volcanic spot with strategic airfields, less than 650 miles from the Japanese mainland. After a bloody campaign, beginning on February 19, in which 6,800 marines lost their lives, Iwo Jima was secured on March 16. Many of the marines whom we had transported to Hawaii were doubtless among those killed or wounded in this bloody assault, and we were certain that we ourselves had missed being a part of this invasion force by only a few weeks. We now began to prepare and train for the invasion of Okinawa, the southernmost island of the Japanese empire. During these training exercises, I was stationed, with a first-aid pack, life jacket and helmet at a battle station located a short distance below the signalmen's battle station topside. Often, as I stood there, I would hear my friend Buckley whistle the opening of the second movement of the Beethoven quartet opus.59, no.1:

to which I would answer:

We even learned how to whistle a section in two part counterpoint from the slow movement of the "Eroica" Symphony of Beethoven:

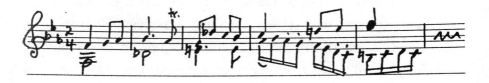

Whistling these bits of music seemed somehow to give us strength and calm our nerves in what was to become our greatest test of endurance in the face of over-whelming danger and fearful stresses, and even now, over fifty years later, the memories of these experiences brings a rush of adrenaline and a cold sweat!

***

On Easter Sunday, April 1, 1945, at 3:45 a.m., general quarters sounded on the USS BUTTE, signaling the beginning of the Okinawa invasion. Our ship was a part of Task Force 58, consisting of over 1,300 ships and 287,000 men. It has been estimated that this invasion force was the largest ever assembled, surpassing even that of the Normandy invasion. The entire operation was complicated by the lack of any substantial mainland supply bases; we were thousands of miles from San Francisco and even Pearl Harbor. The BUTTE carried over 700 marines for the assault on the southwestern shore of Okinawa.

While large machines located on the rear of the ships poured out enormous clouds of white smoke in order to disguise our positions from the air, thousands of army and marine troops disembarked from a huge flotilla of landing craft launched from the hundreds of troop transports massed together for a distance of eight miles in the harbor. Dozens of these landing craft passed beneath our ship en route to the beach where certain death and injury awaited many aboard them. The fourteen-and sixteen-inch guns of ten battleships, including the mighty *Missouri, New Mexico, Wisconsin* and *Mississippi*, and heavy cruisers such as the *St. Louis* and the *Indianapolis*, pounded the hills above the beaches. The sound of their guns was indescribable; we felt the concussions throughout our entire bodies. Shock waves created by the guns' discharge caused the water in front of the ships to boil. The invasion forces encountered only minimal resistance, and by nightfall of the first day of the invasion over 50,000 troops had been put ashore on the beaches.

The following days were strangely quiet, until the morning of April 6, when the first of a series of fanatical suicide attacks by hundreds of Japanese aircraft, the dreaded "kamikaze" (Japanese for "divine wind") were launched against us. As the task force's greatest advantage, its mobility, could not be utilized because we were supporting the invasion and taking on injured troops from the beaches, we were forced to absorb over 1,465 of these attacks over the next few weeks, in which the Japanese pilots deliberately crashed their planes into our ships, which were anchored almost like sitting ducks in the harbor. On several occasions I watched in horror as a kamikaze pilot aimed his plane at one of our ships, and attempted to crash into it. The enormous amount of "flak" thrown up by the ships in the harbor, as they fired a variety of guns at the incoming planes, was simply indescribable.

One afternoon, at a time when we were not even at general quarters, I happened to look up into the sky and noticed a Japanese Zero silently diving toward our ship. It crashed into the ocean less than 2,000 feet off our starboard bow. "GENERAL QUARTERS" immediately sounded and we began firing our twin forty-millimeter antiaircraft guns at the attacking planes. We had four or five gun emplacements, plus a single five-inch gun on our rear deck. The blazing firepower of all the ships in the harbor firing at the incoming planes was deafening, and in the confusion there were instances in which American gunners, in their eagerness to down the enemy pilots, mistakenly hit our own planes. In one instance, one of the pilots, gravely injured, was brought to our ship for treatment, only to die while being attended by doctors and corpsmen.

We also knew, although we were constantly under attack, that the real heroes of this operation were the long lines of destroyers and destroyer escorts which operated at the periphery of the invasion fleets on so-called "picket" duty, often as far away as seventy miles out in the ocean. Their job was to warn the task force of the incoming "bogies," Japanese planes, by spotting them on their radar and flashing the alert to those of us in the harbor. Often, however, the planes would come in so low that they could not be picked up on radar. These ships were the ones that were attacked first, and the crews suffered staggering losses. In addition to the loss of the destroyers *Bush* and *Calhoun,* four other ships were sunk and nine other destroyers, four destroyer escorts and five mine vessels were damaged. The ships which had been hit by the kamikaze pilots reported a total of 94 killed, 264 wounded and 178 missing.

We began to take on severely wounded army, navy and marine corps personnel with various types of injuries. The officer's mess had been converted into a large triage area, where the boats bringing in the injured were hoisted to the deck, stretchers brought into the room, and doctors performed their initial examinations. Within six days the troop compartments were filled with hundreds of wounded men, lying in iron bunk beds stacked three and four high. All of the corpsmen worked hard at keeping the wounded comfortable and in comparatively little pain. At one point, I recall tending to the wounded for almost twenty-four hours straight, without sitting down or taking a break. My fellow corpsmen did as much, and when I was finally persuaded to take a short nap, I fell asleep, not awakening for six hours.

On the morning of April 14, as I stood in the "head" (navy terminology for "toilet") relieving myself, the loudspeaker above me blared: "Now hear this, now hear this: President Franklin Roosevelt died yesterday from a stroke. Harry Truman has been sworn in as President." The man who had led the United States out of the depths of the Great Depression, into recovery, and through the first years of World War II was now gone, at the relatively young age of sixty-three. The other momentous event occurred on May 10, when the official surrender of Germany was announced. It was V-E day, and we were jubilant! If only we could bring the Pacific conflict to an end soon.

53

On about April 15, the USS BUTTE departed Okinawa with 165 badly wounded men, most of whom were in body casts. We were part of a convoy of auxiliary hospital ships and troop transports protected by destroyers and destroyer escorts which made their way to Saipan to deliver the wounded to base hospitals there. We also visited the islands of Ulithi, the Palaus, Leyte and Guam.

At the beginning of June we began the long trip back to Pearl Harbor with another large contingent of wounded numbering over 650 men, many in body casts. Although the war was still being fought in the area around Okinawa, the central Pacific was now considered relatively safe, and troop transports began to sail without accompanying destroyer escorts. Late one evening during our trip back to Hawaii, I happened to come down into the mess hall for a break from nursing duties in the wards, to get a cup of coffee. I was met by a man who had just come off duty on the bridge, who told us something that struck fear in me.

Word had just been received that another troop transport, traveling alone some miles ahead of us, had radioed that they had detected the presence of a Japanese submarine, which had launched a torpedo, and though it missed the ship, its wake was seen in front of their bow! If this report were true, then we might also soon be under attack. How, I thought, would it ever be possible to save and evacuate some 650 injured men, many in body casts, crammed into our holds? The next few hours were incredibly suspenseful, however by daybreak we were obviously out of danger, and the following day pulled into Pearl Harbor where we unloaded all of our patients, including three or four bodies of men who had died during the trip.

Now began a joyous trip to the mainland. The USS BUTTE had been ordered to San Francisco, and we were awarded thirty days' leave before reporting back to the ship in Seattle, Washington. What a glorious sight it was to come steaming under the beautiful Golden Gate Bridge and into San Francisco harbor on that bright, sunny morning of June 18!

The thirty days of leave passed quickly, and I again set out for the coast, boarding a local at the Milwaukee station which traveled north to Aberdeen, South Dakota, where I was to make connections with the Empire Builder to Seattle. As I stood on the platform waiting to board the train a familiar voice greeted me. It was Buckley, traveling on the same train, which was coming from Chicago. In the meantime, he had picked up a few more records, as had I, so that now we could augment our meager collection with the Schubert C major Quintet, Opus 163, a Mozart quartet and later, the Brahms clarinet quintet, a copy of which we purchased in a Seattle record store. The USS BUTTE sailed from Seattle to Hawaii the middle of July, and once more we steamed back into Okinawa harbor the first of August for more combat duty. In the meantime, I had also received a promotion to the rank of Pharmacist's Mate, Third Class.

By this time most of the fighting in our area was over, although we did experience occasional attacks by the kamikaze planes. Organized Japanese resistance on Okinawa had ended already in June, and by the middle of July a major offensive was underway against Japan in preparation for the invasion of Kyusu in

November and the main island of Japan, Honshu, scheduled for March 1, 1946. This final assault was to involve three different armies and supporting echelons from all major bases in the Pacific, as well as the West Coast of the United States. The invasion would never take place.

On Monday, August 6, a lone B-29, piloted by Col. Paul W. Tibbets, Jr., flying from Saipan, appeared over the Japanese city of Hiroshima at 8:15 AM, and dropped the first atomic bomb, wiping out 4.7 square miles of the city and killing or injuring 71,000 people. Three days later, a second bomb was dropped on Nagasaki. We were informed of this new secret weapon only in the most general terms, and one of our corpsmen, a college graduate with a good scientific education, explained, as best he could, the basic principle involved in this deadly new bomb.

On the morning of August 14, the news was flashed to us over the loudspeakers on board ship: "Now hear this, now hear this, the Japanese government has accepted the terms of surrender for ending the war." But, less than five minutes later the loudspeakers squawked again: "Now hear this, NOW HEAR THIS, ALL HANDS MAN YOUR BATTLE STATIONS, GENERAL QUARTERS, THIS IS NOT A DRILL, ALL HANDS MAN YOUR BATTLE STATIONS, GENERAL QUARTERS!" We were still at war, obviously someone had not yet gotten the word. Although this session of general quarters was of short duration, we had an additional two or three alarms in the next few days, until the situation stabilized and finally all armed resistance ceased. On September 2 the Japanese signed the terms of surrender aboard the battleship *Missouri* in Tokyo Bay.

We were certain that from now on, all would be peaceful and we would soon be on our way back to the States. Many were already looking forward to receiving that famous piece of paper called a "discharge." But it was not to be for several more months, and in the events which soon followed, we were to find ourselves in as much, if not greater, danger than we had thus far experienced.

In the middle of September, we were caught in the midst of an intense, extremely dangerous typhoon which had hit the East China Sea and was bearing down on all the ships of the task force. A typhoon in the Pacific is the same storm as the more familiar hurricane in the Atlantic or Caribbean. We were ordered to weigh anchor and put out to sea, facing into the wind.

For hours our ship was hammered by huge waves which threatened to capsize us at any moment. As the bow of the ship lifted, one could look straight ahead and see nothing but the sky, and then, when the bow came crashing down into the trough of the wave, all one saw was a wall of water which inundated the bow of the ship. As the ship hit the bottom of the wave she shuddered almost as if in pain. We hoped the keel would hold together despite all this punishment. The fury of the wind whipping rigging away, and anything else not securely tied down, was never ending; eating and sleeping were almost impossible; we were tossed about as if we were rag dolls, and scores of sailors became seasick. (I considered myself lucky that I suffered only a little minor discomfort. Luckily we no longer had injured personnel on board.)

On October 9, barely three weeks after the first one, we were hit by yet another typhoon, which, because of complications, was even more dangerous than the first. Once more we were ordered to sea, instructed to drop anchor and try to remain headed into the wind. Incidentally, the reason for this procedure is to avoid getting into the huge troughs of waves and capsizing. In many cases smaller ships, such as the top-heavy destroyers and destroyer escorts, were lost under such conditions. Again, sleeping and eating were almost impossible as we tried desperately to ride out the typhoon. Although the typhoon seemed to be subsiding a bit after a day or two, the seas remained very rough.

Suddenly, one day, we had the unmistakable sensation that our engines were no longer running. It was true: Salt water had somehow gotten into our engines, making them useless. We were dead in the water and drifting, totally at the mercy of the storm and perhaps in danger of capsizing! Soon, however, another danger presented itself. It was determined by the navigation division, that we were drifting at about five knots an hour, right toward a minefield, and could conceivably hit one and go down in the storm! Topside, radio operators were frantically trying to get a portable emergency radio to function, in order to send out an S.O.S.

The tension on board was extreme, everyone waiting for the imminent explosion and certain death by drowning in the frigid waters and churning ocean. Hours passed and still we waited. Finally, the next day, the skies began to lift, the seas became calm and we emerged from the minefield, still drifting, but now relatively safe, though still lost at sea. Another twelve hours passed, and the heroic staff of the engineering division finally got one of our engines going again. (We had twin rudders and propellers.) We were finally able to get underway again and limped into Manila, where repairs to the ship enabled us to continue on a number of missions in the Far East.

As I reflect upon what I have recounted here about my experiences during the Okinawa invasion and the typhoons of that fall, of the dreaded, unspoken fear which gripped me and my shipmates during these unbelievable and indescribable times, I marvel at our ability to somehow relegate such terrifying life experiences into the realm of our subconscious. I had given only the most cursory thought to these experiences until I began to write this autobiography. My life seems, somehow, to have been lived with little or no consideration or reflection given to the extraordinary events which formed such an indelible part of some two years of my existence.

Now, thinking through my experiences of fifty years ago, I find myself somehow strangely moved. My life, and the lives of many millions of people, have been changed by what we have experienced. Living such experiences can only make one extremely grateful and appreciative of the life around him: family, loved ones, material comforts and professional success throughout one's life. Such qualities should never be taken for granted.

One is reminded of the ghastly, unspeakable horror suffered by German civilians in the great fire raids of Hamburg and Dresden, of the inhuman suffering of Jews in the concentration camps, of the indescribable suffering of soldiers, sailors and air force personnel during the Korean, Vietnam and Gulf War conflicts.

The sense of self-preservation must evidently be so strong in the human spirit that we continue to summon the strength and the will to survive, which allow us to move ahead in our lives without succumbing, as the result of these experiences, to permanent despair, depression and even the will to live.

Toward the middle of November, we were sent to Manila, in the Philippines, and we again received shore leave to explore this fascinating city. I found the famous bamboo organ there, all pipes were made of bamboo, and managed to play it for a few minutes. Another interesting experience was discovering the rehearsal hall of the Manila Philharmonic, which was, at that time, just beginning to function again. The conductor of the orchestra was Herbert Zipper, a well-known and respected German, who later became affiliated with a music conservatory in Winnetka, Illinois, and lived in the Chicago area for many years.

Finally, in December, we departed from Manila for a long trip back to the West Coast, stopping along the way at Guam and Hawaii. We arrived back at Terminal Island, San Pedro, where we had originally boarded ship, on December 18, 1945. We were now back in the States, and our return to civilian life appeared to be just a few months away. Some of the crew were given leave at this time, in order to get home for Christmas, though I was one among a number of the men who opted to stay aboard ship for the holidays and take our thirty days' leave later. However, before anyone of us was able to depart on leave, a group of high-level navy brass gathered the entire crew in one of the large holds to present us with what they thought would be an attractive offer which we could not refuse.

It seems that the BUTTE had been designated as part of new Task Force 1, which was to be involved in Operation "Crossroads," a series of experimental missions meant to test and examine the effects of atomic bomb explosions on ships. These tests would begin in June of the following year at Kwajalein, in the Marshall Islands, and a crew would be needed to sail the BUTTE to the location.

One can imagine the enthusiasm and excitement which greeted this generous offer, especially as such a commitment would have involved an additional three-year "hitch" in the navy. The majority of us said, "Thanks, but no thanks."

On February 23, 1946, after I had been reassigned and already left her, the BUTTE was ordered to Pearl Harbor and then to the atomic test area, where she was subjected to atomic bombing, and survived. Afterward she "was retained for structural and radiation study at Kwajalein until 12 May 1948, when she was disposed of by sinking," as it is laconically recorded in the pages of the *Dictionary of American Naval Fighting Ships*, volume 2, pp. 182-183.

After receiving two leaves, I was finally ordered to report to Great Lakes Naval Training Station for temporary duty and eventual discharge. I arrived there around March 20. During my free time, I usually traveled to Chicago, about forty-five minutes away on the North Shore electric line. The so-called "Skokie Valley" route of the North Shore entered Chicago at Howard Street, and ran on the elevated structures into the "Loop." Chicago fascinated me. I had never ridden on an elevated train, and thought it was interesting to be able to look into people's apartments from the windows of the train. Little did I know that in less than two years, I would be living here. I was always on the lookout for opportunities to hear music, and often took in concerts at Orchestra Hall.

One memorable musical experience was hearing the great Artur Schnabel for the last time. I had heard him once before in Los Angeles playing a beautiful program of chamber music, which included the G minor piano quartet of Mozart (K. 378). Schnabel played at Orchestra Hall, and I was surprised to run across my old school chum from Sioux Falls, Claire van Ausdahl, who happened to be in town. We had a pleasant reunion.

Because of my intense interest in the harpsichord, culminating in hearing and meeting Ralph Kirkpatrick, I continued looking for opportunities to meet other performers on the instrument. One weekend, I decided to visit the well-known Chicago harpsi-chordists Philip Manual and Gavin Williamson, who had been teachers of men with whom I had studied, J. Earl Lee in Sioux Falls, and Arthur Fraser in San Diego, California. Mr. Lee also had some Musicraft recordings of the Bach double and triple harpsichord concertos by them, although I found the playing a bit pedestrian.

I found the address of their studio, which was located in a lovely south side neighborhood near the University of Chicago, climbed the stairs to the house, and rang the bell. A large, somewhat overbearing black man answered the door, and asked what I wanted. I told him who I was, and that I wanted to meet the two musicians. I was admitted into the front hall, and the man (butler? handyman?) disappeared up the stairs. I looked into the large living room, and was suitably impressed at seeing two beautiful Steinway grand pianos, two large, two-manual Mandler-Schram harpsichords, and a Hammond electric "organ". Presently the officious butler reappeared and announced that the two men were "resting" and were unable to meet me. I thanked him and left quickly.

I then went over to the home of another Chicago harpsichordist, a lovely, gracious woman by the name of Dorothy Lane, who had studied at one time with the two men. The two of us talked for a short while, and I found her to be genuinely friendly and welcoming to this brash young navy man who had come calling. What I could not have known at that time was that Dorothy Lane was an excellent musician and a fine harpsichordist whom I would have the opportunity to hear less than two years later in a superb performance of French harpsichord music, including François Couperin's delightful *Les Fastes de la Grande et Ancienne Ménéstrendise* at Kimball Hall in Chicago. I also heard her in 1950, during the Bach anniversary year, when she played *continuo* for a cantata series at Northwestern University in Evanston, conducted by George Howerton.

One Sunday afternoon, having stayed overnight at a USO facility in downtown Chicago, a part of what is now Roosevelt University, I was walking down Michigan Avenue, looking for a concert. I stopped at a location called the Fine Arts Building, which I thought might be a promising music venue, and entered. I immediately heard some piano playing coming from somewhere a few flights up. Following the sound, I discovered that it was coming from a music studio on the third floor. Sitting outside the studio was a shy, young girl holding one of the familiar yellow Schirmer volumes in her arm. I inquired as to what was going on in the studio. She indicated that this was the studio of Howard Wells, a well-known piano pedagogue, and that a masterclass was taking place. She said she was late in arriving, but was scheduled to perform that afternoon, and invited me to come in and listen. I was immediately taken by her friendliness and accepted her kind offer. At an appropriate moment we entered and sat down. She was presently asked to play her selection, which was the first movement of the Beethoven Sonata in E minor, Opus 90.

After the masterclass was over, the young lady, whose name was Mary Ellen Kindt, invited me to come out to her home. I had never been, as it were, picked up by a girl in my life, and assuming she lived in Chicago, I accepted. However, I was about to discover that she lived in Kenosha, Wisconsin, some sixty-miles north of Chicago, though not far from Great Lakes. The North Shore, which I took to Great Lakes, had direct service to Kenosha as well.

We took the North Shore to Kenosha and were picked up by her father at the station. Though I'm sure her father was a bit nonplussed to find his seventeen-year-old daughter alighting from the train with a sailor in tow, he said nothing as we drove to her home on 35th Street. We walked in the front door and I was introduced to her mother, a lovely, rather intense-looking woman who was a local piano teacher. In the living room were two Steinway grands, and I immediately headed for one of them and began playing, while Mary Ellen went into the kitchen with her parents. I could tell that a rather heated discussion was taking place, but paid little attention to it. A couple of weeks later, when I visited the young lady again, she confided to me that her parents were furious with her for having "picked up" a sailor. In any case, I must have redeemed myself. After a lovely dinner, I played two-piano music with both mother and daughter.

I visited at the Kindts' home several more times, and "Muffy," as she was called by her family, and I got better acquainted. On Sunday evening, May 12, I said goodbye to my new young friend, and, as we drove to the North Shore station in Kenosha, I began to whistle the opening of the Brahms 4th Symphony:

Muffy immediately answered:

And I squeezed her hand tenderly. I knew this would not be the last I was to see of her: She was a musician, a pianist, she was sweet and fun to be around, and I liked her a lot by now.

The following Thursday, May 16, I left Great Lakes on the North Shore and traveled to Milwaukee, Wisconsin. Walking down the platform from the North Shore station, I entered directly into the Union Station, where I boarded the Hiawatha for my last trip as a member of the armed forces, to Minneapolis, Minnesota, to be discharged from the navy. We were ordered to the Naval Personnel Separation Center at Wold-Chamberlin Airport, and on Friday, May 17, 1946, about 11:30 AM, Commander C.E. Austin gave us our final orders: "And now, gentlemen, turn to the man next to you, and shake his hand. You are now both civilians! Congratulations and good luck to you all!"

CHAPTER 3

A COLLEGE STUDENT IN SIOUX FALLS AND CHICAGO; CAB DRIVING IN THE "WINDY CITY" (1946-1951)

In Minneapolis, I checked into the Radisson Hotel on 7th Street Friday afternoon, May 17, and spent some time just soaking in a hot tub, luxuriating on a clean bed leisurely celebrating and enjoying myself, finally drifting off to sleep for a while. How satisfying not having to share sleeping quarters with thirty or more men. What could I do to commemorate this wonderful new freedom as a civilian? What better way than to attend a concert, but not just any concert. I had seen an announcement of a performance of the Bach B minor Mass at Northrop Auditorium on the campus of the University of Minnesota, so after a delicious meal, I hailed a cab and took it to the concert. How appropriate, I reflected, that I should be hearing, on my last day in the service, the same work which, eighteen months earlier, I had heard in Los Angeles, during my early days in the navy. I don't know when I've enjoyed anything as much as I did that performance, and, in addition, I could look forward to the prospect that, on the following day, I would be on my way home to Sioux Falls at last. I could honestly say that I had never been happier in my life.

The next day, after a quick visit with my former orthodontist, whose office was a short distance from the hotel, I boarded a bus to start the final leg of my journey home. The well-known route was like an old friend. I knew every curve in the road, every tree and farmhouse, every town we went through: Shakopee, Belle Plaine, LeSueur, St. Peter, Mankato and on through Fairmont, Worthington, and finally to Sioux Falls. It was almost nine at night before I arrived, but my family was at the station, at 11th and Main, to greet me.

On the very first weekend I was home, I unfortunately backed the car into a telephone pole putting a large dent in the trunk. I hastened to reassure my father that I would pay for the repairs, and felt bad that I had to present him with a coming home present of that nature! Most of the summer I spent just getting used to civilian life again, buying some new clothes, swimming and enjoying being with my new girl friend, "Weesie" Brumbaugh. "Weesie," her given name was, inexplicably, Maurice, was the daughter of the assistant principal of Washington High School. She was a fine musician, with a beautiful voice. She was also a double bass player as well. "Weesie" was extremely intelligent and had a delightful sense of humor. However, by fall, our "summer romance" had pretty much run its course, although we still enjoyed making music together.

I also began studying piano again with J. Earl Lee. He put me to put work on the Chopin Preludes, Opus 25 and the Bach Inventions. The plan was to learn one each per week, but unfortunately nothing much came of it, and after six weeks Lee gave up this ambitious plan and we learned other things at a more leisurely pace. Mr. Lee was to be gone for the year starting in September, so that after the lessons during the summer of 1946, I never had the opportunity to study with him again. I always regretted it.

Spring, 1947, at the Sioux Falls History Club on South Phillips Avenue. Small choral group, here being directed by Dean Arlton, left. The other singers are (standing l to r): Claire van Ausdahl, Roland Arlton, the author, Stan Arlton, Ludwig Wangberg. Women (seated l to r): "Weesie" Brumbaugh, Norma Mitchell, Elise Halvorson, LaVonne Johnson, Shirley Carls and Arlette Peterson.

I entered Augustana College in September as a music major, taking a number of academic courses such as German, history and biology as well as ear training, first-year harmony and again played tympani in the Augustana Symphony conducted by Richard

Guderyahn. I studied piano with Verona Rogness, who replaced Earl Lee while he was in the east on sabbatical.

During the winter and spring of 1946/47 a group of singers began to meet at my house for the purpose of reading through a lot of Renaissance polyphony, including what we called "madrigals." In truth, the majority of these pieces were more in the style of the Italian *frottole*, but in English, usually with a "fa-la-la" refrain and strophically composed. The group was most talented: it included the three Arlton brothers, Dean, Roland and Stan, Claire van Ausdahl, and a number of women, including my girl friend, "Weesie" Brumbaugh, as well as several other students. The three Arlton brothers and Claire all had absolute pitch, so we never needed to depend on the piano, sitting around a large dining room table for most of our sessions. The group also included an excellent horn player and singer by the name of Ludwig Wangberg, without question, probably the most natural talent on the horn I'd ever heard.

"Lud," as he was known, was a student at Augustana, and played in the Sioux Falls Municipal Band as well. My memories of him have always been vivid. On one occasion, during a rehearsal for the Beethoven First piano concerto, the bassoonist, who was, incidentally, his girlfriend, and whom he eventually married, was having a difficult time with a particularly crucial passage just before an important piano entry. "Lud" leaned over her shoulder, sight reading the part, which was in the bass clef and played it on his F horn! On another occasion, I rode with him and another friend returning from a concert by the Sioux Falls Municipal Band, while he played all the important horn solos

(Strauss, Wagner) from the repertoire, without missing a note, as the car careened over rough country roads!

One of my best friends during this time was Art McKenzie, who eventually joined the group and sang baritone with them. Art was a competent composer as well as a horn player. I especially remember one delightful evening during the summer of 1948, after I had been in college already for two years and was home visiting for the summer. Four of us, two tenors and two basses, were sitting in my room. We were discussing the interesting Renaissance practice of using popular tunes of the day, such as "L'homme armé" ("The Armed Man") or "Se la face ay pale" ("If my face is pale") as a *cantus firmus* for Masses. Art asked me for a sheet of manuscript paper, and went off into a corner of the room while the rest of us continued talking.

About twenty minutes later, he rejoined the conversation, and, with a sly grin on his face, announced that he had just dashed off a short "Kyrie" for a Mass, scored for two tenors and two basses, and wondered if we might sing it through. As we gathered around to sight read it, we were astonished at what we saw on the paper: It was the melody of Hoagy Carmichael's "Stardust," set to the words "Kyrie Eleison," in a series of acceptable imitative entries.

One of the highlights of my year at Augustana involved the visit to the campus of the well-known American composer Roy Harris and his wife, Johana, for a week of masterclasses and concerts of his music. Professor Guderyahn had met Harris in Colorado the previous year, and had prevailed upon him to come to Augustana College. At that time, Harris was beginning to be quite popular in America, and had been hailed as the great new

American composer. The Augustana Symphony set to work learning several rather difficult works by Harris, including the "Ode to Friendship," and "When Johnny Comes Marching Home Again," as well as the Beethoven C minor piano concerto, which Mrs. Harris played on the concert. For me, the encounter with a famous, living composer was extremely enriching, and I was impressed by the composer's own somewhat modest, self-effacing personality, and his down-to-earth, easily approachable manner.

Spring, 1947, Augustana College, Sioux Falls, South Dakota. Roy Harris and his wife, Johana, are welcomed by the President of Augustana College, Dr. Lawrence M. Stavig, and Richard J. Guderyahn (left), director of the Augustana Symphony Orchestra.

The entire episode was the highlight of the year for many of us. Little did I know that we would meet again in less than two years.

The reader will recall that in Chapter 1, I introduced Dean Arlton, who had a good deal of influence on my musical development. His younger brother Stan was also a most interesting person, and equally brilliant. Not only was he a good musician who sang and played viola and piano, he had an extraordinary grasp of science, particularly mathematics and was the inventor of a unique circular slide rule. Stan was also a student at Augustana, and later took over the small choral group which I had started after I had left for Chicago the following year.

However, Stan was most known at this time for his outstanding accomplishments as a cross-country bicycle rider. He rode from coast to coast, throughout the Midwest, even riding up Mount Rainier in Washington State on his bicycle. I was totally fascinated by his bicycle trips, and became determined to do something similar. When an opportunity arose to work as a bellboy in a resort hotel in Highland Park, Illinois, in the summer of 1947, I decided to emulate Stan, and ride my bicycle from Sioux Falls to Highland Park, stopping for a few days in Kenosha, Wisconsin, to see my new friend, Mary Ellen Kindt, whom I had met the previous year while still in the navy. The day I was to leave, my father, fearful of what I had undertaken, offered to pay my train fare if I would only reconsider. I was determined to make the trip; however, unfortunately, I had neither the training nor the skill and equipment to successfully carry out my ambitious plan.

73

With great fanfare I departed from Sioux Falls on my bicycle, with a few clothes and a collapsible tent lashed to a carrier on the rear. I got as far as Rock Rapids, Iowa (which is about 30 miles), on a hot, humid morning in June, before giving up and hopping on a train. I did sleep overnight in a field somewhere in Iowa, before finally boarding another train which brought me as far as Lake Geneva, Wisconsin, where I disembarked, riding the final thirty-two miles into Kenosha, so as to give the impression I had ridden all the way.

Unfortunately, my employment at the Hotel Morainne on the Lake in Highland Park lasted just about two weeks, and I returned to Kenosha and made myself a guest of the Kindts. After about ten days, Muffy's mother decided I should try to find a job somewhere, broadly hinting that I could not stay there any longer. At the time I was terribly chagrined, but, upon reflection, realize I must have been totally obnoxious and insensitive. Mr. Kindt had some sort of connection with a firm in Chicago, and managed to put me in touch with the company. I rode the North Shore to the city, and found employment at Chicago Rotoprint, located at 4601 West Belmont.

While working in Chicago I had the opportunity to attend a few concerts at Ravinia Park on the weekends, where the Chicago Symphony played during the summer. Muffy, and often her mother, would meet me at the park and we'd have a picnic while listening to the concerts. I also enjoyed going to Grant Park, but because I worked at night, I could only attend rehearsals in the morning. I have always enjoyed rehearsals, often more than the actual concert, as one has the opportunity to see the inner workings of the orchestra, to hear the music being taken apart, and where the various formal aspects of the work may be more easily delineated.

Muffy was to begin her sophomore year in the fall at Chicago Musical College, in downtown Chicago, and encouraged me to consider transferring there for my second year. She was a piano major, and a student of the internationally famous Rudolph Ganz, a legend in the musical world, and the president of the college. By this time, I knew I was very much attracted to Muffy, and the prospect of moving to Chicago to attend school with her appealed to me. I knew I was not good enough to be a piano major, and had become enough interested in music history and literature to consider the possibility of majoring in "musicology," although I wasn't certain I knew what it entailed. I was soon to have some interesting experiences which would make it clear what was involved.

One morning in the early part of July, after getting off work from my night job at Chicago Rotoprint, I stopped in at 64 East Van Buren St., in downtown Chicago, to see what the school was like. I was instructed to step over to the office of the dean of the college, Dr. Hans Rosenwald, who was also professor of musicology. He was a tall, large, rather formidable looking man with a thick German accent and an almost overpowering presence. I estimated him to be about forty-five years old. I was intimidated and fearful.

Dr. Rosenwald had an impressive pedigree, including a doctorate from Heidelberg University, where he had studied under Heinrich Besseler, with further study in Berlin with some of the legendary figures in 20th century German musicology: Johannes

Wolf, Arnold Schering and Friedrich Blume. In 1936, he had escaped the Nazi pogrom against Jewish intellectuals, musicians, artists and scholars such as Rudolph Serkin, Arnold Schoenberg, Paul Nettl and many others, and, like them, had emigrated to the United States, where he settled in Chicago and began teaching at Chicago Musical College. (Henceforth, I shall refer to it by the initials "CMC.")

"So, you vant to schtudy musicology," he almost challenged me. "Und vhat do you think musicology is?" I tried desperately to explain what I thought it included. He did not appear impressed. He asked, "Haf you schtudied any Ghurman yet?" I answered in the affirmative. "Vell," he continued, "musicology is a very demanding field, und you must be prepared to work hard and study. Not everyone does well, and it requires an enormous amount of knowledge of the repertoire and a grasp of history as well. I tell you what: why don't you attend a few of my classes this summer and see if you think you would like to major in the field. Now vhwere did you say you come from, did you say Dahkota?" "Yes sir, *South* Dakota," I corrected him. End of interview, end of conversation.

The following week I decided to go back to CMC and attend some of the professor's classes. Dr. Rosenwald often spoke without lecture notes, and paced back and forth at the front of the tenth-floor lecture hall, his enormous appearance mesmerizing the students. This morning he was lecturing on the chamber music of Schubert, particularly those works directly inspired by one of the composer's own songs: "Die Forelle" and "Tod und das Mädchen."

"Does anyone here know the Schubert song, 'Die Forelle'?" he asked. No hand in the class of about forty students went up except for mine. Somewhat surprised, Dr. Rosenwald boomed: "OK, come up to the piano and play it!" (Although Schubert's original setting is in D flat major, the setting in the variation movement of the so-called "Trout Quintet" was in D major.) Fearful, I went to the piano and played the first few phrases of the song as it appears in the chamber music version. "Very good," he responded.

Further discussion dealt with some of the string quartets, especially that with the nickname "Death and the Maiden," because of its expanded quotation of a theme from the song of the same name. Again the query to the students: "Does anyone know this song?" Again no hands were raised except for mine. Once more I was called to the piano to play the song. (In this case, Schubert's original is in D minor, though in the quartet setting it is in G minor, and is considerably more expanded, with a second, complementary phrase which becomes the basis for a magnificent set of variations.)

The class ended, the professor disappeared. I then went down to the ninth-floor administrative offices of the college, and suddenly heard a booming voice calling to me from across the room: "You, Sau-ht Dah-kota, come here!" It was Dr. Rosenwald, motioning me into his office! *Now what?* I thought. As a mere visitor to the class, was I not supposed to have volunteered to respond to the professor's queries? He knew only that I was from "Dah-kota," out in the sticks, as it were. Apprehensive, I sat down in the chair opposite his desk. For a moment, he said nothing, puffing in silence on a fat cigar. Then, leaning over, he said in a friendly voice: "Sau-ht Dah-kota, you know a hell of a lot of music! We will accept you here in the fall as a musicology major if your grades are good enough. Get a transcript from your college out in Dah-kota, and have them sent to the registrar's office here for evaluation. I hope to see you here in the fall." Dr. Rosenwald would become, in the intervening years, my major professor, and an important musicological influence in my professional development. I am also indebted to him for securing for me a teaching fellowship at CMC some years later.

The decision to transfer to CMC was, in the final analysis, a good one, and I never came to regret it. The move to Chicago brought me into contact with some of the richest musical experiences I have ever had, and the city has, to this day, a special place in my memories, not only on the professional and academic levels, but also on a more personal one.

I found a cozy basement room in a private home at 64 E. Cedar Street, on the near north side of Chicago, just a half block from Michigan Avenue, and entered CMC in the fall of 1947. This area of the near north side, near Rush Street, was the most colorful part of the city. It was the "bohemian" district of Chicago, and at such locations as "Bughouse Square," as it was dubbed, assorted anarchists, communists and preachers would hold forth daily, often actually standing atop an old-fashioned soapbox! The near north side was also the center of the "alternative lifestyle." On the other hand, directly across from "Bughouse Square" was Newberry Library, one of the finest humanities research libraries in the country, containing a large collection of original musical documents.

Inasmuch as I was a fairly experienced organist, I was able to get a number of positions as choirmaster and organist at churches in Chicago during the years of my residence there. The business manager of CMC, C. Gordon Wedertz, was himself a longtime church organist, and often had knowledge of such openings. Soon after I began my sophomore year at CMC, I accepted my first position, as organist and choirmaster at Forest Glen Congregational Church at Catalpa and Lawler, on the far northwest side. The trip, from Cedar Street, was a long one, involving a subway, elevated and bus ride taking over an hour.

A few months later I got a job as an usher at Orchestra Hall and, except for choir rehearsal night, I worked there for several years. Working at Orchestra Hall provided me with an incomparable opportunity to hear all the great performers of the time, and get paid for it as well. The list of those I regularly was privileged to hear is endless. Some of my most vivid memories were of conductors Dmitri Mitropolis, Artur Rodzinski, Leopold Stokowski, Bruno Walter, Pierre Monteux (who conducted, by memory, Stravinsky's *Le Sacre du Printemps*, the work of which he had, some thirty-five years earlier, given the world premiere in Paris), Fritz Busch (under whom I sang in a performance of the Mahler Second Symphony as a member of the CMC chorus) and Raphael Kubilek.

Pianists included Horowitz, Rubinstein (see chapter 2 for an account of a celebrated encounter with him), Myra Hess, Brailovsky, Rudolph Serkin and many others too numerous to recall here. Especially memorable were Marian Anderson singing Schubert's *Erlkönig*, Myra Hess's riveting performance of Beethoven's Opus 111, the last piano sonata; Bruno Walter conducting some superb performances of Haydn symphonies, Horowitz having a memory slip in a Scarlatti sonata and playing the first half of the bi-partite form over and over again, until he finally remembered the second half. Then there was the night Leopold Stokowski forgot which work was to begin a concert, giving the downbeat for something like the soft, delicate *Prelude* to the third act of Verdi's *La Traviata,* while the orchestra came in with the "*fff*" opening of Dvořák's *Carnival Overture*! (The Verdi was to be the first work *after* intermission!)

In addition to musical performances, Orchestra Hall was also home to the Fourteenth Church of Christ, Scientist, and the hall was used on Wednesday evenings for so-called "testimonial" meetings, during which those who had been healed by praying to God or Mary Baker Eddy were heard. Therefore no concerts were ever scheduled on Wednesdays. On these nights, the well-known Fine Arts Quartet of the American Broadcasting System in Chicago, would perform in the small hall of the Art Institute, across the street from Orchestra Hall. Several of us who were experienced ushers were usually contacted by their manager, Mary Wickerham, for duty at the concerts. It was, for me, a total delight to hear the quartet, which consisted of Leonard Sorkin and Joseph Stepansky, violinists; Shepherd Lehnhoff, violist; and George Sopkin, cellist. I could not have imagined at the time that I would, some twenty-two years later, become a colleague of the quartet, teaching at the same university where they were professors and artists in residence.

My courting of "Muffy" continued happily during this time. She was living in the girls' dorm, on the fifth floor of CMC, and we often attended concerts together. As the end of the school year approached in 1948, I thought it might be appropriate if she came to Sioux Falls for a visit during the summer, meet my family, and see my hometown. This, as it turned out in the end, eventually resulted in a somewhat unfortunate turn of events for me, though I could not have known it at the time. During her stay of about ten days in Sioux Falls, Muffy met all my good friends, including Stan Arlton, Art McKenzie, and my sisters, Libby and Martha.

Art was a tall, somewhat reticent fellow, with a sly grin and a wonderful, dry sense of humor. He was an interesting composer, who had dabbled in serial techniques occasionally, but mostly wrote in a rather conventional, derivative musical style which reminded one of some mid-eighteenth-century composer. He had written a rather impressive "Christe Eleison," and wanted to get a group of singers and instrumentalists together to sing it.

I decided to get together with some of my friends from our high school chamber music group, as well as a number of singers, write out some parts and try to read through sections from the Bach B Minor Mass ("Qui tollis" and "Crucifixus") as well as portions of the cantata "Christ lag in Todesbanden" (BWV 4) and Art's "Christe Eleison." We met in the chapel of "Old Main" at Augustana College, and had some extremely satisfying evenings of music making. The group had no plans to ever perform in public; it was simply our joy and pleasure in music making which brought us together. By now two other wonderful people had become a part of our group. Lillian and Hugo Lutz, brother and sister, joined us as well. They were both students at Augustana; Hugo an art major, and Lillian, a music major. Lillian was a singer, an alto, a sweet, small, dark-haired girl with a delightful sense of humor, extremely friendly and quite musical. Hugo was a talented flutist, and they were the children of a Lutheran pastor in Gary, Indiana. Hugo later became professor of art at Upsala College in East Orange, New Jersey.

In addition to these frequent get-togethers to read through McKenzie and Bach, four of us also tried our hand at some chamber music on one memorable occasion. By then I had had two semesters of cello, as my so-called "secondary instrument" at CMC, and my old buddy from the navy, Dave Buckley, who was in town for the summer, working at the college, played first violin. Art McKenzie was second violin, and Stan Arlton played viola. (Stan was probably the best player in the group.)

One night, as we struggled through, more accurately, "slaughtered," some Mozart, it occurred to us that the beginning of the slow movement of the Beethoven quartet, Opus 132 ("Heiliger Dankgesang") ought to be within our grasp. The entire opening section was basically in open position, at least for me as the cellist, and should be easy enough. As we slowly wound our way through the wonderful, ethereal opening, with much effort and some out-of-tune playing, the door to the room opened, and J. Earl Lee walked in. "Never before have I heard such playing!," he marveled. "It is out of this world!" We had arrived! What praise!

Shortly after I returned to Chicago at the end of August, I was surprised one day to have a visit from Art, who had decided, apparently at the last moment, to come to Chicago and enter CMC. He asked if I would be interested in trying to find a place to live together, and so I moved from my near north side room to a place with Art at 3840 W. Gladys Avenue in the Garfield Park area on the west side. For a number of reasons, we remained here only a few months, and then moved a short distance to 3414 W. Monroe, just west of Homan Avenue. This would be my home for several years to come.

In the fall of 1948 I began to sense that all was not going well between "Muffy" and me, and in November we broke up. I'm sure there is no connection between that event and what happened the following spring: Art McKenzie, my roommate, was beginning to date her. Had he been the right man at the right time, just as we had broken up? Was he getting her on the rebound? I didn't think much of it at the time, and could only admire his taste in women. *All's fair in love and war*, I finally reminded myself.

Meanwhile, life as a student continued, and I became more deeply involved in my musicological studies, as well as enjoying the enriching life experiences as an usher at Orchestra Hall. The musicology students were, by and large, some of the most intelligent, delightful group of people I've had the pleasure of knowing.

My old navy friend, Buckley, was now a student at CMC, also majoring in musicology. Eugene Joseph Leahy ("Joe" to his friends), was a bright young scholar whose specialty was, later, medieval music. I eventually had a course on chant with him. A devout Roman Catholic, and a product of parochial schooling, he read Latin the way others read English. Joe has had highly successful stints as a researcher in Marburg University in Germany as well. He recently retired as professor at Notre Dame University in South Bend, Indiana.

Luise Eitel, a young Jewish girl from Germany, had apparently made her escape from Berlin amid bombing and devastation at the end of the war, ending up in Bonn for a short time before coming to America, and eventually to Chicago, where a cousin, Otto Eitel, was a well-known local hotel owner (his most important property was the Bismarck Hotel). Luise went on to get her Ph.D. at Columbia University with an excellent dissertation on the origins of the song cycle. She later became professor at the University of South Carolina. I was quite infatuated with her, admiring her sharp intellect and wonderfully precise Friedrichstrasse accent.

Other students in our class were Richard Wenzlaff, a clarinetist, who became professor in a Chicago area college and William Sherwood and Dick Kirchoff, both brilliant students with excellent minds. I regret that neither continued in musicology, so far as I could determine. A beautiful black woman, Vada Lee Easter, was also one of the shining lights of our class. I believe she later joined the faculty of Howard University in Washington, D.C.

Many of the CMC faculty were distinguished in their fields. Rudolph Ganz, not only the president of the college, but also the most colorful personality I had ever met, led a general musicianship class that operated somewhat like a piano masterclass in which advanced students performed, often accompanied by delightful anecdotes of his life in music by "Uncle Rudi," as he was called by the students. I was constantly overwhelmed by the man's knowledge of the entire musical scene.

Not only was he a superb pianist, he was also a conductor, a composer and a raconteur of the highest level. At the age of seventy-two he could still jump up on the stage of the recital hall, climb mountains and teach in an animated manner. I recall meeting him one day on the elevator. He announced, with that delightful little lift of his eyebrow, that he had a dental appointment on north Michigan Avenue, and wasn't looking forward to it with much pleasure. He got off the elevator, headed out the door east to Michigan Avenue, from where he strode off north on the avenue. I tried desperately to keep him in view, but he walked so fast, and with such long strides that he had soon left me far behind. He is so well known by his accomplishments that one need only consult a standard music dictionary to read about him.

I studied conducting with Ganz for three years. We were often hampered by not having an actual orchestra to work with, and many of us concluded that the only difference between each year of conducting class is that the anecdotes became ever more hilarious. We often conducted while four of the students played the two Steinways in his studio, reading instrumental parts from the scores.

In my junior year, Ernst Krenek, the Austrian composer, joined the faculty for a year, and it was a great privilege to study some basic composition with him. Krenek undoubtedly had one of the finest minds I have ever known, though his music is not highly regarded by many. My favorite work of his, and one which is not too well known, is the *Symphonic Elegy* for string orchestra, in memory of Anton Webern. It is an intense, highly-charged work. Krenek also had a delightful sense of humor, which often came through in our composition classes.

On one occasion, he set us to work for the better part of a month writing nothing but unaccompanied melodies. Each class would be devoted to a detailed discussion of the merits and weaknesses of everyone's melodies. Day after day we wrote all kinds of melodic lines, mostly tonal, though a few were more atonal. Finally, after over three weeks of writing melodic lines, we were to be introduced to the writing of a second voice. Krenek, his voice very low, and with great seriousness, began. "Now," he said, in his thick Viennese accent, "sie main dieference between vohn und two pah-t writing, ist de presence uff die secund voice."

Dr. Heinrich Fleischer, F.A.G.O., the well-known organist of Valparaiso University, came up to teach two days a week at CMC, and, in addition to private organ students, taught a graduate course on the history of organ music. Fleischer was undoubtedly one of the finest organists and organ teachers I had ever encountered; in addition, he was a fine scholar and knew much music, both vocal and instrumental, of the 17th and 18th century, especially German music. However, what always impressed us students as most amazing, was that Dr. Fleischer was missing the fourth finger of his left hand! He never said anything about it, no one discussed it, and it obviously had little effect on his superb performing abilities. Someone said he'd never heard Fleischer hit a wrong note, perhaps omit a note, but never play a false one. He performed the most demanding repertoire, from the complete organ works of Bach and the majority of early composers as well, to Reger, Liszt, Hindemith, and one of his own favorites, a 20th-century German composer I've heard very little of, Johann Nepomuk David.

One day in class, Fleischer was excitedly discussing pieces from part three of Bach's *Claiverübung*, also known as the "German Organ Mass" or the "Catechism Chorales." He had come to the powerful setting of "Aus Tiefer Not" (BVW 686) with the masterful double-pedal passages. As he sat at the organ, he began playing the magnificent work, meanwhile carrying on an analytical discussion of the piece. Without missing a note, and most of the time not even looking at the music, he continued to talk as he performed the complex counterpoint.

The organ, I regret to say, was an abominable monstrosity: a theater organ, complete with the famous "horseshoe" console with its variously colored stop tabs, and special effects such as "Grand Crash." Nevertheless, Fleischer did the best he could with such meager resources. Apparently the former organ professor had made his living as a theater organist in the days of the silent films, and had rescued this instrument from some Chicago theater when the "talkies" started to become popular.

The widely-respected Mozart scholar Paul Nettl, professor of musicology at Indiana University in Bloomington, traveled by train to Chicago twice a month to conduct two graduate seminars, one on Bach and the other on Mozart. Nettl was quite possibly the most knowledgeable musicologist I had ever encountered. A veritable walking dictionary of music, he could discuss, at length, any number of topics, particularly regarding Mozart, including dates of composition, performance, locales, information about such arcane subjects as the first *Figaro,* or where the manuscript of an obscure work was housed. Nothing seemed to faze him; his was the closest to a photographic memory I'd ever experienced.

Nettl also had a delightful sense of humor. He had written a book titled *Mozart und Casanova,* and could be rather "earthy" in his comments. One Saturday afternoon, his graduate seminars for the day concluded, he sat with me in the ninth-floor reception area of CMC, waiting until time to leave for his train back to Bloomington that evening. We were alone, and after talking for a bit (I no longer recall what we discussed), he fell silent, and after perhaps two minutes, looked up and said, in his thick German accent: "Dehr ah tree kinds of women: the ones you pay, the ones who do it for nutting, but da tird kind iss da best: day ah da ones who pay YOU!" Where the remark came from I will never know. It just sounded so out of place coming from one of the preeminent Mozart scholars in the world!

Another outstanding scholar who taught at CMC was M. Alfred Bichsel, also from Valparaiso University. "Bix," as he was called by close friends, looked and talked like a Chicago gangster, with a clerical collar! He was an ordained Lutheran minister, but with his severe black suit and hat, could have passed for a Catholic priest. He conducted a seminar on medieval music and theorists, Garlando, Franco, Grocheo, de Vitry, Jacques de Liège and others, which was attended by a group of our best graduate students. It was some of the most stimulating instruction I have ever received.

He later became head of the church music department at the Eastman School of Music in Rochester, New York.

One day in January of 1949, Dr. Rosenwald mentioned to me that his friend Roy Harris, the well-known American composer, was to be in town shortly. I responded excitedly that two years earlier, while I was attending Augustana College in Sioux Falls, Harris and his wife had been guests on our campus for a week of masterclasses and performances of his music. Dr. Rosenwald asked me if I'd enjoy coming along for dinner with them on the seventeenth. I was thrilled, as January 17 was also my birthday.

As I continued my musicological studies I became more and more acquainted with a vast body of music of which I had been totally unaware until then. Much of the musical literature of the Medieval and Renaissance periods was new to me, and I gradually added the music of Machaut, Dufay, Josquin and Palestrina to my knowledge of the repertoire. Josquin des Prez was especially interesting to me, and I soon found myself studying not only his sacred works, motets such as the stupendous setting of the 51st Psalm, "Miserere mei Deus," "Tu pauperum refugium" (actually the Secunda Pars of the motet "Magnus es tu, Domine"), "Absalom, fili mihi" the "L'homme armé" Masses and the Missa "Pange lingua," but also his extremely charming chansons: "Basies moy," "Faulte d'argent" and the deeply felt love songs "Plus nulz regretz", "Parfons regretz" and "Plusieurs regrets."

At the University of Chicago, the Austrian musicologist and choral conductor Sigmund Levarie (I was told he had changed it from "Löwenstein" when he came to America) was presenting exciting performances with his *collegium musicum*, of unknown

Renaissance and Baroque masterpieces, as well as Bach cantatas. On one occasion, I heard the first Chicago performance of the Machaut Mass, which left me deeply impressed. Levarie also conducted a superb production of the Mozart Singspiel "Abduction from the Seraglio" (K. 384), with my very good friend from Sioux Falls, William Abbott, in the lead tenor role of Belmonte. Bill was also a student at CMC, and possessed a magnificent high, lyric tenor voice. He lived for awhile with us on West Monroe.

One day I read in the paper that Ralph Kirkpatrick was to play a Bach recital at Bond Chapel at the University of Chicago. The featured works were the two-part Inventions, and the three-part Sinfonias. He was performing them on the clavichord. I decided to attend with a man from Sioux Falls who was then a seminary student at the university. Marvin Halverson was a good friend of J. Earl Lee's also. Bond Chapel is a beautiful, intimate room seating no more than 100 people. Kirkpatrick walked down the inlaid stone floor and sat down at the instrument.

Turning to the audience, he cautioned us to be as quiet as possible, explaining that the sound of the clavichord was extremely delicate. "If anyone chances to cough, it will sound like a thunderclap in here," he added. After the performance, I stepped into a room where the artist was greeting the audience. As I walked up to him, he immediately recognized and greeted me.

***

One night in February of 1949, as I stood at my usher's post on the sixth floor gallery of Orchestra Hall, I noticed a young woman approaching to take her seat. I was totally stunned by her beauty! I didn't think I had ever seen such an incredibly beautiful woman. She was unbelievably fair skinned, with complexion like the driven snow, bright blue eyes, and beautiful, blond hair. She reminded me a bit of the movie star Veronica Lake, who was popular at that time. On two more occasions, this lovely young woman came to the concerts, one time with an older woman whom I took to be her mother. I finally got up enough nerve to strike up a conversation with her one evening during the intermission of a concert. Lutitia Bowen lived on the far north side of Chicago, in an area known as Rogers Park. She was still in high school, a senior at the prestigious Chicago Latin School, and I soon found myself totally smitten with her and determined to court her with all my courage and strength. I could hardly believe that a ravishing beauty such as she would be interested in me, however.

Lutitia was a musician and a pianist who was making plans to go on to college as a music major. Her father was employed by a number of prominent Loop stores as a window display artist. Her mother was Swedish, and had emigrated to America as a young woman many years earlier. (This probably explained the striking Nordic looks of her daughter.) She lavished much attention on her only child, and had already taken her to Europe in the mid-1930s. Lutitia, her mother proudly told me, had celebrated her fifth birthday in a restaurant at the Eifel Tower in Paris. They were members of Fourth Presbyterian Church on north Michigan Avenue, one of the most prestigious churches of Chicago's elite residents, though the Bowens themselves were of relatively modest means. I was always a bit fearful of her mother, who seemed quite possessive and overprotective of her beautiful daughter. I wondered what kind of a mother-in-law she might make. Lutitia was graduated from Chicago Latin School, near Astor and Goethe Street, on the near north side, in June, of 1949, and was accepted at Boston University as a music major, to begin that fall. I had hoped that she might choose CMC, but apparently her mother thought that a fashionable eastern school might be more enriching. I also suspect that she wasn't particularly keen on her daughter's getting involved with some starving music student and probably hoped Lutitia would eventually find some wealthy Harvard Law School graduate.

After Lutitia left for Boston University, I was miserable. I missed her very much and began to make plans to somehow go to Boston and visit her. In the meantime, I had accepted a new church position in a Lutheran Church at Laramie and Hirsch, on the far west side. It was much closer than the job at Forest Glen Congregational and the church building was brand new. Unfortunately, it had only an electronic "substitute" organ, and the church itself suffered from extremely poor acoustics. Although it had a high, slanted roof, the Haddite block out of which it was built soaked up the sound like a sponge. The ceiling also had acoustical tile. The experience of playing in such dead rooms marked the beginnings of my interest in church acoustics. We performed some rather good music as the choir had about eighteen members, many with good voices. The choir loft was in the front of the church, but we were all together, not in those abominable "divided choir" setups so typical of Episcopal churches. I stayed at the church for almost two years.

In January of 1950, during the semester break at CMC, I could no longer bear being away from the lovely Lutitia, and because of a modest tax refund, I was able to scrape together enough money to take the train to Boston to see her. I showed up at the girls' dorm where she was living, and told her I was thinking of transferring to Boston University for my master's. I had written to Karl Geiringer, the senior musicologist at Boston University, and requested an appointment. Professor Geiringer was very friendly and encouraging and I began to plan on entering Boston University to pursue my masters in musicology with him.

Lutitia and I enjoyed several days of beautiful, close intimacy, and also explored the city together. I very much enjoyed trying out the Aeolian-Skinner organ in the Church of the Advent designed by G. Donald Harrison. As the weather was comparatively mild, we walked along the Charles River all the way to Harvard, where we visited the Busch-Reisinger Museum to see the very interesting "Baroque" organ which Harrison had designed for that building in 1937 upon the recommendation and with the encouragement of E. Power Biggs. As we entered the building, I could hear someone playing the instrument. I went up to the gallery and introduced myself; it was the young Boston composer and organist Daniel Pinkham, a harpsichord student of Landowska's and an organ student of Biggs.

Returning to Chicago, I finished my undergraduate degree in June, though my plan to attend Boston University with Lutitia finally fell through when she found another boyfriend in Boston. I always wondered what happened to her, if she continued to be as beautiful as she was when we were going together, and if she eventually married some wealthy member of a Boston Brahmin (or Chicago) family.

During my final undergraduate year at CMC I took a number of interesting academic courses at the University of Illinois Navy Pier campus at the end of Grand Avenue on the near north side. In addition to advanced courses in German and French, I took an excellent course in English literature which stimulated my interest in the works of Chaucer, Spenser, Bacon, Milton and Swift. Two years earlier I had also studied at the University of Chicago, in the then popular Great Books courses, founded by Chancellor Robert Hutchins. In addition to Plato, Aristole and other Greek philosophers, we also studied the writings of Jefferson and other American statesmen. I found it all enormously stimulating and my mind eagerly soaked up knowledge like a sponge.

After I was graduated in June of 1950, Dr. Rosenwald offered me a teaching fellowship at CMC for the following year, while I pursued a master's degree in musicology. In July, I began attending the rehearsals of the Grant Park Symphony, meanwhile continuing as organist and choir director at the Lutheran church on the west side. I have always enjoyed attending rehearsals of all kinds of groups, finding that I could learn a lot about the music from hearing how the group takes the music apart and puts it back together, how the conductor tries to express his ideas on interpretation and what the final product then sounds like.

One morning I noticed a girl sitting near me whom I had seen working in the music accessory department at Lyon and Healy, a large music store at Wabash and Jackson. I didn't know her name, but she had waited on me a few times when I needed to buy music manuscript paper, a baton, or a pitch pipe. I sat down next to her, she recognized me and we began chatting. Unlike the beautiful Lutitia, she was rather plain looking, not ugly by any means, but definitely not a "knockout," though she had that clear complexion I always admired in a woman. She wore glasses, was fairly tall, almost as tall as I was, and her short, light brown hair was straight and parted in the middle. We talked for a few minutes, and I found her quite intelligent and knowledgeable about music. Marge Ford was studying violin, I later learned, and was absolutely crazy about anything having to do with violins: the music, the composers, and the performers. At the conclusion of the rehearsal I walked her to the subway station on State Street and asked her if I might call her sometime. She lived at the exact opposite end of Chicago from Lutitia, the far southeast side, mere blocks from the Indiana state line. Why did I always choose to be interested in women who lived so far away from me? Little did I know then that the girl whom I would someday marry would live over 3,000 miles away from me!

At CMC, my teaching duties included two sections of undergraduate music history, the founding of a *collegium musicum*, and a freshman ear-training class. (This last assignment was because no one else wanted to teach at 6:00 p.m. I was excited, though nervous, about the prospect of actually doing teaching, lecturing on music history, and, as it were, getting my feet wet in the classroom. The reader must remember that some of the people in those classes were former classmates of mine from the previous year. There were about forty-five students in the morning music history course, and on the very first day of class, I found myself confronted by an ominous situation.

I had begun the lecture by observing the manner in which the general history and culture of an era can be mirrored, to an extent, in the music of the time. I pointed out that we gain an understanding of Bach's music by knowing something of the Lutheran church in 18th-century Germany, that Beethoven must be seen in the light of the new ideas of egalitarianism, liberty, and democratic thought which are mirrored in such historical developments as the French and American revolutions, and, in the 19th century, the rise of musical nationalism must be seen as the result of the rise of independent and proud nation states, particularly in central Europe, Russia and the Scandinavian countries. I though I had made a particularly forceful presentation of my ideas and thoughts on the subject as the class came to an end.

A hand went up in the rear of the room. "You know," a young man said, "I don't agree with you at all, Mr. Miller; *as a matter of fact, I think you're all wet!*" I was stunned for a moment: my very first lecture, and already I was getting flak from the students! I remember the student's name to this day: Lambert Bresters. He had a peculiar habit, while he talked, of twisting a strand of his hair between two fingers.

"Well, Mr. Bresters," I said, "why do you think I'm wrong, and what do you think might better explain such phenomena?" Mr. Bresters attempted to clarify his ideas as the students watched and listened intently. (*OK, Miller, get out of this*, they must have been thinking) We talked for a few more minutes and, the class having ended, most of the students left: all except Mr. Bresters. He came up to me at the front of the room and admitted: "You know, I guess maybe you're right; I hadn't quite thought of it in that light." I breathed a sigh of relief and returned to the ninth floor, where Dr. Rosenwald was waiting for me.

"Well, Frahnklien," as he pronounced my name, "how did your first music history lecture go?" "Oh, Dr. Rosenwald, it was just terrible," I answered despairingly. "Some student got up in front of the class and told me he thought I didn't know what I was talking about. He said I was 'all wet!' " "What," he stormed, "who was it, what was his name?" I replied, "Lambert Bresters." He laughed heartily. "Lambert Bresters was just released from Hines Veterans Hospital Psychiatric Ward; I'm afraid he's probably still a little unsteady and unsure of himself!"

I am happy to report that, from then on, I experienced no more such unfortunate incidents, and, as a matter of fact, was extremely gratified doing this type of teaching. The class included a number of very bright, talented students. One student, of whom I am eternally proud to have been the first music history teacher, has now gone on to become one of the three or four outstanding musicologists in the United States. He is also highly respected in Europe for his work in German music and theory of the 17th and 18th centuries. His name: George Buelow, professor of musicology at Indiana University.

***

In the winter and spring of 1951, Marge Ford and I became more and more intimate. I finally asked her to marry me and invited her to accompany me out to Sioux Falls to meet my parents and other family members. She returned to Chicago, and I followed a couple of weeks later. Sadly, however, due to a number of unfortunate misunderstandings, we mutually broke off the engagement the last Sunday of August. It was her birthday. I never saw her again.

Shortly before this unfortunate turn of events, however, I was given a unique opportunity to work with my organ teacher, Heinrich Fleischer, in a very concentrated fashion, when he invited me to come to Valparaiso and work with him on a number of organ pieces. Dr. Fleischer's wife and children were to be abroad for a few weeks and he would be alone in the house. Never very comfortable with the intracacies of domestic life, he proposed that I come down to Valparaiso and, in return for providing a modicum of order in the house, cooking mostly, he would provide me with intense study of the Bach *Orgelbüchlein* while a guest in his home there for several days. My daily schedule consisted of a lesson with Dr. Fleischer in the morning, after which I would retire to one of the organ practice rooms and work on the music. After a noon meal, I would have another lesson and more practice, perhaps with some informal music making, reading through Schubert four-hand music or delightful musical discussions with M. Alfred Bichsel and others. It was, without question, one of the most enriching and, at the same time, demanding few days of my life, and I have treasured the memory of it ever since.

During summer school of 1951 I had continued to work on my thesis, took a few more courses at CMC and finally finished up in August. Meanwhile, I had been offered an instructorship at the college to start in the fall, but declined the offer, sensing by then that I really needed to get out from under the continual influence of just one major professor: Hans Rosenwald. In retrospect, this decision may have been a wrong one, because I had no further means of support, having resigned my position as organist and choirmaster at the Lutheran church where I had been for over two years. Although I now had my master's degree in musicology, I was unemployed, and, in addition, I'd lost my girlfriend. The next four months were to be a period of extreme hardship and depression, during which time I went from one low-level job to another with no prospects of employment in my chosen field.

Why I decided on the first job I took is not at all clear to me: I became a Chicago taxicab driver. (Checker Cab Co., #4268). Although I did enjoy driving, the job itself failed to bring in enough money to pay for anything except rent and food. The only cab drivers who really made a decent living were those who stayed on the street continually, pushing themselves to pick up as many fares as possible. However, my life as a cab driver enabled me to learn every area of Chicago and pick up a number of interesting and colorful individuals from time to time.

After about six weeks of cab driving, I was involved in a serious auto accident as I was taking a woman to Mass at Holy Name Cathedral near Chicago and State. As I drove east on Wacker Drive, going at a pretty good clip, a car suddenly appeared directly in front of me, and I smashed into it broadside as it traveled south on Dearborn, forcing it all the way around in the intersection, until it ended up about ten feet shy of going into the Chicago River! Luckily my passenger was unhurt; I quickly hailed another cab and transferred her to it, before calling police and the cab company. I was cited for failure to yield the right of way, and at this point, I swore to end my cab driving days. Although the officials at Checker Cab encouraged me to simply take a few days off, I adamantly refused to consider it, and now found myself out of work. I was to appear in traffic court in three weeks to answer the charge.

The first week of November I got another job, this time as a bookkeeper in a boiler repair company on Milwaukee Avenue. (Remember, I was the one who had so much trouble with arithmetic as a youngster.) I was miserable trying to concentrate on my job, what with all the hammering and banging going on out in the shop. The days and hours crept by, and I was barely able to continue at times. It was awful.

Sometime in November I appeared at traffic court on south California Avenue to answer the charge: failure to yield the right of way. The judge, sitting at a card table in a dingy basement room, asked the bailiff to call the complainant in the case. The bailiff answered, "I'm sorry, your Honor, the complainant is not present." The judge banged his gavel. "Case dismissed. Next case." I had beaten the rap through good, clean living and fancy footwork! (Apparently, the man whose car I had hit was a salesman, and the car belonged to the company. Although it was a new car, with less than 100 miles, the company probably just collected the insurance on the damaged auto and bought him a new one.)

The bookkeeping job at the boiler repair company lasted until shortly before Christmas, when I finally escaped the scene, and decided to take the train home to Sioux Falls for the holidays. Little could I have known that, quite literally, the entire course of my future would be irrevocably and forever sealed by this one decision; for in what followed, a new and wonderfully exciting chapter in my life was about to begin. I have often reflected on how profoundly my life would be forever changed by this chance trip to my hometown.

CHAPTER 4

A CHRISTMAS TRIP HOME;
GUDRUN; HEIDELBERG UNIVERSITY;
MARRIAGE; MARTIN ANDREAS;
JOE CIPRIANO AND THE UNION
(1952-1954)

Shortly after I arrived in Sioux Falls, I had a call from Stan Arlton, my longtime friend from our Augustana College days. He was in town, he explained, and hoped to touch base with me while there. He planned to be at Williams Piano Company on Main Avenue that afternoon, and wondered if I might meet him there. At the time, Stan was teaching in a small high school in Tripp, South Dakota, about seventy miles southwest of Sioux Falls. I met Stan that afternoon and we reminisced about our activities during the previous two years. He related to me that he had met a young German girl a couple of years earlier, while in Germany, and had discussed with her the possibility of coming to America to attend Augustana College. I recalled that Stan had visited me in Chicago in the spring of 1949, on his way to the East Coast for a flight to

Germany for some sort of youth project whose aim was to assist German young people in reconstructing churches there which had been damaged during the war. He apparently had met the girl during this time.

The previous fall the girl had arrived in Sioux Falls to attend Augustana and Stan thought perhaps I might enjoy meeting her, inasmuch as I spoke some German, and she was a good musician, a cellist, organist and recorder player. I gave it no further thought until, a few days later, in speaking with my aunt Elinor, I mentioned the girl, whose name was Gudrun Herrmann. My aunt recalled having met her, while visiting her good friend June Solberg one day while Gudrun was baby-sitting for the family.

Richard and June Solberg were a delightful couple with three young children. Dick was an ordained Lutheran minister and a philosophy professor at Augustana, and June, together with my aunt Elinor, was active in a number of local civic organizations. One of their sons, David, later went on to great fame as a hot TV personality, who goes by the name "David Soul." He played one of the leads in the series "Starsky and Hutch," a popular police show. Aunt Elinor seemed to think the young lady in question was living in the "Cottage," a kind of overflow girls' dorm at Augustana. I knew exactly where it was, and finally decided to pay her a visit one day.

On January 11, 1952, a crisp winter evening around 8:00 p.m., I stopped in at the "Cottage" and asked if Gudrun Herrmann was there. Presently a very pretty, charming young lady whom I judged to be twenty or twenty-one, appeared. She had an infectious smile, flashing brown eyes, short auburn hair and that beautiful, clear European complexion which I always loved. I explained who I was, and that my friend Stan Arlton had suggested I stop by and introduce myself. I tried out my German on her, hoping to impress her with my knowledge of the language, and in a few minutes was sitting at a piano in the reception area, talking animatedly about music and playing excerpts from the literature: Bach, Mozart and other favorites. I immediately sensed we were on the same "wave length," and her delightful German accent and somewhat shy demeanor instantly attracted me. *Wow*, I mused to myself after I had left and drove home, *that is some gal. I'd like to see her again soon.*

The first picture taken of Gudrun and me, in front of my parent's car, January 15, 1952. Looks like love to me! Check out the bobby sox and saddle shoes! (Note the chains on the tires, a consequence of our famous South Dakota winters).

The following week I called her, and asked if she would like to go out for something to eat some afternoon. I picked her up and we drove downtown to the Palace of Sweets at 11th and Phillips. We must have sat in the booth at the restaurant for four hours talking about music, other interests, future plans and what we wanted out of life. By now I was quite interested in this utterly fascinating girl. I learned that she came from Mosbach, a small town not far from Heidelberg, that her father was a Lutheran minister there, that she had already studied. classical archeology at the University of Göttingen, in central Germany. She read or spoke, in addition to German and English, Latin, Greek, Hebrew, French and Italian. I felt intimidated by such erudition, and wasn't quite sure I was up to her level of accomplishment. Nevertheless, I became determined to get to know her better. Unfortunately, however, there soon arose a slight complication: The young lady already had a serious love interest in Germany.

One day, while we were downtown together, I decided to take Gudrun up to meet my father at the office. He greeted her warmly, having already been prepared by my talking about her often. Speaking German to her he asked: "Wie befinden Sie sich, Fräulein Herrmann?" ("How are you, Miss Herrmann?") This was proper and excellent German, and I hoped she was impressed! In any case, she was soon invited to dinner at our house, to meet my mother as well. It was a very pleasant evening, which even included my father and her waltzing around the living room together. I learned that Gudrun was a dancer, and my father was an excellent waltzer as well.

At the end of the evening, we decided to walk back to the college, and as we walked I slipped my arm through hers in an ever increasingly warm embrace. The gentle snow crunched under our feet, and the moonlight sky cast a glow on the landscape as we walked south on Summit Avenue a few blocks from the college. Suddenly, impulsively, I stopped, swept her up in my arms, and kissed her tenderly. It was almost as if it were meant to be, she melted in my arms and we both stood on the street weaving slightly from the heat of our embrace. Yes, I knew it now, I had fallen head over heels in love with this lovely, young lady!

Now, however, my time to remain in Sioux Falls was drawing to a close, and I had to get back to Chicago. I had a room there for which I was paying rent, and I had to somehow find a job again; anything to make a living. But being in love with a young lady 500 miles away from me was not a pleasant thought, and I thought Lutitia and Marge lived a long way from me in Chicago. My only hope was that she had told me that she had a cousin in Evanston whom she would be visiting over the Easter vacation in March, and perhaps we could see each other again then. I jumped at the prospect, and began making plans to meet her train when she arrived.

Because of my training in the navy as a hospital corpsman, I decided to go to work as a hospital orderly. In the second week of February I found a job at Presbyterian-St. Luke's Hospital on Chicago's near west side. After only a short while I decided that the trip on the bus was too long and expensive, and I began to work at Garfield Park Hospital at Washington Blvd. and Hamline Ave., only a ten-minute walk from my room on Monroe. This work was strictly as a ward orderly and was physically demanding. It included preparing male patients for surgery by shaving the area where the operation would take place. (I don't know who was more frightened, me or the patient, as he saw the razor descending toward his most private parts. I am happy to report that I never "Bobbitized" any of the patients.)

I wrote my beloved Gudrun almost every day, showering her with letters, expressing my ever-increasing love and my loneliness at being away from her. Never, in my life, had I felt such an intense longing for anyone; never had I known such love for a woman. How, I thought, was I ever going to be able to let her go all the way back to Germany at the end of her year at Augustana? I didn't have an answer. She arrived in Chicago to spend the spring break with her cousin in Evanston, another long trip for me from West Monroe Street. We had an absolutely delirious time together, enjoying each other's company in every way possible, attending a beautiful Palm Sunday concert of Bach's *St. John Passion*, in which I was singing with Sigmund Levarie's *collegium musicum* at the University of Chicago, and walking together from place to place. We even attended the "Kino" on North Avenue, the only German movie theater in Chicago. We were now passionately in love with each other.

As it came time for her to leave for Germany again in June, Gudrun made a suggestion to me that sounded extremely attractive. She recommended that I come to Germany in the fall, where we could, *together*, attend Heidelberg University; she was to begin her next year of university study there. Having finished my master's, it was important for me either to begin making plans

April, 1952, Evanston, Illinois. Visiting Gudrun at her cousin Irene's house. We are very much in love by this time!

to find a job in a college or university, or perhaps start work on my Ph.D. What better place to study for a doctorate than a German university? Germany, the birthplace of musicology, was a logical choice. The majority of my professors at Chicago Musical College had all been German or German speaking as well: Hans Rosenwald, Heinrich Fleischer, Paul Nettl, Ernst Krenek.

Now, there was only one small detail to be hammered out: How in the world was I to raise the necessary funds for such an ambitious plan? Obviously, my job at the hospital was not going to make it possible. Finally, I decided to move to Evanston, where Gudrun's cousin lived, and try to find work out there. I had a lucky break. The well-known TV marketing research firm A.C.

Nielsen, was in the process of hiring a large work force for a number of ongoing TV and radio surveys being conducted throughout the United States. I got a job with them, and, in addition began to work a second job as a dishwasher in Tally Ho restaurant on Orrington Avenue in Evanston. Finally, I had obtained a new church job at a far west side Baptist church, where I traveled each week on the Lake Street "L" from Evanston. I would often work all day at A.C. Nielsen, go to work at the restaurant, and then after I was done there, would return to Nielsen to work the evening shift until after midnight. Ah, the things one does for love.

At A.C. Nielsen I met a delightful young married couple who, like me, were trying to earn some extra money by working for Nielsen's. Walt and Midge Wade were both music majors at Northwestern University. Walt was working on a Ph.D. in theory and was an excellent organist. He also did a little composing. Midge was in the music education program, and played the viola. It was good to be able to talk about music with someone again, and I spent many delightful evenings at their tiny apartment above a garage over on Foster Avenue in Evanston. (They were to be very helpful to us later, and have since become our dearest friends.)

Gudrun flew out of Chicago on June 9, sailing on the U.S.S. *Independence* from New York two days later. I applied to Heidelberg University looking forward to joining Gudrun in the fall. Her cousin, Irene Anderson, whose mother, Margarete Lenz, was visiting from Germany at the time, assisted me in writing a formal letter to Gudrun's father in Mosbach, asking for his daughter's hand in marriage. Mrs. Lenz knew Gudrun's father, and feared that he would be none too keen on the idea of his daughter marrying an American. She said she could hear him fume: "Es kommt nicht in Frage!" ("It's out of the question"!)

One day in the middle of August, I received a letter from Gudrun. In stunned disbelief and through tear-filled eyes I read what she had written: She wanted me to know that she was thinking of marrying Norbert Gulba, her German boyfriend, and didn't know whether I would still want to come to Germany. I was crushed. How was it possible, I thought? What had happened? By then I had already received word of my acceptance at Heidelberg University, and had booked passage on a small Dutch freighter for the third week of October. What should I do, simply give up and cancel all my plans? It was incomprehensible to me. After discussing it with Gudrun's cousin Irene, I decided not to give up my plans to attend Heidelberg University, hoping that I could possibly persuade Gudrun to change her mind about marrying her German boyfriend. The opportunity to attend a German university was also an important consideration in my plans. I wrote, begging her not to do anything until I'd arrived and we had had a chance to talk some more. I said that I had been looking forward to the opportunity to go to Europe, and to attend Heidelberg University, and that I didn't want to cancel my plans at this late date.

The trip across the north Atlantic in late October produced a strange sense of *déjà vu*: we were caught in a hurricane which brought back frightful memories of my navy days in the Pacific! (I always claimed I got to Europe on a piece of cheese: The freighter's name was the "Edam"). The ship's speed was about nine knots an hour, and the trip took almost ten days. We entered the Westerscheide passage leading to Antwerp on the morning of October 20, 1952. I couldn't believe it: Europe at last; it had been a dream of mine for years, and now I was there!

The lowlands around me had numerous windmills (something I had never seen), and there was something exotic about the entire landscape which fascinated me. After we docked in Antwerp, I went to the nearest telegraph office to send a wire to Rolf Lenz, Irene Anderson's brother, who was to meet me in Heidelberg. I had assumed that Gudrun would not meet me, and, as a matter of fact, had not even written her to indicate when I would arrive. I wired Rolf when I would arrive and what I would be wearing: "Habe an grauen Regenmantel" ("Wearing a gray raincoat.")

The train from Antwerp would take me to Cologne, Germany, where it was necessary to transfer to another train going to Heidelberg. I arrived in Cologne after midnight, wandering around the station for most of the night until boarding the connecting train to Heidelberg, which made its way along the beautiful Rhine River valley, past ancient castles and vineyards, and through the cities of Bonn, Mainz and Frankfurt, many of which still bore the scars of wartime damage.

As the train began to pull into the station in Heidelberg, I glanced out the window of the compartment. My heart literally skipped a beat: Gudrun was standing on the platform waiting for me! I couldn't believe what I was seeing. I swept her into my arms with tears in my eyes. She introduced me to Rolf Lenz, her cousin, who was Irene Anderson's brother. I couldn't keep my eyes off Gudrun; I thought she had grown even more beautiful than before, and I couldn't believe my luck at being here in Germany with the woman I loved so deeply. She had found me a room in the small suburb of Ziegelhausen, just outside Heidelberg, and would show it to me the following day. For tonight, however, I was to stay at the home of Rolf Lenz, while Gudrun stayed at her grandparents' home, a short distance away.

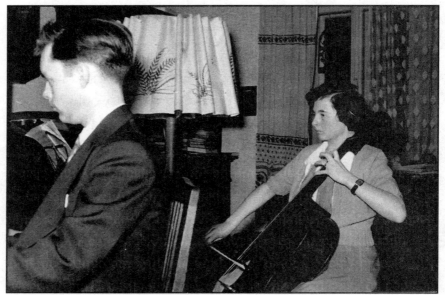

Making music together at Rolf Lenz's house in Schröderstrasse, Heidelberg. I think she looks somewhat like Ingrid Bergmann in this shot.

That evening, I accompanied Gudrun as she played the cello. The piano was a beautiful Steinway in Margarete Lenze's living room. Frau Lenz was a trained singer with a rich mezzo soprano voice. I recalled that on one occasion the previous summer I had accompanied her in Schubert Lieder, and that she and Gudrun had attended one of the rehearsals for Bach's *St. John Passion* which I sang at the University of Chicago in March. Rolf excused himself as we continued to make music together, and soon we were in each other's arms. Yes, she said, I'm glad you're here, and, no, I'm not going to marry Norbert yet. I was in paradise: I was in Germany, with my beloved Gudrun, and still had a chance to marry her.

The following day Gudrun and I took the streetcar out to the suburb of Ziegelhausen, about four miles east of Heidelberg, to look at the room she had found for me. To get to the village, we needed to take a small ferry across the Neckar River after getting off the streetcar. She explained that, as Heidelberg was fairly modest in size (approximately 120,000 inhabitants), and had a large student population, that it had been impossible to find a room in the city itself, and this was the only place she could find that she thought I might like. It was absolutely charming, modern and clean. The room looked out on the Neckar River, which flows through Heidelberg. The Neckar, which connects to the Rhine River at Mannheim, is the main waterway from Stuttgart in southern Germany. Large barges traveled up and down the river at all hours, and I enjoyed watching them go by my window and hearing the low *chug-chug* of their engines, which often lulled me to sleep at night.

Soon I met Gudrun's brother Ludwig, who was a doctoral student in theology at the university. He was extremely helpful to me as I struggled to go through the hoops of the academic life at a German University. Ludwig accompanied me when I went to register at the Musicology Institute of the university, and to meet some of the professors whose lectures and seminars I was to attend.

View of the beautiful Neckar valley east of Heidelberg. On the left is Schlierbach, and on the right Ziegelhausen. Beyond the bridge, on the right side, was located the small chapel in which we were married. Further up the river was "Heidelberger Landstrasse 48A," where we lived.

Thrasybulos Georgiadis, obviously not German, but Greek, was a fine musicologist whose publications were well known in Germany. I had only one course with him, a general survey of music history. Professor Siegfried Hermelink was my major music professor, and, among other courses, I had a seminar on lute tablature with him. This was a field with which I was totally unfamiliar, so that the work was quite challenging. I also had a course in figured bass with him for one semester. Hermelink was a Lassus scholar, and came from Stuttgart. He was a real

"Schwaab," as the Germans say, from Swabia, in southwestern Germany.

I was also enrolled in courses in "Philosophie des Mittelalters" ("Philosophy of the Middle Ages") and "Deutsche Malerei der Gotik" ("German Painters of the Gothic"). I think I may have understood about 30% of the lectures, at least at first. Gudrun assured me that even the German students only understood 50% of the lectures, so arcane and esoteric was the language. Heidelberg University is the oldest university in Germany, and the third oldest in all of Europe, so it has an exceedingly rich history.

The city of Heidelberg was almost completely spared from the destruction which many other German cities suffered during the war, due, in part, to decisions by the American high command to make the city their headquarters during the post-war period. I learned that many citizens were forced to give up their homes so that American officers had places to live. Gudrun's maternal grandparents were among them, and lived now in a small, two-bedroom apartment in the Bergstrasse.

Grandfather Otto Hagmaier was a noble, warm-hearted man who had been a Lutheran pastor with a number of congregations in southern Germany during his active years. He was born and raised in Walldorf, less than ten miles from Heidelberg. (Walldorf, incidentally, was the hometown of John Jacob Astor, who had emigrated to America, and built the famous New York City hotel which he called the "Waldorf-Astoria," combining the name of his hometown with his own.)

Sophie, Otto Hagmaier's wife, was absolutely elegant, well-bred and warmhearted. She reminded me a little of my grandmother. They had adopted a young girl, Anne, many years earlier. Anne lived with them and worked in an office downtown. She was a few years older than Gudrun, and they were good friends. Gudrun lived with them in this tiny apartment while she was studying at the university. Her field was classical archaeology, and she was enrolled in seminars and lectures in her field.

On my second weekend in Heidelberg, Gudrun and I took the train to Mosbach to meet her parents. I was nervous, and somewhat anxious, especially about meeting her father. I had been told that he was a rather stern disciplinarian, formidable and intimidating. As I entered their home, the first person I met was Gudrun's mother. I immediately liked her; plus, in her I saw where Gudrun got her beauty. Frau Herrmann was very good looking, rather delicate and quiet, but I sensed that we would come to like each other. I was particularly impressed, because Gudrun had told me that her mother had studied at the music conservatory, intending to become a professional violinist, and at age nineteen, had already performed the Beethoven F major Romance with the Heidelberg city symphony. She still performed occasionally when a violinist was needed in some musical program in Mosbach.

When her father came in, I saw that he was not the ogre that some had said he was. He was genuinely warm-hearted and friendly, and we immediately understood one another. He was almost bald, slightly shorter than I, and had a handsome moustache and deep-blue eyes. I especially liked his firm handshake and his sonorous voice. When I heard him in church the following

Sunday, I was impressed by his remarkable voice, which easily filled the large church.

I was asked if I would like to play part of the service some Sunday, and was excited about the prospect. Dean Herrmann, for he was dean of the cathedral there, told me what the hymns were to be, and gave me the hymnal. I opened it and discovered with a shock, that it contained only the melody of the hymn. Where was the complete harmonization? I asked Gudrun, who said, in response to my query, that organists were expected to play the "chorale" from this single line. Not only that, they were also expected to improvise a prelude on the chorale with just the single line in front of them. I was taken completely aback. These German church organists must be highly trained musicians. I tried to practice as best I could, until Gudrun, taking pity on me, found appropriate harmonizations for me to play from. In addition, I practiced on some Bach chorale preludes as appropriate to each chorale.

***

The musicology seminars with Professor Hermelink included a number of young scholars who later became some of the most prominent and highly respected of the post-war generation in Germany. Among them were Ernst Apfel, Theodor Göllner, the Schubert scholar Arnold Feil, and Wolfgang Osthoff, son of the highly respected Josquin scholar Helmut Osthoff. In connection with our study of lute tablatures, Professor Hermelink presented each of the seminar participants with a duplicated portion of a manuscript containing tablature. We were to transcribe the music into notation, and, in addition, were given the task of identifying the music, determining where it may have originated, the year of publication and the composer. I was extremely pleased that I was the only one able to solve the problem, and, in addition, found the book in the seminar library from which Professor Hermelink had taken the example.

Of course, not everything I did was that noteworthy. One cold, blustery night, while a group of us studied in the seminar library, we heard the sound of horses' hooves in the courtyard below. Someone on horseback was riding by. Quick as a flash, I tried to show off my knowledge of German poetry, and quoted a line from the opening of Goethe's famous ballad, "Der Erlkönig" ("The Erl King"), which has been set so dramatically by Schubert:

Wer reitet so spät,	Who rides so late,
Durch Nacht und Sturm.	Through night and storm

except that I recited the second line incorrectly. I should have said: "Durch Nacht und *Wind*") ("Through night and wind"). Theo Göllner looked up from his book and sarcastically completed the couplet for me so that it rhymned perfectly:

Es ist der Vater,	It is the father,
Mit seinem Wurm.	With his worm.

The line actually should be: "Mit seinem *Kind*" ("With his child") so as to rhyme with "Wind"("Wind")! Göllner seemed to be saying: "Miller, if you want to quote our German poets, please get the text straight." The room erupted in laughter.

***

Now, as fall turned into winter and our love for each other grew ever stronger, deeper and more intense, there was no longer any doubt that Gudrun and I wanted to get married. In December I wrote my parents, asking them to send me a copy of my birth certificate, and on Saturday, January 17, 1953, the wedding took place. It was my twenty-seventh birthday. (I've always said that Gudrun chose that date so I wouldn't forget our anniversary.)

Gudrun's father officiated at the ceremony, and I was deeply touched that we would be married by the man who was to become my father-in-law. The wedding took place in a tiny chapel in Ziegelhausen, and the wedding dinner was held at the Hotel Schwarzer Adler. It was a lovely celebration, and all of Gudrun's family was able to come. There were many toasts to the bride and groom, and wishes for a happy and prosperous life together.

I had arranged for a trio of two violins and cello to provide the wedding music. The performers were all students from the musicology seminar: violinists Marianne Decoppet from Switzerland, Gustav Mebold from Germany, and Angelika Jacobi, from Poland, an international trio. The organist of the church performed the *basso continuo* parts, and the music itself was by Dietrich Becker (1623-1679), a Hamburg composer who had written it as wedding music for a royal wedding.

January 17, 1953. The wedding party at the Hotel Schwarzer Adler. (l to r, rear): Pastor Otto Hagmaier, Heidi Gulba (Gisela's daughter), Dean Ludwig Herrmann, father of the bride, Gudrun, Franklin, Sophie Herrmann, mother of the bride, Ludwig Herrmann, Gudrun's brother, Hedwig Lenz, wife of Erich Lenz, Gudrun's cousin, Gertrud Hagmaier, Sophie Herrmann's sister, Anne Herrmann, adopted daughter of Pastor Hagmaier and his wife, Erich Lenz and Gisela Gulba, Gudrun's sister. In the front are Karl Otto Herrmann, Gudrun's other brother, Gisela Herrmann, Ludwig's wife, and Rolf Lenz, who is Erich's brother.

Because they had so enjoyed playing for our wedding, the three string players and I decided to undertake a modest tour of the area, performing baroque chamber music in a number of churches. I also performed organ works by Bach, Buxtehude and others on the programs. We played mostly in small towns near Heidelberg: Walldorf, Hassmersheim and Mosbach, and we always had an appreciative audience. One reviewer wrote of my performance that "...his playing was void of the romantic attitude which so often afflicts organists of today. He excelled in strong rhythmic presentation even in slow chorale preludes. That Miller can also master major works was obvious in the *Fantasy in A minor* of J.S. Bach, which became a moving experience." The music critic of the *Rhein-Neckar Zeitung* wrote: "At the organ was Franklin Miller (Chicago), whose playing was simple, not over-powering, especially in the accompaniment and therefore, was very pleasing." (The Bach *Fantasie in A minor* [BWV 904], though considered for harpsichord, is most probably an organ work because of the consistent five-part texture, and the contrasting sections in three voices following strong cadential closes, which seem to call for a manual change.)

In the spring, there was a grand ball, with dancing and all sorts of humorous skits by the students poking fun at the professors. It was the so-called "Faschings-Ball," an annual event held all over Germany, roughly the equivalent of *Mardi Gras* in the United States. This evening is the only time students are allowed to use the familiar "Du" form of the personal pronoun "you" in addressing their professors, and it is always a delightful, informal evening for everyone. As Professor Hermelink was becoming a well-known scholar of the music of Orlando de Lasso (also known by his Flemish name "Lassus"), we decided to put on a little song and dance routine, in part with the following text, sung to the well-known Latin dance tune, "La Cucuracha":

Orlando, Orlando   Orlando, Orlando
Verwendet nie dem Rhumba Takt!   Never uses the
                                      Rhumba beat!

Our Faschings-Ball was held together with the students and professors from the Archeology Institute, where Gudrun was studying. She and I took part in the festivities, but unfortunately, this led to a rather embarrassing incident for her. The director of the Musicology Institute, Professor Georgiadis had shown up at the dance with a beautiful, shiny top hat. Now, anyone who has ever seen a Fred Astaire movie will recall that a top hat can be made to collapse upon itself easily enough, and then snapped out again before being placed on the head once more. However, one must be aware that top hats come in two different styles: collapsible, and NON-collapsible.

As Gudrun, who had perhaps consumed a bit too much bubbly, danced gaily around the room with Professor Georgiadis, she impulsively hit the top of his hat, hoping to get it to collapse on his head. Unfortunately, however, the hat was of the non-collapsible type, and all she succeeded in doing was putting a large dent in the hat. I don't recall what Professor Georgiadis said, but I know that Gudrun was totally chagrined and apologetic.

Despite such an occasional *faux pas* I had every intention of continuing my studies in musicology at Heidelberg University during the summer term. However, a number of complicating factors forced me to alter my plans, first and foremost of which was that Gudrun announced she was pregnant! It now became imperative that I get back to the United States in order to find some kind of job to support my new family. It was also important that our child have the advantage of American citizenship. And finally, my bank account was beginning to decrease rather precipitously and I wasn't certain how or if I could find any work in Germany. One member of the family even suggested I consider working in a nearby mine or stone quarry.

Gudrun now began the application process needed to apply for a visa, and I booked passage on the Dutch liner MAASDAM, departing from Rotterdam on April 14, arriving in New York on April 24. From there I took a bus to Chicago and was able to stay at Gudrun's cousin Irene's home in Evanston, until I could find a room, at 1501 Maple, coincidentally, only half a block from where I'd lived before leaving for Germany the previous October.

Now I began a search for some kind of job. In about a week or ten days, I was able to find work at a carpet store in Wilmette. The job consisted of hoisting heavy rolls of carpets into trucks, some weighing over 300 pounds, and accompanying the carpet layers out to the house where they would install the carpets. We did carpet cleaning as well. I also went over to Tally Ho restaurant, where I had worked previously and was immediately hired again. I was thus able to begin setting money aside in order to find a small apartment and buy a few pieces of used furniture at the Salvation Army in preparation for the day Gudrun would join me.

Meanwhile, back in Germany, Gudrun was in the process of being interviewed and going through a physical examination prior to being issued a visa. She had been cautioned that there was some concern about a premature birth, and she was extremely anxious to be able to get here, in case there were complications. Because of the unbelievable nature of her experiences in the proceedings, we wrote a letter to the *Chicago Tribune* some years later recounting the circumstances of Gudrun's hilarious adventure at the American Consulate in Frankfurt. A feature column in the *Tribune* was called "The Day my Baby was Born," but, because we thought the story so unusual, Gudrun decided to send it in, although the events connected with the birth did not strictly deal with the exact day of the baby's birth, but a time some two months earlier. The newspaper thought it sufficiently unusual and humorous to publish it, together with pictures of her and our son, Martin-Andreas. We pick up the story, in Gudrun's own words, from the pages of the *Chicago Sunday Tribune,* August 30, 1959 edition.

"...I was in Frankfurt, Germany, waiting for emigration clearance to the United States. Suddenly, a question had arisen that might smash all my dreams of being reunited with my husband [and] of having my baby born on American soil.... At the American consulate I had been told that I would have to remain in Frankfurt several days, since there was a question of my being issued a visa at all.... every hotel room was jammed [because of an industrial fair][and] if I returned home...I would forfeit my chance to get a visa and could apply again only after the baby was born. This could mean a wait of up to two years.

"After vainly hunting for a room, I returned to the consulate and asked the receptionist... if they could give me a couch or even a place on the floor where I could rest overnight. And I added timidly that I thought some consideration might be given my special condition. 'Why, that is out of the question!' she snapped. 'You must wait your turn like all the rest. What is this special condition that makes you an exception?'...I explained that I was expecting a child...! With a surprised look, she quickly located my application and thrust it into my hand, directing me to a room down the hall. With a 'thank you,' I turned to leave, glancing at the papers in my hand.

"What I read sent a shudder through me. Under 'General Remarks on Physical Condition,' I was shocked to read this note: 'STOMACH TUMOR. ISSUANCE OF VISA CONTRAINDICATED BEFORE SURGICAL REMOVAL!' How could the doctor who had examined me earlier have arrived at such a wrong diagnosis?...I recalled, too, the remark made by a German medical technician who had X-rayed me that morning: 'Put your chin here, *und bitte, ziehen Sie Ihren Bauch ein!*' ('Please pull in your stomach!')

"My only hope now lay in convincing someone in authority that I did not have a stomach tumor. I rushed to the room down the hall, with barely 15 minutes left until closing time, shoved the papers at a clerk, and gasped: 'There has been a terrible mistake. I don't have a stomach tumor: I'm going to have a baby!' The girl laughed and called an American doctor. He strode over to me, laid a hand on my shoulder, and asked me where my husband was. I explained that he had had to return to America and that I wished to join him as soon as I could so our baby could be born an American. Smiling, he wrote on my application: 'DEFINITE SIGNS OF PREGNANCY. NO STOMACH TUMOR. VISA OKAYED!'..."

Gudrun and her stomach tumor sailed from Rotterdam, Holland, on Tuesday, June 23, a passenger on the NIEW AMSTERDAM of the Holland-America lines. She was met in New York by her mother's close friend Hedi Spiegel, a Jewish woman and former resident of Walldorf who had fled to America in the late 1930s. Hedi had also assisted Gudrun when she first came to America in 1951, and on this occasion drove her to La Guardia airport to catch a flight to Chicago. First, however, she took Gudrun to a women's store to purchase a cooler maternity outfit: The one she had on was 100% wool, and she was sweating like a pig. Two employees of Tally Ho restaurant offered to drive me to Midway Airport on Chicago's southwest side, to meet the flight, and it was a joyous moment when I met my dear wife that evening. Her first request was for a glass of milk to ease a severe case of heartburn. Or was it perhaps a stomach tumor?

I had found a tiny apartment at 1003 Grove Street in Evanston, and our dear friends Walt and Midge Wade, whom I had first met the previous year while working for A.C. Nielsen in Evanston, helped us find an obstetrician for Gudrun. They had just had a baby girl, who had been delivered by a Dr. Valency. He practiced at Swedish-Covenant Hospital in Chicago.

Meanwhile, I continued working at the carpet store in Wilmette, as well as the Tally Ho restaurant. The work at the carpet store was extremely hard on me physically, and, in addition, I was forced to work at the home of the mother of one of the owners, doing chores around her house which had nothing to do with the work at the carpet store for which I had been originally hired. Finally, on Friday, July 24, I complained that I wasn't hired to do housework for a member of the family, and was summarily discharged.

Saturday evening, July 25, about midnight, some weeks before her due date, Gudrun surprised me by announcing that it was now time to go to the hospital. I was frantic, as we had not expected this to happen so soon. Did it have something to do with the ocean trip or the plane flight? In any case, she had been issued the visa only because the indicated due date was not until sometime in September, and travel less than thirty days before a birth is generally not approved. After all, I later reflected, hadn't they been misled into thinking she had only a stomach tumor, and was not even pregnant?

We somehow called a cab (we had no telephone) and drove to Swedish Covenant Hospital at California and Foster. I sat down at the admitting desk for registration, and was asked my place of employment. I had to admit that I had just lost my job, and was out of work. The officials at the hospital were, however, quite understanding, and Gudrun was taken up to the delivery room, while I waited, pacing back and forth, in a nearby waiting room, as is apparently the custom with all expectant fathers. At approximately 5:45 a.m., July 26, a warm, humid Sunday morning in Chicago, our first child, Martin-Andreas, was born. He was an American citizen. Cost of the delivery: $75.

Gudrun came home from the hospital in about a week and started the usual round of feedings every four hours, getting up in the middle of the night, and all the other joys of new parenthood. However, I still had no job and needed to start hustling to find something. In the latter part of August I finally found work as a driver for Elm Hand Laundry on Chicago Road at Main Street, on Evanston's south side. In September I got another church job, at All Saints Episcopal Church at Wilson and Hermitage in Chicago; however, I stayed only there for two months, and in the meantime had quit at the restaurant.

One day in late fall, as I went conscientiously about my laundry truck route, I noticed that a car seemed to be following me a bit too closely. I had driven only three blocks when the car swerved in front of me, the driver motioning me to pull over. What in the world is going on here? I wondered. Had I perhaps gone through a red light, and was this some kind of unmarked police car? He curbed me, pulling directly in front of me, and, getting out of his car, walked back to me. He was a large, swarthy man, wearing a dark Fedora. I guessed he may have come from southern Italy.

"Good afternoon, young-a fella, my name's Joe Cipriano and I'm with the truck drivers union. Let's see your union card." Union card? I thought. I had no union card, and told him so.

"You don't belong to the union, eh? Look kid, Ned Weisbaum (the owner of Elm Hand Laundry) knows dat his drivers gotta belong-a to da union. I want to see you in my office downtown in Chicago with your $50 initiation fee before five o'clock this afternoon." It was now 3:30 p.m.

"I'm sorry, sir," I stammered, "I don't have $50, and I can't meet you at your office. I'm quitting as of this moment." The man was enraged, but I told him to talk to Ned Weisbaum, and I drove off to tender my resignation. I'd lived in Chicago long enough to know better than to get on the wrong side of the union. I returned the truck to Mr. Weisbaum and told him what had occurred, pointing out that I had a family, and wasn't interested in being fitted with a cement overcoat just yet. He scoffed, saying that the union had no authority outside of Chicago. However, I also remembered that a number of my trips to pick up or deliver laundry did include trips into Chicago. This was the end of my laundry truck driving days, and I had to return to Gudrun, announcing that I was again out of work.

On a more cheerful note, we had a most delightful series of experiences in a small choral group which my good friend Walt Wade was putting together. Walt was director of music at the Episcopal Church of the Atonement on north Kenmore Avenue in Chicago. We planned a concert of baroque choral music, to be conducted by Dr. John Ohl, the musicologist at Northwestern University. We met regularly at Walt and Midge's upstairs apartment on Foster for rehearsals for the performance.

The choral group sang two works: a *Missa Brevis* by Dietrich Buxtehude, for five voices (soprano, second soprano, alto, tenor and bass) and Purcell's great funeral anthem, "When we are in the midst of life," with its grinding chromatic basses and hair-raising dissonances. Walt played the C minor passacaglia of Bach (BWV 582) and the A minor *Choral* of Franck, as well as some shorter works. The concert was an unusual success, although the audience wasn't large, and Gudrun and I enjoyed singing in the group, which also included my old navy friend Dave Buckley, and his girlfriend, Marilyn Fillis, as well as a number of Northwestern music majors. Martin slept the whole time in a room off of the sanctuary. Gudrun's cousin Irene Anderson, and her mother, Margarette Lenz, attended, and we were all invited out to Dr. Ohl's house after the program for some wonderful food, drink and conversation.

Events such as these kept us occupied and enriched our otherwise depressing existence. We had no money and I was on unemployment several times. More than once Gudrun walked over to a small butcher shop in the neighborhood to buy ten cents' worth of chicken livers, saying it was for the baby, when it was, in fact, for us. I love chicken livers. Walt Wade had, at one time, worked at a department store in Evanston, and suggested that I apply there, especially as the Christmas shopping season as not far off. I began work in the Men's Furnishings department of Lord's Department Store in the first part of November. The store was within walking distance of our apartment, which made things convenient. I worked at Lord's, except for a few days at Christmas when we took the train to Sioux Falls, until the latter part of August, 1954.

In January of 1954, I accepted a position as organist and choir director at Wheadon Methodist Church on Ridge Avenue in Evanston. The church was not large, had the awful divided choir setup and a mediocre electronic substitute, but there were some excellent voices in the choir. I was quite pleased to be able to prepare a rather good performance of the Schütz *Seven Last Words* on Maundy Thursday. The edition was a fine new one by Richard Gore published by Concordia. The new edition sought to restore the correct pitch level of the work, which was close to G minor, rather than E minor, which the poor Schirmer edition had perpetuated. (In all probably the previous editor had taken a look at the key of the continuo part, which, however, was in so-called "tief Kammerton," and had assumed, incorrectly, that the pitch, a minor third lower than the other parts, indicated that as the key of the work.) I hired a string quintet of Northwestern students (two violins, two violas and cello) to accompany the five-part chorus, and singers in the choir took all the solo parts. A strange coincidence occurred that night: At the same time we were performing the *Seven Last Words* by Heinrich Schütz, Austin Lovelace, at Evanston's First Methodist Church, was performing the *St. Matthew Passion* by the same composer with his choir. It was the first, and probably only time that two major works by Heinrich Schütz had premier performances at the same time, in the same city.

One day in the spring, it became necessary for me to go down to the Loop in Chicago, to register and bring my files up to date at Lutton Music Personnel Bureau in the Lyon and Healy building at Jackson and Wabash. Charlie Lutton was a hard-headed business man with no special sensitivity to "artistic types;" that is, musicians. He ran a business to make a profit, and that was that. I had spoken to him on a number of occasions, so he remembered me as I sat down beside his desk. Nervously lighting a cigarette, he nodded in the direction of the door, where another person was just leaving, after having been interviewed and registered with the bureau.

"Hey, Miller," he ventured, "see that guy who just walked out? Hell, he can't play 'Come to Jesus in whole notes!' " I always wondered after that kind of evaluation what he told the next candidate about *my* abilities, after I had left. In any case, I got my credentials up to date, and told him I was anxious to find a position for the coming academic year. Lutton did send me word of a full-time minister of music opening in Wilmington, North Carolina, and I applied for it, but then decided I didn't want to get tied up in

131

the church music field. As things turned out, however, I did, in fact, finally end up going to North Carolina.

Sometime during the late spring Gudrun informed me that Martin was going to have a little brother or sister. It now became imperative that I find some kind of academic position before the start of the new school year.

In the middle of July, I received a notice from Lutton about an opening at Mitchell College, a junior college in Statesville, North Carolina. They were seeking someone to head the music department, conduct the choral group, teach organ and piano, harmony, music appreciation, and, no doubt, perhaps sweep the floors at night. I applied for the position and flew down to Charlotte, where I was picked up by the president, Dr. John Montgomery, a Deep South resident (from South Carolina.) Montgomery, a chain smoker, appeared to be an able administrator. I was hired. My salary: $2,800 per academic year. (This did not, however, include janitorial duties.) At last I was on my way. I finally had a college teaching position, and best of all, I was chair of the department. All right, so there was only one other teacher, a part-time voice instructor, I was STILL the CHAIRMAN.

The college would assist us with our moving expenses, and I was able to obtain a small apartment just a few steps away from the college. This was an important consideration, inasmuch as we had no car. We began to prepare for our move, and were able to rent our apartment in Evanston to Gudrun's cousin Erich Lenz, who had recently moved to the United States with his wife and infant daughter.

CHAPTER 5

CHAIRMAN OF THE MUSIC DEPARTMENT: MITCHELL COLLEGE, STATESVILLE, NORTH CAROLINA
(1954-1956)

Gudrun and I, with one-year-old Martin, were met at the Charlotte, North Carolina, airport, by Dr. Tunis Romein, the dean of Mitchell College. Dr. Romein was a rather quiet, but extremely personable man, who had a Ph.D. in Education from the University of Kentucky. He and his wife, Sally, were from the Chicago area. I found him to be a most intelligent, well-educated man, with whom I soon became good friends. His book *Education and Responsibility*, an outgrowth of his dissertation, was published during my first year at Mitchell. Romein writes clearly and succinctly about the problem of responsibility, and the ways in which various educational philosophies have attempted to address the problem. The book is not easy reading, but is rewarding in providing insights to the attempts at attacking the philosophical problem of education and responsibility. Romein had a fine mind and was an extremely lucid thinker. It was a joy to have known him, and I only regretted not being able to know him better: In my second year at Mitchell, he left to take a position at Erskine College in South Carolina.

I had rented a small apartment at 119 South Mulberry, only a block from the college, which made things quite convenient for us. Soon after we arrived in town, I also took a position as organist at Trinity Episcopal Church, a tiny parish just around the corner from our apartment, which had a four-rank unit organ by Wicks. Although the instrument was totally inadequate for the performance of any organ works, it did serve me well as a fine practice instrument. When one doesn't have the luxury of forty or fifty ranks of pipes, one is not tempted to "play around" with all kinds of different stop combinations. The only thing to do is get down to work and practice earnestly.

The rector of Trinity was James P. Dees, who, some years later, created a schism in the Episcopal Church by establishing a breakaway denomination known as the "Anglican Orthodox Church," and proclaiming himself its presiding bishop. In 1988, the "International Headquarters" was still in Statesville, located in a house directly across the street from where our apartment once stood. My understanding is that the group is not recognized by the Episcopal Church. There apparently had been evidence that Dees held some racist views, and evidently attempted to somehow mingle them with the beliefs of his new church, though I have no firm knowledge of any details relating to the denomination.

At the college my teaching duties included directing the choir, teaching piano and organ and some low-level theory instruction. The work was satisfying, and I had a few talented students. Nancy

Krider was an excellent organist who performed in a masterclass on one occasion, conducted by my teacher Heinrich Fleischer, at Davidson College, just a few miles from Statesville. I taught piano to a few high school students as well. In the same year I began at Mitchell, Ralph Church was hired as an English professor. He was a fine scholar who was rapidly becoming an authority of the works on Robert Penn Warren and other southern writers.

At Davidson College, I met a young organist who had recently joined the faculty there, and we eventually became good friends. Phil Gehring was a gifted organist, as well as a composer and scholar, and had succeeded Robert Noehren, who had accepted a position as university organist at the University of Michigan. Phil was an organ student of Arthur Poister's at Cornell University, and had recently written a lovely "Missa Brevis," which my Mitchell College choir learned and performed in a number of places around Statesville. The work, in a mildy dissonant, Hindemithian idiom, was very effective and I always felt honored to conduct it. Phil's wife Betty was an excellent violist, and I have maintained contact with both of them over the years.

In the Davidson College chapel, Herman Schlicker had recently installed a large, three-manual instrument which was getting a good deal of attention in the professional organ journals. It was the largest Schlicker in that part of the country as well. However, the instrument suffered unnecessarily by being in a completely dead room. The acoustics were completely unsympathetic to the low-pressure, largely unnicked pipework, with several exposed divisions standing like rows of corn in a field. It was one of the first attempts at this type of installation in the South, and it was one of the first times I had experienced the work of the Buffalo builder who was gaining an important reputation because of his interest in building so-called "baroque" organs. In Charlotte, there was a smaller instrument by the same builder in a chapel attached to a large church, which I played each time I was in town. The company had also rebuilt a fine little tracker instrument in Tryon, North Carolina, which I had the pleasure of examining in 1956.

On March 1, 1955 Gudrun began to develop an insatiable irritation, with itching and a prickling sensation which was driving her crazy. I finally called a taxi and we went over to Davis Hospital to see if she could get some relief during the night. I then went home with Martin. About seven the next morning I was awakened by someone ringing my doorbell and banging on the front door. When I answered the door, Sally Romein stood there, and announced to me that Gudrun had given birth to a girl, and that I was wanted at the hospital immediately! The hospital had tried repeatedly to call me, starting at 1:00 a.m., but the telephone was apparently out of order, and, in desperation, they had called the Romeins, who lived only a few houses away, to ask someone to come over and get me up. Leaving Martin with the Romeins, I went immediately to the hospital, and met my little daughter, who would be named Claudia Renate.

Later in the month my parents visited us in Statesville, pulling up to the front door of the college and waiting for me to finish my day's work. I was surprised to see them, as they'd not given us any indication they were coming, but the best surprise was yet to come. At the end of their visit, as we sat in the living room, my father pulled his car keys out of his pocket and dramatically presented them to me. It was the generous gift of a 1953 Ford. I was extremely grateful, as we had not been able to afford a car up to this point. It made me think I'd really arrived, and we were eternally grateful. A few days later we drove them down to the Charlotte airport for their return flight to Sioux Falls.

Statesville, North Carolina; a visit by the grandparents. The caption on the back of this picture, written by my mother, reads: "Martin had pulled the metal blinds down cutting a gash near his eye, eight stitches, but he wouldn't keep it bandaged! This was taken the night we left, March 16, 1955." (Claudia was two weeks old in this picture.)

At the end of March the manager of the local FM radio station, WSIC, called the college to see if I would be interested in hosting a one-hour Sunday afternoon program of "classical music" from 4:00 to 5:00 p.m. The reader will recall that, as a youngster of ten or eleven, I had developed a great interest in radio broadcasting, and now I was to have an opportunity to fulfill that dream. This was to be the beginning of a very satisfying association. For my "theme song" I chose the slow movement from a little-known symphony by Charles Avison, a minor English composer. (Avison is chiefly known today for his arrangements of Scarlatti harpsichord pieces in the form of *concerti grossi*, as well as some important writings in the field of musical criticism.) The music of the first program, on April 3, 1955, Easter Sunday, was a slightly abridged performance of the Bach *St. John Passion*, sung in English by the Robert Shaw chorale. Initially I sat in a studio to announce the selections, while the regular announcer played the records from the control booth. Soon, however, the announcer showed me how to run the turn-tables, volume controls and microphone switches, and I began to do the shows myself.

One afternoon the regular announcer was somehow delayed arriving at the station at the conclusion of my program, and the engineer came running into the control booth to tell me I would have to announce the station break, read a commercial, and flip a couple of switches to connect WSIC to the Mutual Broadcasting Company for a network show. I was a bit nervous, but the engineer said that he'd heard my voice, which seemed quite pleasant and ideally suited for broadcasting, and he said he'd help me. At the conclusion of the program, I did what he had directed, pushed some switches and got the station connected to the network program. Two weeks later I was offered a job as announcer on the station, working from 6:00 p.m. to midnight each night. During the course of my evening shift, most of the programs were network feeds, but after 10:30 p.m., I hosted a show called "Midnight Melodies," during which I played all the new hits by Elvis Presley, Bill Haley and the Comets, The Four Freshmen and rock, country and Top 40 groups of the time.

March, 1956, Statesville, North Carolina.
Radio announcer on station WSIC.

However, I was now faced with a slightly sensitive dilemma: How could the young, upstanding chair of the Music Department of Mitchell College, in the habit of promoting only the "great" music of the "classics," Bach, Beethoven and Mozart, possibly be identified with such low-brow stuff as rock music, blues, country and other musics of popular culture? I decided to slightly disguise my name, by referring to myself on the radio by the handle "Frank Miller," hoping that no one would be the wiser. Needless to say, it didn't take long for some people, especially my high school piano students, to catch on to my identity. As a matter of fact, it would actually come in handy on occasion: My young female high school students could be persuaded to practice diligently if I would promise to play for them the latest rock tune on my evening show, especially if I dedicated it to their favorite boy friend over the air!

In September, Gudrun decided to take a trip back to Germany to visit her parents and introduce the children to their "Opa" and "Oma" there. Unfortunately, however, we had to sell the car my father had presented me in order to finance the trip. We traveled by train to New York, and I put Gudrun and the two children on a Holland-America ship bound for Rotterdam. In October, I spent $150 and bought an old Chevrolet from one of the announcers at the radio station. The next eight months were lonely ones for me, until I could be reunited with my family. Gudrun wrote me beautiful, intimate letters to help me keep up my spirits, and in June of 1956, I borrowed a car from a friend and drove to New York to meet them. Our return trip to Statesville was a joyful reunion for us all, and I began to look for another position in order to better my academic standing and, I hoped, increase my modest salary. (I had received a munificent increase of $200 in my second year at Mitchell.)

In July, I was notified of a vacancy at Hendrix College, in Conway, Arkansas, which sounded promising. Although it didn't include teaching music history, there were courses in choral literature, teaching of organ and directing two choral groups, which I thought would be pleasant. More important, it was a four-year college with an excellent reputation. The school was under the aegis of the Methodist Church, and also included the minister of music post at Pulaski Heights Methodist Church in Little Rock. Most important, the salary of $6,500 sounded particularly attractive, being a distinct improvement over my present position. I applied for the position, and was invited to the college for an interview. I was met at the Little Rock airport by Dr. Matt Ellis, the president of the College, and driven to the college campus in Conway. The interview was perfunctory, and I thought it a bit peculiar that the only person with whom I spoke was the president. I met none of the music faculty, not even the chair of the department; later, I would come to understand the distinctly political reason for this, though at the time I could not have known the true nature of it. I was offered the position on the spot, and I returned to Statesville with the good news. Although we would still be in the South, and still would feel a bit out of place as "Yankees," I did not consider it a disadvantage. I would soon have a distinct change of heart.

CHAPTER 6

HENDRIX COLLEGE, CONWAY, ARKANSAS AND PULASKI HEIGHTS METHODIST CHURCH, LITTLE ROCK
(1956-57)

After assuring ourselves that our household goods were packed and ready to go, we departed from Statesville, North Carolina, late in August of 1956 to take up residence in Conway, Arkansas, where I had accepted a professorship at Hendrix College. The trip through the scenic Appalachian Mountains in western North Carolina and eastern Tennessee was beautiful. We stopped in Cookeville, Tennessee to see our dear friends Walt and Midge Wade, whom I had first met in 1952 when I was working for A.C. Nielsen in Evanston, Illinois, and Walt and Midge were students at Northwestern University. Walt was now professor at Tennessee Technical University. They had a daughter, Ann, who was almost the same age as Martin. Both children, you may recall, were delivered by Dr. Valancy at Swedish Covenant Hospital on Chicago's north side. Many years later, Ann, then a college student, was killed tragically in a fall from a mountain in southern Germany, where she had gone to work during a summer vacation.

Her parents were devastated. They had three other charming girls who have since become successful in their chosen professions. Two of them are now married and have produced a number of grandchildren for Walt and Midge to enjoy.

Conway, Arkansas was a sleepy little town of about 9,000 but with three colleges: Hendrix College, Ouachita Baptist College and Arkansas State Teachers College. As our furniture had not yet arrived, we stayed for a few days in what passed for a motel; they were called "tourist homes." In those days, the nationwide networks of Days Inn, Comfort Inn, Motel 6, Howard Johnson and dozens of others, were just starting to be established, and our overnight accommodations did leave something to be desired. However, I was impressed that the president of the college, Dr. Ellis, stopped by to see how we were getting along, asking if we needed anything. In a few days our furniture arrived and we moved into a small, two-bedroom duplex at 1617 Caldwell. We were to have some interesting experiences in Conway which made a lasting impression on us.

Hendrix College was a small, Methodist school with quite a respectable reputation. There were approximately 500 students in the college, which was situated on an attractive campus at the northeastern edge of the city. The music department consisted of seven professors, and I had been hired as director of the choral groups as well as organ instructor. I also inquired about the possibility of teaching the music history courses. Dr. Ashley Coffman, the chair of the department realized that, as a musicologist, I was best qualified to teach in this area, and indicated to me that the person who had taught the courses in the past did not really enjoy it, and would be more than happy to be relieved of the burden.

A few weeks later, in speaking with some of the students, I was told that the former instructor, a fine musician and an excellent pianist, but with no training in either musicology or music history, usually walked into the classroom at the beginning of the semester and announced: "I'm just as bored teaching this stuff as you are having to take it, so let's just make it easy on ourselves." I was often to be confronted with this type of attitude toward historical studies in music in other institutions as well.

I have always failed to understand why music history courses, which really require a rather high level of specialized skills, as well as a broad knowledge of general history and culture, oftentimes seem to be entrusted to studio teachers, pianists, bassoonists or singers who are shy a few hours of a required teaching load. Administrators will argue that they have all had music history courses in school, even in graduate school, so they should be able to teach it. Using this kind of logic, I should then be capable of teaching the cello; after all, I had a year on the cello as my "secondary instrument" during my undergraduate days at Chicago Musical College.

The position at Hendrix College also included the job as minister of music at Pulaski Heights Methodist Church in Little Rock. The first time I walked into the church, my heart sank as I saw that the building was constructed of that awful Haddite block which, a few years earlier, I had experienced in Chicago. Haddite block is a rather inexpensive pressed Italian stone, quite porous, and it soaks up sound like a sponge. The church itself was a beautiful building, with a high roof, but also with the abominable divided choir setup found in Episcopal churches. It is without question, one of the worst designs for music making that can be imagined. No orchestra would put up with such conditions: Half the choir is on one side of the center aisle, and the other half on the other side. It is never possible to achieve any type of balance in such a situation, and the arrangement in which half of the group sings across the aisle to the other half results in much of the sound getting cancelled. The absolutely dead acoustics just compounded the difficulty of producing any kind of quality musical results. The final blow was discovering that the organ was one of those ghastly electronic substitutes. I always called them "toasters" or "refrigerators," but a musical instrument they were not. (In all fairness, however, I should report that the church replaced this electronic monstrosity some years later with a good pipe organ; as I recall they purchased a three-manual Schantz.)

The organization of the choral groups was ambitious: The church had what I called a "womb to tomb" choir system. There were four different choral groups: a children's choir, a junior high girls' choir, a high school choral group, and a senior choir. Facilities were impressive; rehearsal rooms abounded and the budget for purchase of music was generous. Looking back on it all now, I realize how frantic all this activity was, and how much sheer energy it took just to keep the entire enterprise going. I was totally overwhelmed by the amount of work I had to do: directing four choral groups and preparing and directing the music for each week, in addition to my full-time position at Hendrix College, which included two choral groups there, several classes in music

145

history, choral literature, eight or ten organ students, plus a *collegium musicum* which I organized on my own. We often traveled two or three times a week between Little Rock and Conway, and this was before the days of the interstate.

Luckily Gudrun, a good musician, had had considerable experience conducting a girls' choir in Germany, so I gave her the responsibility of directing the junior high girls' choir. She had some music scored for three-part girls' voices, but it was all in German, so we set to work translating the texts into acceptable English. I'm afraid Gudrun was not too happy working with the girls, who were less capable and less willing to work hard as her students in Germany had been. (She received no remuneration for the work.)

At Hendrix, I had several excellent organ students. Jerry McSpadden and Robert Burton were two of the most gifted students I had ever taught, and they were capable of playing the major works of the French school: Langlais, Messiaen, Dupré and others, as well as the major Bach preludes and fugues. Unfortunately, the organ at Hendrix College was totally inadequate. It was a small sixteen or seventeen rank Kimball; however, the instrument was installed in an excellent acoustical space, in the college chapel, and actually sounded better than it was. Even the larger school auditorium, which had an electronic "substitute," possessed such excellent acoustics that the electronic sounded almost acceptable.

I conducted some run-of-the-mill performances of Handel's *Messiah* and Mendelssohn's *Elijah*. Both performances utilized members of the Pulaski Heights Methodist Church choir, who joined the Hendrix choristers. A number of excellent soloists gave highly creditable performances as well. In the spring, the Hendrix College Choristers took an extended tour throughout northeastern Arkansas, and I was introduced to the Bible Belt mentality. At the high schools where we sang, I was informed that people did not applaud sacred music, and I had apparently committed the unpardonable sin of encouraging the students to applaud sacred music, oh, shame! I simply could never understand this strange mind-set, which resulted in a visit, to my home, of a professor of religion at Hendrix, who told me quite pointedly that my instruction to the students to applaud sacred music, was not acceptable behavior, and could not be tolerated.

I had another peculiar experience when I conducted Mendelssohn's *Elijah* at Pulaski Heights Methodist Church. The Hendrix College Choristers had joined the church choir, and the groups were spread out on both sides of the divided chancel, half on one side, half on the other. The only way I could conduct them was to stand in the middle of the aisle where all the singers could see me. This resulted in a severe reprimand from the pastor of the church, who reminded me that one does not stand in front of the cross for any reason. I don't see how I could have conducted the music in any other location, and I thought it quite odd that the Methodists, so proud of their Protestant heritage, would be so tied down to liturgical correctness that they would be offended by such supposedly "high church" prohibitions. In addition, the performance took place completely outside the confines of any church service.

147

We also began to be bothered by what had to be one of the most difficult attitudes we encountered in the South: People seemed to resent the fact that I was from the "North," and reminded me that "you Yankees really ruined us in the War Between the States," as they referred to the "Civil War." I'm sorry, I would answer, I wasn't even around at the time, and I could not be held personally responsible for something which occurred almost one hundred years earlier. I have never been able to understand such attitudes, but I knew that I was not happy in such a situation, and it soon became apparent that we would have to somehow get back to the Midwest, in spite of some superior students and fine faculty members at Hendrix College.

Because she was an excellent cellist, Gudrun was invited to become a member of the Little Rock Philharmonic, a mostly amateur orchestra, though some of its members came from nearby colleges and universities, including Hendrix. Gus Rudolph was the conductor. Gudrun became assistant principal 'cellist and also played in a smaller, more select chamber group which performed baroque literature, such as the Brandenburg Concertos and other literautre for small groups. All of this activity entailed even more trips to Little Rock. (Seated directly behind Gudrun was the young cellist Charlotte Moorman, who eventually went on to a highly publicized career as an avant-garde musician famous for all sorts of shocking public appearances with Nam June Paik, the Korean composer.)

One day Gudrun received a letter from a young, ambitious concert pianist from her hometown in Germany. The man was soon to arrive in America, and was hoping to be able to play some

Conway, Arkansas, April, 1957. "Mommy is practicing cello."
Martin looks on as Gudrun, looking rather pregnant again, works
on the Bach Brandenburg Concerto #3 for a concert by the Little
Rock Philharmonic.

concerts in our area. He wondered if we would be kind enough to arrange some appearances in and around Little Rock. So now, in addition to all our other responsibilities, we had to take on this additional one, in which I became, in effect, a concert manager for a man whose playing I had not, until then, even heard. Helmut Braus turned out to be a wonderful pianist, a sensitive and superb musician. He played several concerts in the area.

In November, Gudrun became pregnant with our third child, and, although she continued to play in the orchestra, she began to gradually curtail her activities. In March of 1957, I was informed that my contract would not be renewed, and eventually determined that the position at Hendrix was only meant to be a one-year position, though no one had apprised me of this. As I understood it, the son of one of the college dorm mothers had his eye on the job, and had apparently expected to return to the school after getting his master's degree from the University of Arkansas. (I now understood why no one but the president of the college interviewed me.)

On one occasion, I recall a visit from an old-fashioned, circuit riding Methodist preacher, who was somehow connected with Hendrix. After a pleasant visit with us one night, just as he was departing, he queried me: "Say, Miller, what church do you go to?" I answered that I was an Episcopalian, to which he retorted: "Oh, that's all right, we'll make you a Methodist one of these days."

One of the few wonderful people whom we met while in Conway was a music professor at Arkansas State Teachers College, on the opposite end of town. Tom Higgins, a fine pianist, was also, without question, one of the zaniest, most delightful men I'd met in many years. Exceptionally well educated in literature, philosophy and art history, as well as in music, he had a good command of Latin and French. His specialty was the music of Chopin, and he later published a number of first-rate scholarly studies dealing with the composer's music. I think if it had not been for Tom, his wife Jane, and their children, Gudrun and I would have just about gone stir crazy in that place where I swore they rolled up the sidewalks at night. Tom was the only person in whom I could confide my problems, and he was always sympathetic, suffering under the same kind of stifling, narrow-minded, provincial mentality as we were. Unfortunately, we didn't have an opportunity to get to know the Higgins' very well, as we were to leave Conway soon after the birth of our third child.

Gudrun entered the hospital in Conway on July 23, 1957, and little Doris Christina, another "preemie," at only five pounds, two ounces, was born that evening at 8:00 p.m. Luckily, we were at the new hospital, which had been open only a week; the old hospital was not, and would have been unbearable in the heat. Often temperatures were over 105 degrees, and, in addition, it was humid. Gudrun suffered a slight stroke during the birth and was partially paralyzed for several days.

At this point, I had no job, and no prospects for one. We had no money, Gudrun was still in the hospital, and I was trying to keep house for four-year-old Martin and two-year-old Claudia in the oppressive summer heat. In addition, Blue Cross was threatening to deny our claims for Doris's birth as I was no longer connected with the college. I recall, that at night, I would often step into the kitchen to get something to eat, and when I turned on the lights, could hear the scurrying of dozens of cockroaches which covered the sink and cupboards in the room. It was a very depressing time for us all.

Since I had been informed of my contract nonrenewal, I had been in the process of writing over 235 different colleges and universities throughout the country inquiring about possible faculty openings. I typed each letter on my manual typewriter, and included my *curriculum vitae* as well. Out of 235 schools, I received only about five positive answers, but even these said that, while I seemed qualified, they had just hired someone. In one instance, I actually drove to a school in Missouri and appeared without an appointment for a position I had seen advertised. I was never given the opportunity for an interview by school officials. I was registered with Lutton Musical Personnel Service, Hughes Teachers Bureau and the College and Specialists Bureau, all in Chicago. It was the middle of July, and the summer hiring period was almost over. I was desperate.

Shortly after Doris was born, my parents paid us another visit. My father was appalled at our strained finances, and loaned me $1,000 in order to tide us over until I got another teaching job somewhere. At this point, I think I would have taken anything, except that I no longer wished to stay in the South. I had covered a map in different colors to indicate those areas where I would absolutely never consider applying: the entire area south of the Mason-Dixon line, which I dubbed "TOTALLY UNACCEPTABLE." Other areas, such as the majority of the Midwest and mountain states were generally acceptable, with a few "acceptable with reservations" on the West Coast, East Coast and desert Southwest.

During the second week of August, I received a notice of an opening at Howe Military School in Howe, Indiana. They were looking for a man to direct the sacred music program of the school, train two choirs, play the organ at daily chapel services and teach some piano and organ. The salary was $4,500 a year, and included preparing a small choral group for some type of summer pageant which took place outdoors at a camp grounds a few miles from Howe. The military school was connected with the Episcopal Church.

As there were no other prospects at the time, I applied for the job, and soon received a letter from the commandant of the school, B.B. Bouton, Colonel Inf., N.G. He wrote that he was pleased to hear from me, inasmuch as a teachers bureau had recently reported that they had no candidates for the position. He also liked the idea that I was an Episcopalian, though he was concerned that the rather elementary nature of the position might be less than I would care to consider. At this point, I figured that "beggars can't be choosers," and took the train to Chicago on August 19 to meet the colonel and his wife in the University Club at Madison and Michigan the next day.

CHAPTER 7

HOWE MILITARY SCHOOL
(1957-1963)

I met Colonel Bouton and his wife at the University Club in Chicago. Bouton appeared to be a stiff, formal man devoid of any personal warmth. I later determined that he was somewhat parsimonious as well. A few years after I had left Howe, I read in the paper that he suffered a fatal heart attack while attending a Notre Dame football game in South Bend.

Following a long trip on the Indiana Toll Road, we arrived at Howe, Indiana, a wide spot in the road with a population of about 800; that is, when the military school of approximately 300 students was in session. In his letter, Colonel Bouton had indicated that "...the organ although it has a beautiful tone, also has a somewhat limited console, I am informed." That was, without question, the understatement of the year. The instrument was a 1903, fourteen-rank, tubular pneumatic Kimball, in poor condition, incapable of playing much of anything. The stop knobs pulled out by the foot, and one of them had been broken off. The colonel went on to say: "...I hope that sometime in the near future some improvement can be made in this direction, but it would not be immediately." Nothing was ever done about the condition of the instrument while I was there.

On the other hand, the chapel itself was an absolute gem of a building. I have never seen anything like it in this country. Stepping into the building, one could easily imagine himself in an English monastery chapel. Dark wood stalls with elaborate carvings and a stone floor almost gave the impression of some kind of medieval building. All the seats in the nave of the chapel faced toward the center aisle, and there was a handsome, white stone altar at the far end. The building seated about 250, and also had a commodious rear gallery seating another fifty people, though it was normally not used, being reserved for visiting parents, usually on the weekends. It was, without question, one of the loveliest buildings I have ever been in.

A small choir rehearsal room was located off the chapel, and there was a collection of choir and service music, much of it mediocre, together with a few volumes of third-rate organ music. In the gymnasium about a block away were the piano studios, six small practice rooms with upright pianos. It was obvious that the school considered the study of any kind of music as a totally unimportant and frivolous subject, not on the same plane of serious study as the sciences, military discipline, endless parade drills and "ath-e-letics."

After we had taken the tour, Colonel Bouton and I returned to his office and sat down. It was a strange meeting. At no time did he ask me whether I would be interested in the position, nor did he indicate that he was even interested in hiring me. After about ten minutes of banter, I finally had to come right out and ask him if he were offering me the position. Somehow I finally sensed that he was, and a contract was then drawn up and signed.

A young woman in the office told me of a small apartment a mile or two out in the country, which her father owned, and which he would be willing to rent to us. She took me out to the house, which was in a lovely wooded area near the Pidgeon River, and showed me a small, two-bedroom apartment situated above a double garage, which would be adequate for our needs, at least until we had an opportunity to find something a bit larger, perhaps a house.

This was to be the beginning of what, in many ways, was the most depressing and frustrating period of my life so far. I appeared to be falling farther and farther behind in my efforts to teach music history and musicology at the college or university level. For the next few years we were to suffer some family crises and subsistence-level living, which were extremely depressing. However, certain clouds do have a silver lining, and, as it turned out, there were a number of promising developments which would take place, after a few years, that were quite exciting, so it was not totally desolate. At least, I thought, we were only three hours from Chicago, where we still had friends, as well as Gudrun's cousins Irene Anderson and Erich Lenz. Most important for me, I think, was that we were now back in the North, with all the other "Yankees." Less than a week after we left Arkansas, National Guard troops, on orders of President Eisenhower, were called to Central High School in Little Rock to escort black children into the newly integrated school.

156

We traveled over the Labor Day weekend, arriving at Howe to stay at the same small motel where I'd been during the interview. After a few days our furniture arrived, and we moved into the small apartment above the garage. The area was quite isolated except for two families on either side of us. The woods were full of wild animals whose calls could be heard at night, and trains whistled in the distance as they traveled from Fort Wayne north to places in southwestern Michigan. It was rustic and peaceful. I recall arising very early one crisp fall morning, and, with Gudrun, watched the first man-made satellite, the Russian "Sputnik," streak across the darkened skies over northern Indiana.

The work at the military school was not demanding, consisting of two short daily chapel services, one at noon and one at night. The services, a shortened form of Evensong, required three hymns, a prelude and a postlude. On Sunday, the entire corps attended the Eucharist, celebrated only by the priest. The Northern Indiana diocese of the Episcopal Church was, as one priest in Arkansas characterized it, "sky high." This was the first time I had ever seen such things as genuflection, Sanctus bells and even incense. I half expected to see rosary beads. It was the closest thing to a Roman Catholic Mass I'd ever experienced. I learned what the term "Anglo-Catholic" meant.

Two priests were in charge, one for the "lower school" (fifth through eighth grades), the other for the "upper school" (ninth through twelfth grade). Robert Murphy was the priest in charge of the upper school. He was a short, sweet, lovable man, a heavy smoker, and had a relatively good singing voice. The usual Sunday service music consisted either of chant, or the Healy Wilan

157

setting of the Communion service. Occasionally I would prepare the choir to sing an anthem. The school was not in session over Christmas, although there was a special "Boar's Head Dinner" in the dining hall shortly before Christmas. I prepared the choir, which sang the usual carols and other appropriate music.

The piano instruction was a joke. Not only did the boys have no interest in studying piano seriously, they never practiced except for the thirty minutes they came over to the studios for their lesson once a week. Except for some low-level instruction at Mitchell College, I had limited experience teaching piano students. Rather than a diet of John Thompson Book II, "Floating Locomotives" or "Bells Through the Trees," I tried to introduce some of the better students to Bartók's *Mikrokosmos,* usually with little success. Because I was required to work on Sundays, I was allowed Wednesdays off. For the first two years I had no organ students, but a high school student finally started studying organ with me in my third year, until he was expelled for stealing another boy's watch one day.

In contrast to the unstimulating nature of the academic instruction, there were several rather intelligent and witty faculty members. Allen Gates, a teacher of English, became one of my closest friends and later was extremely supportive in a number of my musical enterprises on campus. He had an apartment in a run-down campus building, and had, as I recall, traveled extensively in Europe, where his father had been in the army. It seems to me that he had also lived in Berlin at one time. Others were Arthur Worrell and John Finch. John was from England, and was a beacon of enlightenment and erudition for me, as well as being musically literate. He died tragically in a dorm fire at Cornell University a few years later, while attempting to save some students. Warren Haas studied Proust and other 20th-century writers, and certainly seemed out of place in such an atmosphere. The place of music, of any type, always took a back seat to other endeavors, especially "ath-e-letics." The intellectual and artistic atmosphere was indescribably bleak and I soon was suffering from an acute case of *ennui*.

In February of 1958, Gudrun began to experience severe digestive problems, with bouts of intense stomach pain. Although our doctor in Sturgis, Michigan, just across the state line, assured her it was only gastritis or something similar, she insisted upon a thorough examination. Finally, she was admitted to Sturgis Memorial Hospital the middle of February for a cholecystotomy. The doctor admitted it was the largest case of gall bladder disease he had ever encountered. (We reverently preserved the gallstones for several years in a Mason jar.) While Gudrun was hospitalized, I frantically tried to balance taking care of three small children, ages four, three and eight months, while attempting to fulfill my teaching duties. In addition, we were again financially strapped, and I hadn't even started to pay my father back the money he had loaned me the previous year in Arkansas.

Shortly after Gudrun's operation, we were asked to vacate the apartment, the owner claiming he needed it for a member of his family. We then found a small, two-bedroom bungalow at 209 W. Electric Court, in Sturgis, which is eight miles north of Howe. I commuted twice a day to Howe for the next six years. In March Gudrun announced that she was again pregnant, barely fifteen months after Doris was born. The gall bladder operation had apparently upset some rather delicate calendar calculations.

Sturgis, Michigan, a pleasant little town of 12,000 just over the state line, was five miles north of the Indiana Toll Road, and is best known as the home of the Kirsch Company, manufacturers of drapery and curtain rods. The small house on Electric Court was barely large enough for us, and we were too poor to even afford a telephone. In Sturgis I became acquainted with a first-rate musician and organist, the kind of person I would never have expected to find in such a small place. Myron Casner, F.A.G.O., A.R.C.O., had moved to Sturgis from St. Louis, Missouri, where I believe he had been organist and choirmaster at one of the large Episcopal churches there, perhaps even the cathedral. The story I was told is that he had been persuaded to come to Sturgis by the owner of the Kirsch Company there, to take a position as organist and choirmaster at St. John's Episcopal Church in Sturgis, and teach music in the local high school. Casner was a composer as well, whose music has been published by Concordia in St. Louis. He was the owner of a one-manual harpsichord by the British builder, Robert Goble, and had also rescued a delightful one-manual-tracker organ from a Catholic church which was being demolished, and had, with the help of Jerry Adams, a local organ builder, set it up in his living room.

In 1960 I began studying with Casner, and was able to practice regularly at the church, which was just a short block from our house. The organ at St. John's was a fairly good three-manual Wicks of about thirty-five ranks, although the church was rather small. I mastered the first movements of the Bach C major and C minor trio sonatas (BVW 529 and 526), an awesome achievement for me, as well as parts of the *Clavierübung*, Part III, including the so-called "Credo Fugue" ("Wir glauben all' an einen Gott")[BVW 680], the "Kyrie, Gott Vater in Ewigkeit", (BVW 669) and some other things from the Orgelbüchlein (BVW 599-644).

***

As Gudrun's due date in December approached, we began to think seriously about having a telephone installed, inasmuch as she might have a need to get in touch with me at school, eight miles distant, should I be teaching. The telephone company man appeared at the house around 8:45 a.m., Thursday, October 30, and began installing the telephone. After he had been there less than thirty minutes, Gudrun began to feel the first, unmistakable pangs of labor, and we quickly arranged for an elderly neighbor lady to come over and watch the three children, while I made the first call on the newly installed telephone to school, to say that my wife was going into labor. Again, we had not expected this, as her due date was still at least a month away.

There was a further complication. Every time Gudrun had gone for pre-natal checkups, she always asked doctors about the possibility of a multiple birth, as she knew it ran in her family. (Her aunt Gertrude and uncle Werner were twins.) In every case, she was assured that no second fetal heartbeat could be detected. We left for the hospital, which was a mere four blocks away, and she continued in labor until about 12:15 p.m.. As Dr. Allen Brunson, our doctor, was delivering the baby, he exclaimed suddenly to Gudrun: "Why, Mrs. Miller, I believe there is a second baby here!" Half-dazed, groggy, in pain, Gudrun answered: "Dr. Brunson, please don't make jokes with me at a time like this."

It was no joke: Gudrun was having twins! And they were almost six weeks premature. Each weighed barely three pounds, and they were immediately placed in incubators. As she came out of delivery, Gudrun was smiling at me, and Dr. Brunson broke the news: I was the father of twins! After Doris had been born, we had fully intended to discontinue contributing to the population explosion, and had no plans to have more children. I suppose precisely because we wanted no more children, we were now presented with not just one, but, two. The next day, she underwent a tubal ligation. (The reader should recall that this was long before the days of the "pill," vasectomies, or Roe vs. Wade.)

One Saturday morning, as I was conducting a choir rehearsal down at Howe, I was called out of the rehearsal by an emergency telephone call. Running into the office, I heard a sobbing Gudrun tell me I had to come right home: She had just gotten a letter from her mother informing her that her father had suddenly died. I immediately dismissed the boys and hurried back to Sturgis, having also located Father Murphy, who happened to be in town at the moment. He accompanied me to our house, and comforted Gudrun in her grief. It was to be the first in a series of family deaths with which we would be confronted during the next ten years.

We could hardly stay in the small two-bedroom bungalow with five children, and around November 20, I was able to find a larger house for rent about seven blocks away at 204 W. Congress Street, and planned to make the move the day before Thanksgiving, on November 26. However, fate has a way of upsetting one's plans, and in what followed, all the best-laid plans went for naught.

My daily schedule at school called for me to go to work around 8:30 a.m., teach piano all morning, play the noon chapel service for the "lower school," and then go home in the afternoon, returning at 5:00 p.m. for a daily choir rehearsal and 6:00 p.m. evening chapel service for the high school students. I often took Martin with me to the evening services, just to give Gudrun a brief respite from having to care for all three children. He would sit quietly beside me as I played the service.

On Tuesday evening, November 25, Martin had gone with me and, as we drove north to Sturgis on the main road, State Highway 9, I noticed a car coming from the crossroad to the east. As I was on the state highway, and the driver was on an unmarked country road, he had to observe the stop sign at the intersection with the main road. Unfortunately, he failed to stop, and drove right out into the intersection, where he plowed into the right side of the car, causing me to lose control, veer off to the right, and strike a tree by the side of the road. This, of course, was long before the days of seatbelts, and although the car was badly damaged on the right side, we were luckily uninjured, except for a cut on his forehead, which Martin sustained when he was thrown against the dashboard. We now had no car, the twins were still in incubators in the hospital, and we were supposed to move to a new house the next day.

Wednesday, November 26, dawned cold and blustery, and it was already snowing. The movers arrived and began loading the van. As they were finishing their work, we put three-year-old Claudia and sixteen-month-old Doris into an ancient baby buggy, which I had recently purchased for the staggering amount of five dollars, while Martin, five years old, trudged along in the falling snow with me and Gudrun, who had been released from the hospital less than a month previously. We walked the half-mile to the new house in a heavy snowstorm.

Arriving at the new house, we were met by the movers, the furniture was unloaded and we began unpacking our belongings. Now, however, we had a new problem. The movers pointed out that there was no city gas line into the house with which to hook up our gas stove. Unknown to us, the house had, some years earlier, been moved to the site from another location, and had never been supplied with city gas. The stove had to be hooked up to a tank of propane gas, located outside, at the rear of the house. Unfortunately, the connector on our stove did not fit the line leading from the propane tank into the house, so we had no gas in the house, it was too late in the day to get someone to install the correct one, and tomorrow was Thanksgiving Day. Frankly, I wasn't quite certain what we had to be thankful for at this point. Seeing our plight, the owner of the moving company took pity on me and went back to his office, where he found an electric hot plate for us to use until the gas could be hooked up. Thanksgiving Day dinner consisted of cans of spaghetti warmed up in a saucepan on the electric hot plate.

The day after Thanksgiving, we got the stove hooked up, and by the following week, the Ford garage in Sturgis had repaired the car enough so that I could drive it, although the right front side was still smashed in, the door was inoperative, and the right front headlight was secured by duct tape. This is the car I drove for the next five months. The first week of December the twins, having now reached five pounds, were finally released from the hospital, and shared a bedroom with Claudia and Doris. One must remember, incidentally, that Doris was still in diapers, making it necessary for Gudrun to wash as many as eight loads of diapers daily, hanging them to dry on the line. (Again, this was long before the advent of disposable diapers.) At this point, we finally broke down and bought, for the first time in our lives, an appliance on the installment plan at the nearby Montgomery Ward store: it was our first clothes dryer.

Daily schedules included alternate feedings, every two hours: When one twin was finished, the next one needed to be fed. We both shared in these tasks, day and night. By March of 1959, it had become clear that Gudrun was reaching a point of despair with the daily schedule of caring for three small babies, in addition to getting Martin, now in first grade, and Claudia, in kindergarten, off to school each day. She desperately needed to get some respite from the unceasing burdens of caring for five children, six years old and younger. Just at this time a fortunate turn of events occurred.

I had had an opportunity to meet the director of the Sturgis Public Library, Joe Kimbrough, and, as we talked together one day, I told him something of Gudrun's educational background, her mastery of six languages, and her need to get out of the house, if only for a few hours a day. Joe indicated that he had need of a typist and general desk clerk at the library for three hours a day,

November, 1959, Sturgis, Michigan. The twins are just one year old here. The children are sitting underneath a portrait of the aged Heinrich Schütz.

and, if she were interested, to stop by and discuss the matter with him. As the library was only two blocks away from the house, Gudrun jumped at the chance, and was soon working a few hours each day at the library, while I stayed home with the babies during my free time in the afternoon. The arrangement worked out well: it brought us a little extra income, it provided Gudrun with a change, allowing her to get out of the house each day, and it also started her out in a field which later burgeoned into a profession which eventually provided her with a great deal of personal satisfaction.

Gudrun continued to work in the library, gaining more and more competency and experience, for the rest of the time we were in Sturgis. Joe was a splendid mentor and a sheer delight as a human being, and his knowledge and dedication to the library profession was a source of inspiration and joy to her. He later moved on to ever more prestigious library positions at Lansing, Michigan; Denver, Colorado; and finally, as director of the Minneapolis Public Library.

My days were filled with an unending succession of uninteresting work involving training recalcitrant and unwilling choir boys, daily playing an ancient wreck of an organ, and trying to teach piano to boys who didn't care to learn. I tried to present some lectures on music to classes of the cadet corps, and some of us founded a small group, consisting of faculty members and advanced students, who regularly met to discuss some of the great ideas of history. Lectures on a number of interesting topics preceded weekly discussions. Because of her doctoral studies in archeology at Göttingen, Gudrun lectured on the Dead Sea scrolls, which had recently been discovered, and others talked about new developments in contemporary art and film, the works of Joyce and Proust and British playwrights of the 20th century. The group was one of the bright spots in an otherwise sterile and unstimulating atmosphere.

I believe this period in my life represented the deepest depression I had ever experienced, and at one point, I even contemplated suicide. Here I was, in my mid-thirties, with a master's degree in musicology, and post-graduate study in musicology at a German university, an increasingly broad knowledge of the field, a burning desire to teach in a college situation, to do research, to somehow accomplish something in my life, and I was stifled, discouraged and frustrated at every turn. My dear friend Tom Higgins, from our old days in Conway, Arkansas, writing in answer to a desperate letter I had written him, attempted to cheer me up, begging me to think of my wife and children's welfare. He urged me to try and get out of the depressing atmosphere at Howe, and begin work on my doctorate.

One thing which gave me great satisfaction was my work on an annotated translation of an important book on the organ from the 16th century. Arnold *Schlick's Spiegel der Orgelmacher und Organisten,* (mirror of organ makers and organists) is probably the earliest treatise on the design and construction of the organ. Only one copy of the original, published in Mainz in 1511, was known to exist, and was in the British Musuem, where it had been purchased, as a part of the *Nachlass* (estate) of the Frankfurt antique lover and antiquarian Paul Hirsch. Unfortunately, however, I was unable to consult the work, and was working from a somewhat modernized version, published by Ernst Flade in 1932. Although I knew this was not the preferred way to go about such things, I got to work on it, and proposed to Arthur Howes, the editor of the *Organ Institute Quarterly,* that he consider publishing it. He was very encouraging, and in 1958 the first few chapters appeared in the journal. Further submissions followed at irregular intervals until the complete translation (with the exception of some non-musical material) was finally published five years later. The translation is almost as much Gudrun's work as mine, and, together, it afforded us an opportunity to do something of a scholarly nature, which provided a wonderful respite from the daily round of babies, washing clothes, and disciplining children.

At this time, I decided to turn my attention to pursuing a Ph.D. Although I had given some thought to the University of Michigan, I was interested in working with a musicologist at Michigan State University in East Lansing. There had been a somewhat tricky chapter in my Schlick translation which dealt with tuning and temperament, and in the course of doing research, I read some of the writings of J. Murray Barbour, who was considered at the time one of the world's outstanding authorities in this area. (He was responsible for the *MGG* article on "Temperament.") Barbour taught at Michigan State University, so I wrote him about my desire to pursue a doctorate in musicology. He replied that, unfortunately, they did not yet have a Ph.D. program in musicology, but he invited Gudrun and me to come to East Lansing and discuss my interests with him and to see the campus. We were treated very cordially by Walter Hodgson, the department chair, and Dr. Barbour, who took us to lunch at Kellogg Conference Center on campus. They both indicated that the doctoral program in musicology would shortly become a reality, and encouraged me to begin my work as soon as possible. It would be another three years before I could actually begin, but the prospect sounded very attractive to me, and the thought of returning to the classroom as a doctoral student was most welcome.

In September of 1959, a new member of the faculty afforded me a good deal of enjoyable company. John Henry was a quiet, highly sensitive, well-educated Bostonian, apparently as out of place at Howe as John Finch, Allen Gates and I were. What especially pleased me about meeting John, however, was that he was a devout lover of the harpsichord and its music, and had recently ordered a beautiful French double from the workshop of the highly-esteemed Boston builder Eric Herz. Herz had worked for a while in Frank Hubbard's shop before striking out on his own. The instrument was delivered around the first of the year in 1960, and I could hardly wait for its arrival. After a hectic trip to Chicago, in the middle of a snowstorm, John and I picked up the instrument in my new Ford station wagon and returned to campus. For the next eight months I had the distinct and unending pleasure of playing it anytime I wished. It was, without question, the most beautiful looking and sounding harpsichord I had ever played. It had an especially interesting stop, the *peau de buffle*, in which the strings were plucked by soft buffalo leather. It was a beautiful sound. On one occasion, a group of us played a program consisting of trio sonatas by baroque composers and some solo literature. Myron Casner played both harpsichord and recorder, and Gudrun played recorder, as well as cello, while I played continuo in the trio sonatas. Jerry Adams of Sturgis also played recorder. It was probably the most elegant, distinguished music making that had ever been heard on the campus of Howe Military School.

***

On Monday, February 8, 1960, the Board of Trustees of Howe Military School, at their regular quarterly meeting, announced a major building program which was to include the construction of a new chapel for the school. The benefactor, a wealthy industrialist

Christmas, 1960, Sturgis, Michigan. Singing around the Advent wreath. (l to r): Claudia (I think!), Gudrun, Karin (I think!), Martin and Doris.

December 25, 1960, Sturgis, Michigan. Sitting patiently under the Christmas tree, waiting to open their presents. (l to r): Karin?, Gisela?, Doris, Claudia, Martin. (I always had a difficult time telling the twins apart, until Karin fell down the basement steps one day and split open her forehead, requiring three stitches to close up the wound. From then on, she would push her hair back to show me the scar whenever I asked, "which twin are you?")

171

from the Detroit area, whose son and grandson had both attended the school, was already a major financial "angel" to the school, having made substantial gifts in the past, including a number of campus buildings. The school newspaper, The *Howe Herald,* whose faculty advisor was my good friend Allan Gates, reported, in its next issue "...The chapel will be built on the south campus...[and] will have a seating capacity of 500 with a choir and organ loft at the rear of the building. A new pipe organ will be ordered with delivery not expected for at least 16 months...."

I was stunned. I was ecstatic. I couldn't believe this exciting prospect. I was told I would be closely involved in the design of the organ, and in the choice of a builder. I drove home that afternoon in a state of euphoria. As I came into the house, I called to Gudrun with the exciting news. I simply couldn't contain my enthusiasm, and we both were elated. I was pleased to note that the architect and the bishop of the diocese, Reginald Mallett, had made the wise decision to place the organ and choir in the rear gallery, where they could then operate as an integrated unit, leading and supporting congregational singing from behind and above. It couldn't have been a wiser decision, and I was grateful to the bishop for this excellent choice.

The Right Reverend Reginald Mallett was tall, slim and handsome, balding, and extremely commanding in appearance. He had a bright, pink complexion, piercing eyes, and one was never in doubt as to who was in charge when one spoke to him. He was also a superb diplomat. When the wealthy benefactor had originally proposed the building of a new chapel for Howe School, a story was told about the discussions which were supposed to have taken place between the bishop and the benefactor. The man proposed that the new chapel be named after the bishop's wife, Lucy Murchison Mallett, who had died the previous year. Told by the bishop that the Episcopal Church does not name churches after individuals, the benefactor was supposed to have harrumphed, a bit offended: "What's wrong, Bishop, don't you want *my* church?" The bishop, ever the consummate diplomat, reportedly then recommended that the new church be named "All Saints Chapel," which, we were to assume, would include his wife as well.

Now began the exciting prospect of drawing up a stop list, deciding what type of action, i.e., mechanical or electric, would be used, contacting various builders, determining an approximate cost for the instrument, and establishing time frames for delivery and installation, based on schedules relating to the construction and finishing of the building. In the course of the next six months, I had the pleasant task of corresponding with a number of builders whom I was convinced would build us an excellent instrument. My file regarding the instrument, correspondence with builders, sketches of proposed cases, recommendations to the architect, Carl B. Marr of Detroit, Michigan, as well as the on-site construction firm, is over three inches thick. The entire project represented, for me, one of the richest and most fulfilling experiences of my life thus far.

However, more important than any of these aspects of the project was the opportunity to come to know a man whose friendship, superb musicianship, worldwide reputation, and visionary artistic excellence has meant more to me than anyone I have ever had the honor of knowing: Robert Noehren, the distinguished organist of the University of Michigan, one of the supreme artists of the recital world, and a fine organ builder, as well. I have always marveled at my luck in meeting someone with the international reputation which Bob enjoys: He has been to the organ world what Rubinstein, Horowitz or Ashkenazy are to the piano world, or Perlman, Zukerman or Stern are to the violin world. I have always felt humbled and in awe at his accomplishments, and yet, he has never failed to impress me with his humility and modesty, and his ability to be a friend as well as a distinguished colleague.

After several more months and a considerable number of consultations among the architect, Bishop Mallett and the benefactor, the decision was made to award the contract to Noehren. My own preferences were for a simple instrument suitable for accompanying the cadet corps in hymns and service music, and the performance of much of the organ literature. As such, the instrument would have no swell box, no combination pistons, indeed nothing but a rich and varied stop disposition without spending money on extras. This decision proved to be a wise one, as all the limited funds could now be spent on the most essential components of the instrument, namely, pipes.

The two-manual instrument of thirty-five ranks, would utilize a case front, in the manner of Dom Bedos, in which the Principals, or Prestants of each division would form the facades: Pedal in the middle, Great to the left, and Positiv to the right, each with its own distinctive proportions.

Great	Positiv	Pedal
16' Quintadena	8' Metal Gedackt	16' Subbaß
8' Principal(prospect)	8' Gemshorn*	8'Principal (prospect)
8' Rohrflöte	8 Gemshorn Celeste*	4' Octave
4' Octave	4' Principal (prospect)	2'Octave (extension)
4' Spitzflöte	4' Rohrflöte	V Mixture
2-2/3' Nasat	2' Octave	16' Posaune
2' Octave	1-1/3 Quint	8'Trompette (bottom 12 from Great)
2' Waldflöte	III Cymbal*	4' Clarion (extension)
III-V Mixture	III-V Scharf	
8' Trompette	II Sequialtera	
	8' Cromhorne	
	Tremulant	
	*indicates preparations	

Couplers

Great to Positiv   Meidinger blower in case

Great to Pedal   Tilting tablets

Positiv to Pedal

Jerry Adams, who had worked for Noehren for some years, and was an excellent woodworker and carpenter, as well as a bright young organ builder and organist, was given the task of building the 16' Subbaß in his own shop right in Sturgis. The lumber used in the mouths came from a beautiful stand of walnut trees on the property of the Howe quartermaster, and I had the distinct pleasure of watching the construction of the rank week by week in Jerry's shop, just a few blocks from my house. When the rank was finished, Jerry and I loaded it carefully into my spacious station wagon, and transported it down to the chapel to await the rest of the instrument, which arrived the last week in July of 1961.

Day after day, Noehren sat patiently in the gallery during hot, humid weather, carefully voicing each of the almost 1,700 pipes in the organ, so that the sound "fit" the building. He had initially put the pipes "on speech" in the shop of the Dutch builder Verschueren, except for the reed stops, which came from another source.

The instrument was a great success and the dedicatory recital, which took place on the evening of October 27, 1961, included a large contingent from Chicago, Kalamazoo, South Bend and Detroit. Noehren actually played two separate programs, the second one on Sunday morning preceding the actual dedication of the instrument. Although I was aware that the absence of such amenities as a swell chamber, or registers such as a celeste or a flute harmonique might not make the instrument amenable to works such as the Franck *Chorals*, or the larger works of Widor, Vierne and other French composers, I was particularly pleased, and pleasantly surprised at how well some Brahms chorale preludes, the Mendelssohn 6th sonata, the Franck *Prelude, Fugue and Variation*, and the finale from the Widor Sixth Symphony sounded on the instrument, during the course of the weekend.

In the remaining two years I was to be at Howe, I enjoyed some of my most satisfying experiences playing the organ, and actually made some private recordings on it. Noehren himself made a recording for Lyrichord on it, which included the entire

Noehren organ in All Saint's Chapel, Howe Military School, Howe, Indiana. Installed in 1961, the Principals form the front of the cases: Pedal in the center, Great to the left and Positiv to the right in the smaller case.

Opus 122 chorale preludes of Brahms, divided between the Howe instrument and a smaller one he had built for a Lutheran church in Lincoln Park, Michigan. In addition, Noehren spent a good deal of time in Howe making recordings of north, central and south German organ music. Unfortunately, however, these tapes have never been released, and I regret, to this day, that no one has ever had the opportunity to hear them. I hope that someday we shall have the pleasure of hearing these recordings.

I also inaugurated a series of modest recitals by a number of excellent regional organists: Myron Casner, of Sturgis; Charles

Hoke, of South Bend; Wyatt Insko, a former Noehren student, then organist of Fourth Presbyterian Church in Chicago; and E. Thompson Bagley, an English instructor at Howe, who was an accomplished organist as well. In addition, my good friend Walter Wade played in the series.

Meanwhile, I began to feel more and more that I simply had to try and stay abreast of developments in my field of musicology. I had continued my membership in the American Musicological Society, and was aware of the various meetings of the Midwest Chapter of AMS. Gudrun and I began to attend some of them; that is, when we could afford to find a baby sitter willing to stay overnight with five small children.

The spring 1961 meeting of the Midwest Chapter of AMS was to be held in Ann Arbor, and as Bob Noehren had been asking me to come over and take a look at the console of the new Howe instrument, which he was then building in his shop, I decided to combine a visit to see him and Eloise, his wife, with the conference. It was to lead to the most important and productive meeting in my professional life up until that time.

After the first session of the conference on Saturday morning was over, I left and started walking around in downtown Ann Arbor, visiting the record and bookstores. As I walked, I noticed a couple ahead of me whom I had seen in the lecture the previous hour, and I introduced myself. He was a musicologist on the faculty of St. Mary's College in South Bend, and she was a singer. Hanns-Bertold Dietz, a native of Dresden, Germany, had met his wife, Julie, in Austria, I believe at the Mozarteum in Salzburg, where both were apparently studying one summer. Julie was from

Goshen, Indiana, and later they married, returning to Indiana, where Dietz entered Notre Dame University in South Bend, studying with my former classmate and teacher, Joe Leahy. Dietz was awarded the master's in musicology there in 1954. He was also an organist. The obvious parallels to my own life, and my marriage to a German immediately became obvious, and the three of us immediately felt a sense of comradery. Like my close friend Tom Higgins, Dietz had an absolutely wicked sense of humor, a man who tossed off one-liners with great ease, and was the epitome of graciousness and cordiality as well. If he'd not become a musicologist, he would have made a dynamite TV talk-show host. In addition to this, he was handsome, charming and had his own airplane. We walked for over an hour together, exchanging addresses and phone numbers, determined to meet again. I invited them to drive up to Sturgis and be our guests for dinner. "Bertl," as I called him, and I were to become good friends.

A few weeks later Bertl and Julie came over to Sturgis, and we had a delightful dinner together at Patterson's, an excellent restaurant which Gudrun and I patronized on special occasions. Vowing to continue seeing each other, we began making plans to drive down to Goshen, where they lived. Goshen was only thirty-five miles from Sturgis, and the Dietze's could see that we were starved for some kind of intellectual and musical stimulation. Bertl provided me with a wonderful antidote to the barrenness and frigidity of Howe. Of course, our children were excited about the possibility of being invited to go up in Bertl's plane, and, as they had three children, including a girl Claudia's age, she was invited to stay over the weekend at their house on one occasion.

About this time, Gudrun applied for American citizenship, and, with Jerry Adams' mother as her witness, appeared at the Branch County courthouse in Coldwater, Michigan, on May 29, 1962, to take the oath of allegiance to the United States, thereby becoming an American citizen.

That summer, I began my first work toward my Doctorate, studying with J. Murray Barbour, Gomer Jones, Paul Harder and Richard Klausli. I also became acquainted with the man who would become my so-called "Doktor Vater," Professor Hans Nathan. Probably the most fascinating person with whom I worked there was not a musicologist, but a theorist and composer, Gomer Jones, a purebred Welshman with an incredible ability to excite students about music. He had a seemingly inexhaustible knowledge of the standard literature, playing much of it at the piano by memory. Most important, he always gave one the impression that he loved music very much, and wanted to share his love and knowledge with students. He became, for me, a teaching model whom I hoped to emulate. Sitting at the piano in class, he could lecture on any aspect of the rhythmic, melodic or harmonic structures of the music, often singing along in a high, rather penetrating voice. My only regret is that I was never able to take his course on the Bartók Quartets, which many graduate students pronounced his best presentations. He could be rather "earthy" at times, and, on occasion, swear like a sailor, but I came to love his approach, his enthusiasm and his encyclopedic knowledge.

Dr. Barbour was entirely different. His lectures were dry as dust, he had a somewhat soft voice, and lacked any kind of conviction or liveliness. He was probably the most boring professor I have ever had. I also received the only "C" I ever got in graduate school, in his course on "The Acoustics of Music." Most of it was mathematics, geometry and logarithms, and I was petrified, having done so poorly in mathematics in high school!

Gomer Jones also conducted a large choral group composed of both graduates and undergraduates, who needed to take an "ensemble" course in order to fulfill curriculum requirements. This was a rather motley group of students, but it did allow me to learn some repertoire, including a work which I have since come to believe is probably the greatest choral work, even one of the best pieces of music of the 20th century: Stravinsky's *Symphony of Psalms*, which I was privileged to sing under the inspired direction of Robert Shaw, together with the Bach *Magnificat* and the Schubert G major Mass.

My work at Michigan State during the summers of 1962 and 1963 was some of the most stimulating of my life, and provided me with an intellectual and emotional outlet in marked contrast to the sterile atmosphere of Howe. It gave me an opportunity to stretch my horizons once more, to gain a host of new musical insights and to enrich my mind by contact with some excellent faculty and bright, intelligent students. I also studied organ with Professor Corliss Arnold.

On Saturday, March 23, 1963, I was to drive to Chicago, at the invitation of Wyatt Insko, who had been one of my featured recitalists on the new Howe organ, in order to play an exchange recital the next day at his church, Fourth Presbyterian Church on North Michigan Avenue, but unfortunately, I had car trouble on the way. Wyatt picked me up at the Ford garage in Michigan City, where the car had been towed from the Indiana Toll Road, and together with his associate at the church, Beth Paul, we drove back to Chicago. Beth was an exceptionally gifted organist and a former student of Noehren's at Ann Arbor.

I stayed Saturday night with Gudrun's cousin Erich Lenz, in Evanston, and Wyatt, Beth and I went out to the Lenzes' for supper, after I had spent most of the afternoon practicing at the church. About 8:30 p.m. the telephone rang. It was Bertl Dietz. He told me he was in Sturgis, visiting Gudrun and wondering where I was. (Dietz, of course, is a great kidder, and wasn't in Sturgis at all.) However, he very much needed to get in touch with me to discuss something of great importance, hence the call to me in Chicago.

It seems that he had just been offered a musicology position at the University of Texas in Austin by Paul Pisk, who was retiring, and Dietz was wondering if I would perhaps be interested in his job at St. Mary's College in South Bend. I could hardly believe my ears, and stammered that I most certainly would be interested. Dietz had apparently become well acquainted with Pisk at the national convention of the AMS in Columbus, Ohio, the previous winter. Pisk had been the first doctoral student of the Innsbruck musicologist Wilhelm Fischer, while Dietz was his last. We would be in touch over the next month.

In the first week of May, Gudrun and I drove over to see Bertl at Saint Mary's and meet the department chair, Dr. Louis Artau.

The campus of St. Mary's College, on the north side of the city of South Bend not far from the Indiana Toll Road entrance, is lovely and the physical facilities were spacious and modern. Gudrun had accompanied me, and wasn't quite certain whether she should come in to the interview with Artau, but he cordially waved her on in to his studio. Although the meeting with Dr. Artau was friendly, I wasn't quite sure what to make of him. I judged him to be about sixty years of age. He was a small, intense, chain-smoking man of somewhat enigmatic disposition. He seemed genuinely fond of Dietz, however, and would be pleased to welcome me as a member of the faculty, should I be offered the position. Both he and Dietz were good friends of my old CMC classmate and friend Joe Leahy, who taught at nearby Notre Dame University. Artau was also pleased to hear that Gudrun was a librarian, and suggested that she talk to Sister Rita Claire, the library director, about the possibility of employment on her staff. I left my *curriculum vitae* with Dr. Artau.

After the meeting with Artau, the three of us headed to the administration building, where I was to meet the academic dean. The experience of meeting a Catholic nun was new to me, and I wondered what it would be like. Sister Mary Alma impressed me as being a no-nonsense, straight-shooting administrator of unquestioned ability. A few years later, I would experience these qualities in a most impressive manner. The meeting was perfunctory, and in fifteen minutes she had concluded the interview, and we were on our way over to the library. Sister Rita Claire was a kind, sweet, approachable woman, obviously a sound library professional, and was interested in hearing that Gudrun would be interested in finding work at the library.

On May 18, I received the official job offer from St. Mary's College, for an initial one-year appointment at the assistant professor level. My salary the first year was $6,200. However, far more important than the salary was the fact that I was now back in college teaching, working in the field for which I had been trained, music history and literature, and we were moving to a large city, with all its amenities. Shortly thereafter, Gudrun received an appointment as assistant librarian at St. Mary's College. It was to be the most satisfying period of our lives thus far.

CHAPTER 8

ST. MARY'S COLLEGE, SOUTH BEND, INDIANA
(1963-1970)

As we lived less than an hour from South Bend, we drove over occasionally on the weekends to examine some rental properties in the area, as we began to make preparations for the move at the end of August. I spent the week at Michigan State in East Lansing, working on my doctorate, and drove home on Friday afternoon, after my last class.

Toward the end of the summer we found a comfortable home at 704 California, on the north side. The house was conveniently situated less than two miles from the college, and nearby was the St. Joseph River, and Leeper Park. It was the first one we had lived in which contained four bedrooms, a real luxury for us. Unfortunately, however, we only had one bathroom, which caused a few traffic problems in the mornings as the five children got ready for school. However, nothing could dampen my enthusiasm about having landed this great new teaching position. I also chuckled when it was pointed out to me that I, as a non-Roman Catholic, had the largest family of the lay faculty members, most of whom were good Catholics!

St. Mary's College is under the aegis of the Sisters of the Holy Cross, and had been established as an "Academy" in 1844 at Bertrand, Michigan, just across the state line. The institution eventually moved to its present location ten years later. Hence, the school had a venerable history, and has continued up to the present day as a top-notch educational institution for women. Standards were high, the students were motivated, and the faculty was superior. My memories of St. Mary's College, and the time we spent there, are among the most satisfying of my early teaching career. I shall be eternally indebted to Hanns-Bertold Dietz for his assistance in providing me the opportunity to make this move, just at this critical juncture in my academic career.

Father and mother with me and my family, 1963, standing near the Toll Road entrance.

My teaching duties at St. Mary's were almost ideal: I was responsible for all the music history and literature courses, two sections of a "music appreciation" course, which I have always enjoyed teaching, several excellent organ students, and occasionally some theory. In my third year, I enjoyed teaching 16th-century counterpoint for a semester. The music faculty consisted of seven members, including two or three Sisters, one of whom taught theory as well as providing organ instruction. Another one was responsible for the music education area. After my first year, Kay Valaske, a striking-looking woman with a rich mezzo-soprano voice, was hired as assistant professor of voice and director of the girls' glee club. My office was on the first floor, down a long hall in the new music wing of Moreau Hall, the fine arts building, which contained two auditoriums, the Art Department and a number of other faculty offices. A large music lecture room with a grand piano and stereo equipment, was on the ground level of the building.

I was asked to serve on a number of faculty committees, and to take part in numerous classes in the so-called "Christian Culture" curriculum directed by Dr. Bruno Schlesinger, a charming, highly-cultured man from Vienna, with whom I very much enjoyed working. Another delightful faculty member was Dr. Artau, my chair, who came to be a most fascinating and understanding friend as well. Artau had two beautiful nine-foot Steinways in his small, modest home on the east side, and I often spent wonderful evenings with him discussing a variety of topics of mutual interest, not always music. Artau was a complex, often mystical human being, whom I came to love. He could be rather circuitous in his conversation, and one needed to continually pay attention when listening to him. I considered him extremely sharp intellectually, and sensed that nothing escaped his attention.

Another great advantage of being now in South Bend, was the availability of a good university library. My old friend and fellow classmate from CMC, Joe Leahy, had worked industriously for many years to build up the music collection in the Notre Dame library, and it was a sheer delight to be able to use the facilities at the school. My entire life was now beginning to have meaning again, and the satisfaction which I felt in teaching at a first-rate college with highly motivated and industrious students, brought me untold joy and pleasure. Within two years I had become happier and more fulfilled than at any time in my life until that point.

Administration building of St. Mary's College, South Bend, Indiana.

Friday, November 22, 1963 was our monthly faculty meeting, and we gathered in the science building to hear the usual announcements, discussions and pending decisions of various kinds. We sat in the steep rows of the science lecture hall as Clarence Dineen, a distinguished professor of biology, and president of the faculty that year, presided over the meeting. At approximately 1:10 p.m., he was momentarily interrupted by someone standing outside the front door of the room, who gave him an urgent message. Professor Dineen returned to the podium at the front of the room and announced: "I have just been informed that President Kennedy has been shot in Dallas, Texas." There was a stunned silence, and then Dineen went on to observe that "I'm sure everything will go on all right." Recalling the previous death of a president in office, of Franklin Roosevelt, he was certain that there was nothing to worry about, and continued on with the meeting.

I looked around the room and noticed several of the Sisters appearing to bow their heads in prayer. One was fingering her rosary beads. The meeting ended, and I left school to pick up the twins, who were being cared for at the home of a French professor, living just around the corner from us. As I came into the house, the wife of the professor was watching the TV. Walter Cronkite had just announced that President Kennedy had indeed been assassinated. The woman was in tears. I picked up the twins and went home. Because we did not own a TV, I listened to the radio for reports. It was announced that students were being dismissed from school and, as I drove over to Muessel School to pick up our three other children, church bells all around town began to ring. I don't remember ever being so strongly affected by an external historical event of this magnitude before. I attempted to explain to the children what it meant, though the younger ones probably didn't comprehend the full impact of what had taken place that day.

In 1964, I accepted the position of organist and choir director at Trinity Episcopal Church, in Niles, Michigan. Niles is approximately eleven miles north of South Bend, just inside the Michigan state line. The church was quite attractive, and had a decent three-manual Schantz of about forty ranks, probably ten or fifteen years old. Unfortunately, however, it was another example of the "divided choir" setup which I so dislike. The senior choir was quite good, and we did some excellent choral work. A junior choir was also semi-active. Claudia and Doris eventually became members of this group. The rector of Trinity, Father Vincent Anderson, was an absolutely charming man who shared a birthday with Gudrun. The time I spent at Trinity was fulfilling indeed, and the people in the parish were warm and friendly. I stayed at Trinity until we left for East Lansing in 1967 to begin my residency for the doctorate.

In May of 1964, I received a rather ominous telephone call from my mother: Father had been diagnosed with bladder cancer, and was to shortly undergo exploratory surgery at McKennan Hospital in Sioux Falls. My father was a heavy smoker and I had become aware of such risks to his health. As soon as I could get a flight, I flew out to Sioux Falls and was met by aunt Elinor at the airport with the news that my mother was now also in the hospital. My mother had always been rather unstable in extreme emergencies, and the strain of my father's illness had caused her to suffer a severe angina attack. Her room was next door to my father's at McKennan Hospital. I spent several days in Sioux Falls, but knew then that when I said "goodbye" to my father it was to be the last time I would ever see him.

Meanwhile, exciting plans for a trip to Germany that summer had been developing. We were to drive to New York, where my good friend Dean Arlton, from my high school days at Augustana College, was to meet us. Dean was now on the faculty of The King's College, in Ossining, just north of New York City. The plan was to leave the car with Dean for the summer, while we were all in Germany. We left South Bend the middle of June for a delightful three-day journey to Ossining.

June 21, 1964. Ready to leave on Lufthansa for Frankfurt from New York's Idelwild Airport. (l to r): Claudia, Doris, the twins, Martin, Gudrun.

Soon after we arrived in Germany, I decided to buy a used Volkswagen Beetle, into which we crammed all five children: Martin, Claudia and Doris in the back seat, with the twins in the small section behind the seat and the rear engine compartment. Incredibly, we traveled all over Germany, Switzerland and France this way for two months.

My mother-in-law had assisted me in purchasing the sharp-looking red Beetle, with a sunroof. Proudly I drove up to her house, and excitedly proclaimed that I had gotten a very fine Volkswagen, with "einem Schiebedeckel." I had tried to say "a sliding roof," or sunroof. After some hilarious laughter on the part of all those present, Gudrun explained to me that I had said I'd bought a Volkswagen "with a toilet seat cover." What I should have said was, "ein Schiebe*dach.*"

August, 1964. The morning ritual: getting "Brötchen" (German hard rolls) and milk. In front are Claudia and Doris; the twins are holding on to their "Oma." In the background is the famous red Volkswagen with the "toilet seat roof!"

Gudrun and I had tickets to the Ansbach Bach Festival, at which harpsichordist Ralph Kirkpatrick was to perform. You may remember that I'd had two friendly meetings with Kirkpatrick, one while I was in the navy. Kirkpatrick was to play all six of the Bach English suites (BWV 806-811), and, in addition, there would be a performance of The *Musical Offering* (BWV 1079), one of my favorite works of Bach, during the festival. We stayed at a charming little *pension* in Ansbach, which is about seventy-five miles from Mosbach, for the duration of the festival. After Kirkpatrick's performance, which, as always, was beautifully done, we took him out for coffee and had a delightful visit. Kirkpatrick was always cordial to me, and I felt honored to know him. I would have another opportunity to speak to him before his death some twenty years later, in 1984.

One of the areas of my research dealt with the life and works of the German composer Johann Caspar Ferdinand Fischer (c. 1665-1746). Although the first edition of *MGG* does not list a birth date or place, I had already determined that he was born in Czechoslovakia, near what is now known as Karlovy Vary (in German Karlsbad). Just outside of Karlovy Vary is a small suburb called Fischern. People often took the name of towns they had been born in, though this was less often the case in the 17th century, than it had been during medieval times. Nevertheless, it was worth a try, and if I could locate birth or baptismal records in Fischern showing that Fischer had been born there, I might be able to clear up the question. This required that I apply for and be issued a visa for admittance to Czechoslovakia, as it was under communist control at that time. Before we left South Bend in

June, we received out visas, and began to plan a trip to Karlovy Vary.

Leaving the five children in Mosbach with my mother-in-law, and her sister Margarette Lenz, who, having lived in America, knew some English, Gudrun and I drove to the German-Czech border at Cheb (earlier Eger, which I recognized as the birthplace of Rudolph Serkin), and drove to the resort city of Karlovy Vary. We checked into a run-down hotel on one side of the Cheb River which runs right down the middle of the city. We felt extremely ill-at-ease as our passports were taken from us when we registered for our room. The room itself was enormous, but nothing in the bathroom worked, there was no running water, and the toilet didn't flush. We were informed that they were awaiting spare parts, which were apparently hard to come by.

Karlovy Vary is, next to Marianské Lazné (Marienbad), the best known of the resort spas in western Bohemia. The high mineral content of the waters nearby attracts hundreds of people who come to "take the waters" here, and they walk up and down the streets, on both sides of the river, sipping the healing waters from pots filled with long spouts. One evening during our stay there was to be a concert by a visiting orchestra. When I inquired about getting tickets, I was told they were sold out, but perhaps they could find two seats for the visiting Americans. As a matter of fact, we were even offered better seats than we originally got, so pleased were the officials to have American tourists in their midst. What was the program? Well, what else but Dvorak, several of whose Slavonic Dances were programmed. I have never heard the music performed with such verve and dash: it was in their blood, I concluded.

We then attempted to examine birth records there as well as in Fischern. We met with a completely uncooperative attitude by bureaucratic functionaries in both places. It was totally frustrating. When I inquired about additional information concerning Fischer, I was reminded that the Margräfin of Baden, who had a summer home in Karlovy Vary, had had her main castle in Rastatt, south of Karlsruhe, and perhaps I would have success there finding information about Fischer.

I did some more research on Fischer in Sokolov (earlier called Falkanau). Walking into a library there one afternoon, I inquired of the attendant sitting at the desk if he spoke German. He drew himself up proudly and exclaimed, "Ich bin doch deutsch; mein Name ist Zimmermann." ("But I am German, my name is Zimmermann.") In this part of the country many Germans had crossed over into the country when it had been invaded and made a part of the Third Reich. When the Communists took over, immediately after the close of the war, and closed the borders, these Germans had no time to flee back to Western Germany, and were now stuck in Czechoslovakia.

Unfortunately, we were unable to track down any more information about Fischer, and, after spending several hours in the library, we thanked our host, and started to leave. As we reached the ground floor of the building, the wife of the librarian met us, begging us to take her along in the luggage compartment of our car, back across the border. I certainly would have been happy to do it, but I didn't like the idea of being thrown into some communist jail and precipitating an international incident, so I had to turn her down. However, the meeting made a deep impression upon us, particularly when we saw the miles of electrically fortified barbed wire and the watch towers, where guards were probably watching us with binoculars as Gudrun snapped photos out of the window of the car.

After visits to a number of places, including the baroque church of Vierzehnheiligen ("Fourteen Saints"), one of the great masterpieces of the architect Balthasar Neumann, and to the city of Bamberg, where we saw the crypts of Uta and Eckahard in the outstanding gothic cathedral there, we finally returned, after almost a week, to Mosbach. My mother-in-law was awaiting us as we came in the door. She announced, with a sly grin, that Johann Caspar Ferdinand Fischer had just arrived for a visit. What in the world was she talking about? She said he is in the living room, and as we walked in, there he was, in person, Hanns-Bertold Dietz and his parents! We were totally surprised, not having any idea that he was even in Germany. It was a joy seeing him again as it was the first time we had seen him since we had left Sturgis the previous year, and we all had a great time together. We also enjoyed meeting his parents as well. The three of them were on their way to somewhere near Stuttgart, and just decided to stop in that day. I later thought how providential it had been that we arrived back in Mosbach just that day.

In August, we left for Ettenheim, near Freiburg, to visit my brother-in-law Ludwig, who had a Lutheran parish there. We stayed in Ludwig's house there while they were on vacation. The house was very large, with room for all seven of us. It was a

"Eine Rose zwischen zwei Dornen!" ("A rose between two thorns"). Standing with Gudrun and Johann Caspar Ferdinand Fischer, a.k.a. Hanns-Bertold Dietz, on the marketplace in Mosbach. Note the famous "Fachwerk" ("Fieldwork=half timbered) buildings in the background.

delightful time for all, and my children got a chance to meet their cousins. Almost every day Martin rode a bicycle all the way to the Rhine River, which was the French border.

I also planned to examine some of the organs of Andreas Silbermann, brother of the great Gottfried Silbermann, who had settled in Strasbourg, and built a number of organs in southern Baden. Not far from Ettenheim, was the small village of Ettenheimmünster, where Silbermann had built a modest two-manual instrument in the French style. It had the typical disposition which his father, Andreas, followed:

Grand Orgue	Positif	Pedal
8' Montre	8' Bourdon	16' Subbaß
8' Bourdon	4' Prestant	8' Octavbaß
4' Prestan	2-2/3' Nazard	8' Trompette
2-2/3' Nazard	2' Doublette	4' Clarion
2' Doublette	1-3/5' Tierce	
1-3/5' Tierce	III Cymbale	
III Fourniture	8' Cromorne	
V Cornet	8' Bassoon	
8' Trompette	Trembulant fort	
	Trembulant doux	

The instrument would probably not be particularly effective in some of the typical north German organ works, which really require a much larger pedal division. For the French, the pedal functions most often as a *cantus firmus* line using long chant quotations over faster, colorful manual passages. At the time I first saw the instrument, it was in the process of renovation by the excellent Strassburg firm of Mühleisen, who were also responsible for rebuilding Silbermanns at Marmoutier in France and Meissenheim, just a few miles distant from Ettenheim. I was able to see the "guts" of the instrument, and also to come back a few days later and see the finished product. It had a delightful sound in the typically reverberant church. I recorded some Pachelbel, Bach and other composers on it.

The most exciting visit I made was the day my brother-in-law and I hauled the recording equipment over to the famous organ by

August 14, 1964, Ettenheimmünster, Germany, at the newly rebuilt console of the 1769 Johann Andreas Silbermann organ. (Renovation by Mühleisen of Strasbourg, France.)

Case of the Andreas Silbermann organ in Ebersmünster, France, built between 1728 and 1732.

Silbermann at Ebersmünster in France. Originally built by Andreas between 1728 and 1732, it was subsequently renovated by son Johann Andreas in 1748, and finally by the grandson Jean Josias Silbermann in 1782. Although the case is magnificent, the organ was not in very good condition, and the reeds were often badly out of tune. The priest at the church observed wryly that if France weren't so intent on joining the nations possessing nuclear weapons, they might have enough money to repair and renovate their organs and other national treasures. As we recorded, we were constantly serenaded by swallows which dwelt in the high rafters of the church. I did notice that they only twirped and trilled when I played French music. When I played Bach they were silent. (They also always started their trills on the upper auxiliary, they certainly knew Baroque performance practice.) I recorded music by Lebègue, Titelouze and Bach on the instrument.

One day we drove over to Marmoutier, where there is another Silbermann organ, almost a twin to the Ebersmünster instrument. It is only slightly smaller, the Ebersmünster organ having an additional 8' Vox Humana on the Grand Orgue, and an 8' Trompette on the Recit. Unfortunately, the priest was gone for the day and I had no opportunity to play the instrument; however, as it is almost identical to Ebersmünster, I wasn't too disappointed, and the church, a wonderful combination of the so-called "Crusader" style of the medieval period, and more modern, Renaissance elements, especially the interior, was a fascinating visual treat.

I needed to do research in Rastatt, the residence of Johann Caspar Ferdinand Fischer, in order to ascertain some relevant details of his life. Gudrun and I walked through the cemetery in

Rastatt and located several gravestones with the Fischer family name, including what must be the gravesite of the composer. There was also a son by the same name, which caused some confusion as to the exact date of the father's death. I also played a small organ in the royal chapel there purported to have been played by Fischer, but I didn't believe it.

One interesting result of our quest regarding information about the life of Johann Caspar Ferdinand Fischer, was meeting someone who attempted to assure me that he was already working in the same area, and had materials on Fischer that he would soon publish. I was to watch for the research to be published soon, I was told. I am still waiting. However, one interesting piece of information I gleaned from my conversation with the man, was his recommendation that I do some work on a composer who, he maintained, came from Mosbach. His name: Joseph Martin Kraus. As it turned out, of course, Kraus came not from Mosbach, but from Buchen, perhaps fifteen or twenty miles northeast of Mosbach. This started me on a small research project dealing with Kraus, whom we shall have an opportunity to meet in a later chapter of this narrative.

One bright, sunny day in the second week of August, we decided to get in the car and drive to Switzerland, to show the children the Alps and the beautiful scenery there. From my brother-in-law's house in Ettenheim, where we were staying, it is less than two hours on the Autobahn to Basel, and we thought that would make a pleasant day trip. After we left Basel and began to see the mountains of the Berner Oberland looming in the distance, we decided to just keep going toward them. Higher and higher the road ascended, and narrower and narrower it became. I finally decided that we were now hopelessly lost, and as it was getting dark, we thought it only prudent to try and find some place to spend the night. We were so high that it was possible to look down into the valleys and see clouds *under* us. We finally came down off the high mountain road and reached a much larger and more substantial highway, which took us directly into Lungern, on the Lungern See (lake). We had left without planning to stay overnight someplace, so we didn't have much money or provisions. We pulled in to a small hotel on the main street, and asked for the cheapest rooms they had. We found them: they were on the top floor of the building, with no running water or toilet. It was clean, and we didn't mind dodging the clotheslines in the attic.

The next day we drove over to the lovely Lauterbrunnen Valley, via the city of Interlaken. Not far ahead down the valley we saw the mighty peaks of this most dramatic and breathtaking area of the Berner Oberland: the Eiger, the Mönch and the highest of them all: the Jungfrau. Years later, I would return to this area again and again, so beautiful and spectacular is the scenery. By the time we got to Basel again, we were extremely short on cash, and finally went to a bakery there and bought seven German hard rolls, which served as our lunch on the last day in Switzerland. But the trip was worth it, and the children were enthusiastic about what they had seen.

We returned from Germany on August 26, leaving immediately for South Bend after retrieving my car from Dean Arlton in Ossining. Shortly after we arrived back in South Bend, I had a call from aunt Elinor, who gave me the sad news I had been dreading: My father had died on September 5. The next day I flew out to Sioux Falls for the funeral.

***

In my second year of teaching at St. Mary's, Louis Artau stepped down as chair of the Music Department, and Sister H. succeeded him. She was an excellent, rather demanding theory teacher, and also taught some organ, as well as directing the Schola, a small group of girls who regularly sang for Mass on holy days and various saints' days. Sister was rather overbearing in appearance; someone once observed that she reminded them of a 32' Pedal Principal entering the room.

One day as I sat in my office preparing for a class, I could not help overhearing a somewhat heated discussion taking place between Sister H. and Kay Valaske, the director of the girls' glee club, outside Miss Valaske's studio a few doors down. As far as I could determine, there apparently was a conflict regarding the scheduling of a TV appearance by the girls' glee club, together with the Notre Dame glee club which Miss Valaske, with great effort, had been able to arrange. A program of music with the combined forces of both groups was obviously a *coup* for the choral groups of the music departments of both institutions, and there was much interest in their joint appearance. However, it appeared that the day which had been chosen happened to fall on some kind of saints' day, and Sister H. was upset that she would not have the use of the girls in the Schola to sing a Mass at that time.

"Why, Sister, you have known for some time that the program was scheduled to be given on this date. We can't change it now. There is no way we can ask the Notre Dame glee club director to reschedule this," Miss Valaske insisted.

"Miss Valaske," Sister H. replied, "I need those girls to sing in the Schola for this Mass!"

"But, Sister, I just can't get along without them; I must have them to sing at this program," Kay Valaske answered somewhat impatiently. Sister H., becoming ever more agitated, finally exploded in a paroxysm of anger, in a voice which could be heard all the way down the hall.

"Miss Valaske," she practically shouted, "you are placing yourself above Jesus Christ Himself!" and slammed the door to her office.

To the best of my knowledge, the girls' glee club did, indeed, honor their commitment to the Notre Dame glee club, and sang in a fine program of music.

Kay Valaske presented some excellent choral music, and I was pleased to be able to accompany them on the organ on a number of occasions, including a beautiful Fauré *Requiem* at one concert. Unfortunately, the instrument was another electronic substitute of little worth, and even worse sound. (A fine harpist also took part in the Fauré.) O'Laughlin Auditorium, in which the instrument was situated, was a handsome venue seating 1,300, and was the site of large theatrical productions and academic-related occasions.

Probably the work involving the largest number of performers was a flashy production of Benjamin Britten's *Noye's Fludde*. It involved singing actors, a chorus, an orchestra of strings, brass, handbells, recorders (Gudrun played in the performances) organ and piano. I have always considered it a rather "cutesy," too-precious work, with little lasting merit, despite the huge forces needed to perform it, and I have never heard of any other performances. The production, which had a run of a week, was conducted by Bart Wolgamot, a young man whom Sister H. apparently considered to be some kind of up-and-coming prodigy. He did have a rather pleasant, high, light tenor voice, and, as it turned out, we later had some delightful musical experiences together.

In a short time, I began to think of forming a *collegium musicum* to perform medieval and Renaissance music, and as there were a number of good recorder players on campus, as well as a couple of violinists, and a good cellist, we developed a fine group who eventually performed some very refreshing music. My good friend and colleague Joe Leahy, at Notre Dame, had started a similar group, called "Camerata," in which we played on occasion. There were a number of excellent performers in this group. Yolanda Davis was a superb gambist who also played rebec; Marie Hardy and Elizabeth Hatch also played gamba, and Tom Heck played a guitar altered to a lute tuning. Palmer Cone and I played harpsichord. Palmer had an interesting two-manual instrument in his home in Elkhart, where I visited several times.

One *collegium* program that we did at St. Mary's was, for me, especially memorable. In addition to a number of instrumental works, we performed Monteverdi's beautiful *canzonetta* "Chiome d'oro" for two tenors and two concertante instruments (we used recorders, with Gudrun playing one of the parts). The work, from

Book VII of his collected madrigals, was unknown to me at the time, and I found myself totally enthralled with its delightful ritornelli and ostinato bass line. The two tenors were Father Patrick Maloney of the Notre Dame faculty and Bart Wolgamot, the "boy genius" who conducted the Britten work. I became determined to get better acquainted with more of Monteverdi's madrigals, canzonetti and the various "Scena" in the later Madrigal books. It was one of the greatest delights of musical discovery I had ever made.

As I got to know the school, the procedures and policies of the administration, and the internal lineup and group dynamics of its structure, I began to think that the political parties of this country could learn something from the orders of the Roman Catholic Church. I began to see that there were a number of competing factions or parties at work within the college, but I didn't realize the complexity or the depth of these divisions until somewhat later, when I would be directly affected by them.

At the end of May, in 1965, I received an extremely disturbing letter from the president of the college, in which I was informed that my contract was not likely to be renewed after June of 1966. I was thunderstruck. What had I done to deserve this notice of non-retention? I responded to the president to say that we had come to enjoy our association at the college, that my work was highly satisfying, and that I had hoped to continue. In inquring as to the reasons for this decision, I was told, in subsequent correspondence, that Sister H., the department chair, had reported instances of disagreement with her about rules and procedures in the department. I had never recalled any disagreement with the chair of the department, and finally stopped in to her office to say how very sorry I was about this possible course of action. I asked sister if she would be kind enough to point out where I had erred in the execution of my duties.

"Well, Mr. Miller," she said, "it was reported to me that one day in class you put a record on the player, and it was not the piece of music that you had said it was." I was almost speechless.

"You mean, Sister, that I am being given a notice of non-retention just for THAT?"

"Oh," she replied, "there have been other things, too, but I can't remember them anymore."

I was dumbfounded at this totally arbitrary attitude, and at the prospect that, once more, I would be forced to seek employment at another institution. In the summer of 1965 I returned to Michigan State University to continue my doctoral course work, still smarting from the injustice of this decision.

However, something happened that summer which gave credence to my belief that there was a good deal of political infighting and power struggles that were taking place within the order of the Holy Cross. It should be borne in mind that the mother house of the order was on the campus of St. Mary's. I had, on a number of occasions had the pleasure of having in my classes sisters who held high posts in the order, especially Sister Hilary and Sister Maria Assunta (who was utterly charming, and played folk guitar as well). The librarian, Sister Rita Claire, was also a very dear person, and extremely supportive of Gudrun's work in the library.

In July of 1965, a so-called "General Chapter," equivalent to a national convention, took place on the campus of the college, in which an election of officers to the highest posts in the order took place. Without going into details, suffice it to say that an entire faction of the school, including the president and vice president, was removed from office, and a new group of administrators, from the provincial of the Midwest province on down, took over. In short, one faction, which also included among its adherents the chair of the music department, were all replaced, and another faction, which included Sister Hilary and my dear friend Sister Maria Assunta, who became the new vice president, was now part of a new "management team." Simply put, a *coup* had taken place.

Of course, I had no way of knowing any of this, and in August, I happened to speak to Sister Rita Claire, informing her that, unfortunately, it appeared that Gudrun and I would not be returning after the 1965-66 academic year. Sister seemed rather perturbed and, fuming under her breath, took off in the direction of the administration building. Nothing more was ever heard of the matter, and in February of 1966, I received a contract for the following year, with a substantial salary increase. The letter was signed by the new president of St. Mary's College, Sister Mary Grace, a lively, able administrator.

One of the most fruitful results of my association with members of the new "regime" was an opportunity to help choose an organ for St. Joseph's Chapel, of the Postulate-Juniorate building on campus. Sister Hilary, who often visited my music history classes, approached me one day to inquire about the possibility of acquiring a small instrument for the new facility. Before I could even answer, however, she made it clear that she would not be interested in "one of those electronics." If I hadn't thought it improper to do so, I would have hugged her on the spot. Here was someone who knew and appreciated the value of a real musical instrument for the small chapel, a beautiful example of simple, modern architecture, seating only 150 people. Sister cautioned me that there was only a limited amount of money available, and she hoped that I could suggest something within their budget. There was an adequate niche in the rear of the acoustically excellent room which could house a small, simple instrument of very modest proportions. I recommended a one-manual tracker instrument by the German firm of Steinmeyer, and negotiations were commenced. One of the colleges most faithful supporters was a South Bend business man who owned a fleet of long haul freight lines with overseas connections. He offered to cover the complete costs of shipping the instrument from Steinmeyer's shop in Oettingen, Bavaria, to St. Mary's College. The organ, a gift to the school by Mr. and Mrs. Julius L. Tucker of South Bend, was dedicated in honor of Sister Mary Peter, of the order. The instrument had the following disposition: 8' Gedeckt, 4' Rohrflöte, 2' Principal (prospect), and a small spiky little two-rank Scharf at 2/3'- 1'.

On July 30, 1967, I played a dedicatory recital on the instrument, which included works by Charles Wesley, a Toccata and the Kyrie "Orbis Factor" from Frescobaldi's "Fiori Musicali," three *manualiter* chorale preludes by Bach, the Brahms chorale prelude on "Selig sind sie," and three short pieces in the Dorian mode by the modern German composer Hermann Schröder. The organ was a real joy, and the music came off with great effect. The warm, unforced sound of the Gedeckt and the Rohrflöte were welcome and enveloped the player in a lively ambience, and with the addition of the 2' Principal and the Scharf, provided a wonderfully joyous sound for the singing of the sisters.

***

For us one of the highlights of the summer of 1967 was the visit of my brothers-in-law Ludwig and Karl-Otto, and Karl-Otto's wife, Gudrun, from Germany. They arrived the last week of July for a ten-day stay with us. It was without question one of the most joyful times of our stay so far in South Bend. None of them had been to America before, and there was much to experience, as they learned of such delights as Dairy Queen treats, the great distances one must travel in America, and our customs and traditions.

Only a couple of experiences can be related here. We were anxious that our visitors have an opportunity to visit the big city: Chicago, and, leaving the children at home and hoping they wouldn't wreck the house while we were gone, we set out for the Windy City, which would also include a visit to Gudrun's cousins Erich Lenz and Irene Anderson in Evanston. We checked into one of the tonier motels on Lake Shore Drive north of the "Loop," and Ludwig promptly got his first taste of a distinctly American amenity: The bed in his room had one of those vibrating mattresses which work by inserting a quarter into an appropriate slot by the bed. He was absolutely fascinated by it, feeding twenty-five cent pieces into it and enjoying the soothing sensations.

We went down into the "Loop" to visit the premier department store of the city: Marshall Fields, at State and Randolph. Entering an elevator, we began chattering away in German, with the fellows making sly remarks and in general poking fun at Americans and their peculiar ways. I cautioned them to watch what they were saying, pointing out that, especially in Chicago, you never knew who might understand what you were saying, as the city had a large German population. Just then the elevator stopped at the next floor, and, as the door opened and people stepped out, a middle-aged, somewhat portly woman turned around and said, in perfect German: "Ja wohl, das ist bestimmt wahr; ich habe alles verstanden, guten Tag." ("Yes, that is definitely true; I understood everything you said, good day.")

***

I was, by now, firmly involved in activities in the Midwest chapter of the American Musicological Society, chairing program committees on several occasions, and regularly attending both the regional and national conventions. Our circle of colleagues expanded to include a number of people who became, for us, some of the dearest friends we had known. Ed Kottick, an excellent musicologist, and superb recorder player from the University of Iowa, became a part of our extended family, and he and Gudrun enjoyed talking about recorders and recorder music. Others included Bunker Clark, Dan Politoske and Milton Steinhardt from Kansas; Andy Minor, from Missouri; Alexander Main and Herb Livingston, from Ohio State; Frank Kirby, from Lake Forest College; Paul Revitt, from the University of Missouri-Kansas City;

211

Bill Porter, from Northwestern; and Don Foster, from the University of Cincinnati. In addition, we always enjoyed the company of the "elders of the clan" such as Hans Tischler of Indiana; Ed Lowinsky of the University of Chicago; Gwynn McPeek, Bob Warner and Louise Cuyler from Michigan; and the ever-gracious and lovely Carol McClintock and her charming husband, Lander (an absolute double of "Colonel Sanders" of KFC fame.) In 1965, my good friend Bertl Dietz and I drove to Ann Arbor for the fall national convention of AMS there, and in 1966 Gudrun and I took the train to New Orleans to experience the delightful ambiance of that unique city during the national convention held during the Christmas holidays.

Breakfast at Brennan's, with Bloody Marys and oysters on the half shell, and the Preservation Hall jazz ensemble led by Sweet Emma Barrett and featuring the inimitable Humphrey brothers, Percy on trumpet and Willie on clarinet, were highlights of the convention. A chance dinner conversation with Warren Kirkendale established our parallel paths in life: He was a Canadian who had married a German girl, Ursula; I was an American who had married a German girl. This was also the last time I had an opportunity to see and hear one of the leading figures and founding fathers of American musicology: the delightful, courtly and always lively Charles Seeger.

At St. Mary's College, political and personnel crises began to develop during 1967. A number of music department faculty members began agitating to replace the chair of the department, by seeking a new, external chair. The man chosen to become the head of the department, in the fall of 1967, was Dr. Willis Stevens, an excellent pianist and a student of Edward Steuermann's at Juilliard. His playing of Schoenberg's works was extraordinary; however, unfortunately I had no opportunity to get to know him during his first year, as I had, in the meantime, been awarded a leave of absence from St. Mary's for the academic year 1967-68, in order to fulfill residency requirements for the doctorate at Michigan State University. I have always been grateful to the college for this wonderful opportunity.

In August of 1967, the seven Millers put much of their furniture in storage in South Bend, hooked the car up to a U-Haul trailer and took off for East Lansing, Michigan, where we moved into student housing in Spartan Village at Michigan State University for a year. *Spartan* Village was well named, as our tiny, two-bedroom apartment was barely room enough for five growing children and their parents. I had to persuade the housing authorities to allow me to keep our hide-a-bed so Gudrun and I would have someplace to sleep, Martin having taken one of the bedrooms, while the four girls were jammed into two sets of iron bunk beds in the larger of the two bedrooms. On the other hand, the year the seven of us lived in East Lansing has always seemed to us wonderful; we grew closer together as a family, and I recall no insurmountable problems or other inconveniences which we suffered. Gudrun was able to find work in the library of Michigan State University, where her growing skills in the area of serials were put to good use.

Some of the most stimulating work I did at Michigan State was not with anyone in the musicology area, but in the music theory area. I will always be grateful for the classes I had with Paul

Christmas, 1967, East Lansing, Michigan. Martin and Doris both studied violin at one time, though both gave it up. The twins are singing out of a book of German Christmas songs.

Harder, certainly one of the most brilliant teachers I have had. Harder was a small, neat man with whom I always enjoyed working. He had a certain kind of understated modesty to everything he did, but I learned much from him, both in class, and also in some very intensive work in advanced harmonic analysis.

Theodore Johnson was a violinist, but his competence in music theory was awesome. He was not a demonstrative teacher, but I think I learned more about 20th-century music from him than from anyone with whom I studied. His command of structure, harmonic language and analysis was superb, and his lectures on such works as the Ravel Quartet and Bartok's *Music for Strings, Percussion and Celeste* were highlights of my year there. I also had some enriching, though extremely demanding private work with him in which I worked through, in great detail, the Beethoven quartets of the Opus 59 set. Not a detail escaped Dr. Johnson's critical eye as he went over the results of my harmonic and structural analysis of the music.

My "Doktor Vater" was the unforgettable Hans Nathan, unforgettable because he was such a strange, enigmatic, and, in some ways, thoroughly frustrating teacher. He seemed to spend most of his time trying to be humorous and, at the same time, completely unpredictable. I sensed there was an unfortunate streak of paranoia in his make-up as well. (I was aware that he had suffered grievously: His parents were said to have perished in a Nazi concentration camp.) I don't know whether I actually learned very much from him, though I'm certain I must have. In essence, I wrote my dissertation without any substantial assistance from Dr. Nathan. He had wanted me to write on some aspect of 20th-century music, and had suggested I do my dissertation on the music of Luigi Dallapiccola, not one note of whose music I knew. I told Nathan I was a keyboard player, I knew my Bach, and I read and spoke German. He finally allowed me to write on the keyboard music of Georg Andreas Sorge, a well-known theorist and contemporary of Bach's. Sorge's music was obscure, unknown by anyone. I had first heard of Sorge many years earlier while teaching at Mitchell College in Statesville, North Carolina. One day I drove over to Winston-Salem to visit the Moravian archives, then being administered by Don McCorkle, who became the preeminent scholar of this music in America before his untimely death in 1978. Don showed me a good deal of material, but something which caught my eye was a manuscript of "Die geheime (sic!) gehaltene Kunst der Mensuration der Orgel-Pfeiffen" ("The secretly received art of measuring [i.e., scaling] organ pipes") by Sorge. To my knowledge, this was an *unicum*, and got me to thinking of the keyboard music of this composer, which had, until then, been totally neglected.

Some of the doctoral students at Michigan State were extremely bright. One of the finest, a man with a brilliant mind, for whom I developed enormous admiration and respect, was Alfred Fisher. He came from the Boston area, and I found him probably the most gifted fellow student I'd ever known. He was, in addition, a warm, friendly human being, always ready with an encouraging word or a compliment. I considered it a great privilege to know him. Widely read in a number of disciplines, Al was also an excellent composer, and many years later, I had the opportunity to arrange for a performance of his "Six Aphorisms" for piano.

Continuing to attend meetings of the Midwest chapter of the AMS, Gudrun and I took the train to Columbus, Ohio, from East Lansing for the 1968 spring meeting of the chapter there. While we were there, we were invited to join several colleagues for dinner one evening but, inasmuch as we had no car, we decided to accept a ride from one of the local hosts for the meeting. Hilde Junkermann, a recent graduate of the school, had returned to campus for the meeting, and she and her good friend Olga Buth, the music librarian of The Ohio State University, were kind enough to give us a ride to the dinner.

216

Hilde was a fascinating, truly inspiring person to know. Born and raised in Göttingen, Germany, the daughter of a distinguished professor of pharmacology at the university there, she had married an American doctor at the age of nineteen, eventually settling in Columbus. They had three children, but unfortunately, the marriage had ended in divorce, and, at almost forty-five years of age, she returned to school, earning a bachelor's, master's and finally, a Ph.D. in musicology at the university after she had already turned fifty. I thought this a truly remarkable achievement and had great respect for what she had done. She was now on the faculty of Case Western Reserve University in Cleveland. Hilde was no bigger than a minute, but she had such incredible energy, and such a sharp mind that she was, at least in my book, ten feet tall. I could not have known at the time that our paths would cross again soon, resulting in a rich and long-lasting friendship.

***

In the fall of 1968 we returned to St. Mary's College, as per the agreement I had concluded with the school at the time I was granted the leave of absence. We found a wonderful, large home for rent at 312 W. Marion Street in South Bend, which had been designed by a student of Frank Lloyd Wright's. The unmistakable lines of the house, which emphasized the horizontal planes, and with the typical Wright window decorations, were aesthetically appealing, and for the first time in my life, I finally had a private study. It was an airy room at the rear of the house, which looked out on a lovely back yard.

The house which we had rented was owned by Katherine Jackson, whose father had, at one time, been the mayor of South Bend. "Kah-tie," as she preferred to be called, had seriously studied piano as a young girl, and, when she moved the following year, bequeathed to me a large collection of music, including the Schnabel edition of the Beethoven sonatas, and many other volumes of Brahms, Chopin, Schubert and Bach. It became a rich and enduring addition to my library. We also bought some pieces of furniture from her, including a huge, dining room table and six cane bottom chairs for the unbelievable sum of $35.

The 1968 mid-winter national convention of the AMS was held at Yale University, and as I'd never been in that part of the country, I decided to go. I had also been asked to serve on the program committee of the Midwest chapter, together with Emanuel Rubin, from the University of Wisconsin-Milwaukee. One evening, as I browsed among the various publishers' exhibits at the convention, a voice greeted me from behind. I turned and saw, to my pleasant surprise, that it was Ralph Kirkpatrick, whom I had last seen four years earlier in Germany. (Kirkpatrick was a faculty member at Yale.) It was good to see him again, and we enjoyed discussing a number of interesting musical topics. He had seen, in the volume *Doctoral Dissertations in Musicology,* that I was now at work on the keyboard music of Georg Andreas Sorge, and was very interested in the project, encouraging me to finish the dissertation and perhaps consider publishing some of the best works some day. I am still considering the suggestion.

Some time in 1969, I learned of the presence of an excellent harpsichord builder in Three Rivers, Michigan, and became

218

determined to visit the shop of E.O. ("Bud") Witt. In September Gudrun and I visited him out in the country west of town, and were impressed by the quality of his workmanship, which was impeccable. The upshot of this visit resulted in my placing an order for an instrument with him, to be finished in about a year. The instrument was, in general, a copy of a 1769 harpsichord in the Yale University collection, probably by the French builder Pascal Taskin. (Recent investigation has cast some doubt on the authenticity of the instrument as a pure Taskin, however.) It would have a disposition of two 8' foot strings, a 4' rank, a divided lute, and would be a single-manual instrument.

My own conviction is that fully 80% of the literature is perfectly playable on a single manual instrument. The only works which call specifically for a two manual instrument are the Goldberg Variations (BWV 988) of Bach, and a few pièces croisées by François Couperin. Even the *Concerto nach Italiaenischen Gust* (BWV 971) or the opening Prélude of the G minor "English" suite (BWV 808), by Bach, both of which illustrate the Italian ritornello concerto principal applied to the keyboard, can probably be performed on a single-manual instrument. In addition, the Scarlatti sonatas, with only three exceptions, are completely within the capabilities of a single-manual instrument, as Kirkpatrick's thorough studies have concluded. The model which I ordered would be an ideal *continuo* instrument as well, and one of my ambitions was to perform this type of music. At last, one of the greatest dreams of my life was about to be realized. My mother-in-law assisted me in purchasing it.

My work at St. Mary's continued with great satisfaction for me, and I became involved with some excellent catalogue revisions in the musical offerings which had been proposed by Willis Stevens. These ideas came to fruition in a series of advanced courses in medieval and Renaissance music which provided me with enriched opportunities to expand my knowledge and teaching capabilities. I had eager, enthusiastic students, and I was able to explore many new fields of study. It was some of the most enriching teaching I had ever experienced. In addition, I was awarded tenure, effective the academic year of 1969-70.

St. Mary's College, 1966. Examining a Josquin motet, while hearing a recording in the music library. At the left is Mary Pat Conlin, the others are unidentified.

Although the college was absolutely first rate in every respect, I began to consider some summer teaching opportunities in the Midwest. St. Mary's College had no summer instruction in music, and, with a growing family, I could use some extra income over the summer months. As a member of the program committee for the Midwest chapter of AMS, I was in charge of one of the sessions at the fall, 1969 meeting in Chicago. One of our traditional social occasions is always the *hora felix*, or happy hour at the end of the Saturday afternoon sessions. As I stood at the bar munching finger food and conversing with the well-known Indiana University musicologist Hans Tischler, I mentioned my interest in teaching during the ensuing summer session somewhere, and wondered if he knew of any such opportunities. He thought he might know of something, and indicated that he would write me when he got back to Bloomington.

The first week of November, I received a friendly note from Tischler directing me to write to Emanuel Rubin, Chairman, Dept. of Music, University of Wisconsin, Milwaukee. Having served on a program committee with Manny already, we were somewhat acquainted. Tischler had mentioned that Rubin was looking for "somebody to teach music history (two courses: covering both ancient and modern music) and a course in bibliography." This sounded quite exciting, and, with the easy access to the Indiana Toll Road and I-94, I thought I could make the trip in about three hours, provided I didn't get delayed in traffic on the Dan Ryan or the Kennedy in Chicago.

I wrote Rubin a short note telling him of my interest in teaching in the summer sessions at the university, and received an enthusiastic letter from him saying how pleased he would be to support my candidacy for the summer position. In subsequent correspondence I suggested that we get together to discuss his needs for the summer session during the AMS National Convention, which was taking place in St. Louis over the Christmas holidays, and which I planned to attend.

In the meantime, I received some disturbing news from my sister Martha in California, informing me that mother was not well, and was in the hospital out there. After my father had died in 1964, mother had eventually sold the house in Sioux Falls, and moved to a retirement community in Pacific Grove, California, run by the Episcopal Church. Martha and Libby, my other sister, had assisted mother in the transition to Canterbury Woods and lived only a few hours away from her. The facility is located in a scenic area, not far from Carmel, site of the famous Bach festival each summer, and mother seemed to enjoy it. In 1968, shortly after we returned to South Bend, she had visited us, and we began to make plans for a joyful family reunion in San Francisco over the Christmas holidays of 1969. Mother was to take care of our fares, and arrangements were to be made to secure hotel accommodations for those of us who couldn't be put up at Martha and Jim's house in Piedmont, a small East Bay community.

Another call about a week later by Libby brought me the sad news that mother had died that day, November 18. Now the question arose: what were we to do about the planned trip to San Francisco for Christmas? We all agreed that we would go ahead with the plans, inasmuch as that was what mother would have wanted. Although the Christmas celebrations were a bit muted, it was good to see my sisters again, and, most important, that my children got to finally meet all their California cousins: Jim and Sam MacIlvaine, and Dick and Chuck Soper, four handsome, good-looking fellows whom my girls thought were "really neat guys," as one of them expressed it. Aunt Elinor had sent us all tickets to attend a wonderful performance of the delightful stage show, "You're a good man, Charlie Brown," based on the Charles Schultz comic strip characters. The children were ecstatic.

The day after Christmas members of the family settled the trust and estate distribution of mother's will, and two days later we flew back to Chicago, where Gudrun and the children transferred to a flight to South Bend, and I went on to St. Louis to attend the AMS convention and meet with Manny Rubin to discuss the proposed summer teaching assignment. I told Rubin that I would be arriving in time to attend a concert by the "Studio der frühen Musik," the Munich-based early music group directed by Tom Binkley. Unfortunately, the weather had turned extremely bad, and an ice storm had caused a long delay in arriving at the convention hotel, so I heard only the final few minutes of the concert.

At the conclusion of the program, I sought out Rubin, and we sat down in a quiet spot at the back of the hall where the concert had taken place. We began to talk about plans for the upcoming summer session, and, after a few minutes Manny, almost casually, dropped the bombshell: he mentioned that there were plans in the works to add another musicologist to the department, and wondered whether I might be interested in applying for the position. I could hardly believe my ears, and hoped that Manny hadn't noticed how I was shaking with excitement as I answered in the affirmative. He said he would be in touch with me after he had returned to the campus. I could hardly wait until I reached my room to call Gudrun and tell her the news about a possible job opening in Milwaukee. Of course, if a position were to be approved and funded, the search for a suitable candidate would be a national one, and there was no expectation that I would be chosen. At this point, it was nothing but a distant possibility, but certainly something to hope for.

Flying back to South Bend at the conclusion of the conference, I found myself sitting across the aisle from Edward Lowinsky, of the University of Chicago. I have always had the utmost respect for his scholarship, and it was a distinct pleasure and honor to speak with him. At the time, Lowinsky was in the initial planning stages for the 1971 Josquin conference in New York. He graciously invited me to be his dinner guest at O'Hare after we arrived, and we discussed matters of mutual interest. He was particularly interested in a Dutch early music group I had heard in concert at Notre Dame, as one of the important issues to be addressed at the Josquin conference was the question of performance practice in the composer's music. After we had finished dinner, I drove Professor Lowinsky to his home on the south side of Chicago, where I enjoyed a tour of his extensive library. He reminded me that everyone starts out modestly. He said that when Bücken's monumental series of monographs *Handbuch der Musikwissenschaft* began to appear in installments beginning in 1927, he had painstakingly bought them, one at a time: "Drei Mark im Monat!" ("Three Marks a month"), as he proudly recalled. It was indeed, a stimulating and inspiring visit with one of the great minds in musicology.

In January I was informed that my summer apointment had been approved, and I began to make plans for the courses I was to teach. At this time, I also officially applied for the permanent position and was soon informed that my application had been selected for consideration by the search committee. I heard nothing more for almost two months, but in March, I was invited to Milwaukee for a personal interview with the search committee. I had apparently made the cut, and was one of three final candidates for the position.

On Monday, March 23, I had a very friendly and encouraging interview with Manny Rubin and members of the search committee, consisting of Professors Muskatevc (therapy), Suchy (theory), Abram Loft (second violinist in the Fine Arts Quartet, and a Ph.D. in musicology from Columbia), and Clyde Brockett, the other musicologist on the faculty. The Music Department of the University of Wisconsin-Milwaukee is a part of the School of Fine Arts, and I was also interviewed by the dean, Professor Adolph Suppan. The department consisted of approximately thirty-five full-time faculty members and over 350 undergraduate and graduate students, housed in a handsome, new, four-storied structure containing studios, classrooms and faculty offices. One thing I missed was a performing facility for the larger ensembles such as the band, orchestra and choral groups. The only venue was a small, 330-seat recital hall, and a somewhat larger hall containing steeply-raked seating, which was shared with the department of theater and dance.

After my interview, I wandered about the halls looking at the facilities. I stopped in at "Nat" Brockett's office and we chatted for a few moments. He offered me the use of his apartment for the summer term, but I declined his kind invitation, as I planned to place an advertisement in the Milwaukee Journal shortly.

Serendipitously, I stumbled into the recital hall and found the Fine Arts Quartet about to rehearse. The quartet had joined the faculty at the founding of the School of Fine Arts in 1963, and were now artists in residence. As Loft had just met me during the interview, I was introduced to the other members of the group, which included Leonard Sorkin, first violin; Bernard Zaslav, violist; and George Sopkin, cellist, and invited to stay and listen. I was greatly impressed, not only by their playing, but also by their friendliness. I recalled how wonderful it had been during my years as a student in Chicago to be able to usher for their programs in Fullerton Hall at the Art Institute. The heady prospect of joining them as a colleague was extremely attractive to me.

That evening, again fortuitously, Rubin's *collegium musicum* was to give a program, and I attended. The concert was extremely well done, and displayed a lot of talent among the students. A wide range of music was heard, from the Easter sequence, *Victimae paschali laudes* of Wipo, through Isaac, Palestrina, Caccini, Lassus and Bach. A large number of historical instruments were available, including recorders, sackbuts, gambas, a hochdiskantfidel and a large double harpsichord by William Dowd. Some exquisite singing by Kathy Haaker, Pat Humphreys and Bob Koopman was also welcome and well received. The one glitch in the program was a temperamental slide projector used for some illustrations, which malfunctioned at one point. However, the musical portions were superlative. I was particularly impressed by the playing of string players Peter Parkman and Kenton Meyer. Rubin had spent lots of time training his group, and it showed. After the performance I was invited to join all the performers at a local watering hole on Oakland Avenue, called "Kalts."

The next morning I returned to South Bend to await a decision. I was extremely fortunate to have made it this far in the deliberations of the committee, and I was grateful to Manny Rubin for having given my candidacy serious consideration. I was to be as indebted to him as I had been to Bertl Dietz for recommending me for the St. Mary's College position seven years earlier. Rubin was an extraordinarily capable administrator, with a grasp of the intricacies of arcane and convoluted bureaucratic procedures which bordered on the metaphysical. He was also one of the first persons I knew who had, early on, recognized the pervasive and crucial importance which the then-new technology of computers would have on our lives.

On Monday, April 27, I received a letter from the dean of the School of Fine Arts offering me the position at the University of Wisconsin-Milwaukee. I could barely believe my good fortune; (Some years later, I would learn that I was one of seventy-eight candidates for the position.) After so many years of frustrating existence, with the exception, of course, of my highly satisfying seven-year tenure at St. Mary's, I was about to join the faculty of a large, urban university with a student body of over 25,000, a music department with some high-powered and much-respected faculty members, talented students, and a city with many amenities and advantages. Milwaukee, after all, was the thirteenth largest city in the United States, and, even more important, it was said to contain the largest Germanic population of any city in the country. Gudrun would, I was sure, feel very much at home there.

The following weekend, Gudrun and I drove down to the Midwest chapter meeting of the AMS, being held in Cincinnati. As we drove southeast on Interstate 74, outside of Indianapolis late Friday afternoon, we happened to catch a news broadcast telling of student demonstrations against the Vietnam war taking place on the campus of Kent State University, in Kent, Ohio, a few hundred miles northeast of our location. The National Guard was being called out, and it was reported that the situation was becoming serious. We could not know that, on the following Monday morning, four students would be shot to death on the campus by members of the National Guard.

Saturday morning, after I had registered for the convention and was waiting for the first session to begin, Manny Rubin walked up to me anxiously and asked: "Well, Franklin, are you to going to accept our offer?" I was only too happy to answer in the affirmative, and Manny immediately walked across the room to inform Nat Brockett. Only later did I find out that he also informed Hilde Junkermann, who was also in attendance at the meeting. (The reason for this will become clear in a moment.)

On Friday morning, May 16, we piled all five children into the station wagon, and took off for Milwaukee. We checked in at the Park East Hotel, and Gudrun and I went up to the university to look things over, and, particularly, to explore the library, inasmuch as Gudrun was hoping to find employment there. What we had not counted on was that this was the height of the student antiwar demonstrations underway at a number of colleges and universities all over the country, in part, generated by the terrible shootings two weeks earlier at Kent State University. The entire campus was shut down, and it was impossible for us to get into the library. We were practically ushered off the campus by police.

I called Manny Rubin to tell him we were in town to look things over. He said he was glad I had called, as there had recently been a most interesting development: a week after I had accepted the appointment to the faculty, "Nat" Brockett had submitted his resignation to take a position at the University of Kentucky.

The Executive Committee of the department had then recommended to Rubin that he offer this second opening to the number-two candidate. It turned out to be none other than Hilde Junkermann. So now, not only did I have a new and exciting position, I also had the pleasure and honor to look forward to working with a colleague for whom I had the highest respect and admiration. In subsequent years, I would come to consider Hilde the second most important woman in my life, next to Gudrun.

I drove up to Milwaukee about a week before my summer appointment was to begin on June 21, in order to work in the library preparing for the courses. The work was immensely satisfying to me, the students serious and intelligent, and the entire experience stimulating and fulfilling. Kenton Meyer, whom I had admired for his work in the collegium concert I had heard, was in one class, as was Peter Parkman. Joanne Koehn, a singer, was one of the bright lights of the class, and Jo Ellen Snavely, the wife of the clarinet professor, was finishing up her master's degree. The students were dedicated, talented and motivated. I thought it was some of the most exciting teaching I had ever done. The only weakness I found dealt with the music holdings in the library, which seemed quite weak and with lots of *lacunae*. (One day I looked in vain for a score to Berlioz' *Symphonie Fantastique*). The library did have a few *Gesamtausgaben,* but was deficient in a number of areas. I later learned that, only the year before, the library moved over from the music building, into the main library, where its budget could now be subsumed under the general library budget, rather than be funded solely by the Music Department's base budget. I hoped this meant that we would be able to initiate a plan to purchase much needed materials. Indeed, this became one of my priorities in subsequent years.

During the summer I began house hunting. I was fortunate to find a highly competent real estate broker, who also just happened to be a fine musician. Charlie Koehn was a tall, handsome, balding man with a magnificent bass-baritone voice. I could almost have believed that Mozart had created the role of Sarastro in *The Magic Flute* just for him! (Charlie had, as a matter of fact, sung the role in a number of German opera houses during his residence abroad, before returning to Milwaukee and going into real estate full time, meanwhile continuing to appear as a soloist locally in opera and oratorio. His wife, Joanne, also a fine singer, was in my summer classes at UWM.)

After looking at a number of properties, we finally found a large house at 3015 N. Hackett Ave., barely three blocks from school. The house, typical of the eastside, had four bedrooms and a bath-and-a-half on the second floor, with a fifth bedroom on the third floor with a sink. Although there were some drawbacks to the house, namely an outdated kitchen, and an unheated basement, we were satisfied that we had made the best choice for the money. I was also thankful that the modest inheritance I had received allowed me to make a substantial down payment.

A number of UWM music faculty members lived on Hackett Avenue. Ruth Wilson taught music appreciation courses; Bob Thompson was the bassoon professor; Jeff Hollander was a fine pianist; Israel Borochoff was flute professor, and Katja Phillabaum taught part time in the Music Department as a piano instructor. Her husband was a brilliant professor in the Theater and Dance Department. (We came to call ourselves "the Hackett Avenue mob.")

The house was only four blocks from Lake Park, a beautifully planned complex by the well-known Milwaukee landscape artist Frederick Law Olmstead. A stone's throw beyond that was Lake Michigan, which Manny Rubin assured me was like a natural air-conditioner: the area near the lake was always cooler in the summer, and stayed generally warmer in the winter.

Before I left Milwaukee at the end of summer school, I submitted an offer to purchase, and made an initial "earnest money" deposit on the house, before returning to South Bend to begin preparations for our move. After a few further negotiations with the seller, Charlie Koehn called to let me know that my counteroffer had been accepted, and that the closing was scheduled for August 27. Meanwhile, I had a letter from "Bud" Witt, my harpsichord maker, informing me that the instrument was finished and ready to be picked up. I was excited and happy to be able to look forward to a new house, a new academic appointment, and a new harpsichord. The years I would spend at the University of Wisconsin-Milwaukee turned out to be the most fulfilling and satisfying of my entire life, and the experiences, both inside and outside the classroom, provided me with great joy and a sense of accomplishment.

CHAPTER 9

UNIVERSITY OF WISCONSIN-MILWAUKEE
(1970-1986)

As the seven Millers departed South Bend on Tuesday, August 24, 1970, and headed for the Indiana Toll Road on the trip to our new home in Milwaukee, Wisconsin, there were a number of tearful children sitting in the back of our nine-passenger Plymouth Fury II station wagon, amid suitcases, boxes, a broom and vacuum cleaner, and other odds and ends. Yes, it had been an exciting, fruitful seven years at St. Mary's, the children had made a host of friends in South Bend, and it was a painful time for them as it became clear that we were now all embarking on a journey to a strange city, with no friends as yet. Doris and the twins were still in grade school, and would attend Hartford Avenue school, adjacent to the university campus, while Claudia, a sophomore, and Martin, a junior, were to attend Riverside High School, a short distance from the house.

The first few nights in Milwaukee we stayed at a comfortable motel on Port Washington Road, where the children relaxed around the swimming pool, and on Thursday morning, August 27,

233

Gudrun and I sat down at the offices of East Federal Savings and Loan at the corner of Oakland and Locust with James Last, of the bank, our attorney, Clyde Paust, the seller, Mrs. Philip Harland, and Charlie Koehn, my realtor, to close on the house we had bought on Hackett Avenue. I couldn't help but reflect that, at the age of forty-four, this was the first house I had owned, and it was a large step for me.

Gudrun had been hired by the director of the UWM library, Mark Gormley, as a foreign language bibliographer, and I enjoyed knowing that both she and I were again working at the same institution.

On Saturday, September 19, Martin, Claudia and I drove over to Three Rivers, Michigan, to take delivery of the harpsichord. When we arrived back in Milwaukee, Martin and I unloaded my new prized possession, and set it up in the living room. Eventually it would end up in the dining room, which had a lovely hardwood floor.

***

The University of Wisconsin-Milwaukee had been created in 1956 out of the amalgamation of the former Wisconsin State Teachers College and the buildings of Downer College, located in a pleasant northeast side location, just a few blocks from Lake Michigan. The school had grown enormously in less than fifteen years to encompass many new buildings, a student population of over 25,000 enrolled in undergraduate, graduate and doctoral programs, and a faculty of 800. The Music Department was a part of four subdivisions within the School of Fine Arts, including

Theater/Dance, Film and Art. It was the only one of its kind in the Wisconsin system. The Music Department was expanding, and in 1970 alone added ten new faculty members: a new choral director, a band director, orchestra director, two piano professors, a voice professor, a bassoon instructor, a theory professor and two musicologists.

They also added a second theory professor that year, due to a last-minute resignation: On the first day of class, I was told that a member of the theory faculty had calmly walked into the department chair's office, and announced: "I quit." He then walked out the door, never to be seen again in these parts. He was apparently quite a "character." He belonged to what might best be termed the Nam June Paik or Ken Friedman school of musical composition, which included lots of chance operations and "happenings." The story I heard was that, one day, in a large music theory class held in the recital hall, he calmly proceeded to strip down to the buff, presumably to illustrate some kind of arcane, metaphysical musical axiom. Just at that moment, so the story continued, a middle-aged spinster who was a music theory faculty member, happened to step into the recital hall. The resulting confrontation brought about a hurried visit to the department chair's office and a frantic call to campus police who, unfortunately, arrived on the scene too late to "expose" the perpetrator. Yes, I thought, this was going to be an interesting place in which to work.

I found the students mostly talented, hard working and serious. Many of them later went on to illustrious and responsible positions in major symphony orchestras or as professors at academic institutions. John Sherba became the second violinist of the famous Kronos Quartet, which specializes in modern and avant-garde music. Kenton Meyer, after completing a musicology doctorate at Iowa, is now music librarian at the Curtis Institute in Philadelphia. Kevin Stahlheim is extremely active in the Milwaukee area as the director of "Present Music" and together with his gifted wife Karen Beaumont mounts highly successful programs of contemporary music. Jim Wierzbicki has contributed numerous articles to the *New Grove Dictionary of American Music*.

Mary Natvig, an excellent violinist, who later went on to pursue a Ph.D. in musicology at Eastman, is now associate professor of musicology at Bowling Green State University in Ohio, and presently treasurer of the Midwest chapter of the AMS (1999-2001). Other talented students were Susan Sleight, who became a faculty member of a music conservatory in Chicago, and Richard Piipo, an extraordinarily gifted cellist with whom I had the honor to perform a beautiful program of chamber music. Dick is, I believe, head of the string department at Wayne State University in Detroit. Other talented students who enriched my life at UWM were the Due sisters, Kathie, a pianist, and Chris, a violist; Ed Gogolak (a superb recorder player with whom I performed many fine programs of baroque chamber music); sisters Mary Norquist, a violist, and Margaret, a cellist, whose older brother John, just recently (April 2000) won reelection as the very capable mayor of Milwaukee. Mary is a faculty member at Lawrence University in Appleton, Wisconsin, and Margaret is principal cellist of the Mexico City Symphony.

The faculty itself I found to be, without exception, superior in every respect. Over the years there have, of course, been numerous changes in the make-up of the department, as individuals have retired or resigned. Although we were unable to keep him here, James Tocco was unquestionably one of the most gifted young pianists it had ever been my pleasure to hear. His recording of the Chopin Preludes, Opus 25, is one of my prized possessions. The members of the Fine Arts Quartet were outstanding as persons and performers. My friendship with them resulted in some of my most precious memories. I later had the distinct pleasure and honor to be asked to write program notes for their concerts after Abram Loft had left the quartet in 1979. Other fine faculty members were Armand Basile, whose sensitive performance of the Beethoven G major concerto, Opus 58, was a highlight of an all-Beethoven concert in September of 1970, during the composer's bicentennial. The program also included a performance of the Ninth Symphony utilizing performing resources of the Madison campus as well. Gunther Schuller conducted the concert, for which I supplied program notes.

Some of my most satisfying experiences were with my dear friend Hilde Junkermann. The three of us, Gudrun, Hilde and I, often had dinner together, and in 1977 made a memorable transcontinental trip to attend the IMS meeting at Berkeley. Many times we traveled together to the various meetings of the Midwest chapter of AMS. Hilde served as secretary of the chapter for two years as well. She was a demanding teacher with very high standards, and students worked hard for her. Now living outside Memphis, Tennessee, and almost ninety, retired for many years from UWM, she still actively pursues musical activities and is mentally indefatigable.

Another very dear freind, and one of the great stars of the UWM Music Department, is John Downey. Both John and his wife, Irusha, were classmates of mine at CMC in the late forties. (I used to kid John that I dated his wife before he did, though that was not literally true.) Irusha, who worked in the music library at CMC while we were both students there, sometimes provided me with valuable assistance in translating troublesome passages written in German. Like my wife, Gudrun, Irusha is something of a linguist, having a command of six or seven languages. She was born in the Russian Ukraine. (N.B. Less than a week after I had finished writing this autobiography, Irusha died very tragically and unexpectedly, at the age of 70, on Sunday, June 18, 2000.)

John is a superb composer, whose works have appeared under the imprint of a number of major publishers. There are, in addition, several CDs of his music available. One of this best works is *Edge of Space*, a fantasy for bassoon and orchestra, recorded by our own Robert Thompson, with our former orchestra director, Geoffrey Simon, conducting the London Symphony Orchestra. One of my favorite works is the second string quartet, commissioned by the Fine Arts Quartet and recorded by them some years ago.

One of the first events of the fall to engage my attention was a meeting of the Midwest chapter of AMS, which took place on our campus in October. Manny Rubin asked me to be in charge of local arrangements. Over seventy-five people attended, including most of our colleagues from throughout the Midwest. One evening we hosted a reception at our home for the entire group. My old friend from the Conway days, Tom Higgins, was in town and also attended the meeting. As he and others, including Gwynn McPeek, with his ever-present pipe (and its accessories), Carol MacClintock (who was chapter president that year), Ed Kottick, Frank Kirby, John Suess, Hans Tischler, and other assorted luminaries of the chapter sat in my living room that evening, I announced gravely that we were about to be treated to a serious lecture by a famous German musicologist who had recently discovered a totally unknown cantata by "Johann Sebastian Bach, written when he was three years old, perhaps even before..." As we all sat expectedly, the voice on the tape began: "Gut efening, I am in die 'OO ES AH', zent on a goodwill mission by zie Bundesrepublik vest Deutschland, vich ist trying to further cement...if zat ist de right wort...I don't haf my dictionary..." We listened, and it soon became apparent that we were hearing a wonderful comedy routine by Peter Ustinov, spoofing musicology. The room erupted in laughter; John Suess was convinced it was actually his Yale "Doktor-Vater," Leo Schrade, speaking. Others doubled up in hysterics! (McPeek, sitting in front of the fireplace, almost dropped his pipe.)

***

I soon began to be asked to provide harpsichord *continuo* parts for many local instrumental and vocal concerts, including performances of Handel's *Messiah*, chamber music presentations by faculty members and students, and, later, in a small chamber group organized by Manny Rubin. The members of my *collegium musicum* were excellent players and singers, and I think one of our most successful programs occurred on the occasion of a program in 1971 commemorating the 450th anniversary of the death of Josquin. The concert, on May 29, however, had one rather unfortunate drawback: because I had not carefully timed the selections, the program lasted until 10:30 p.m.! In addition to a large dose of Josquin, including two motets "Tu pauperum refugium" (the *secondo pars* of "Magnus es tu, Domine") and "Ave Christe, immolate," the Kyrie and Gloria from the "Missa Pange Lingua," nine *chansons,* both played and sung, there were also madrigals by Wert and Monteverdi, a Buxtehude Latin cantata ("Aperite mihi portas justitiae"), a great favorite of mine, and, finally, a long solo cantata for soprano, with trumpet obligato, by Alessandro Scarlatti ("Su le sponde del Tebro"), beautifully sung by Kathie Haaker. It was an ambitious program; the intermission wasn't until 9:40 p.m.

***

I had arrived at UWM during the height of the antiwar feelings engendered by our involvement in the Vietnam war. Demonstrations took place regularly, and, naturally, my son, Martin, then going on 18, became actively involved. Letting his hair grow to inordinate lengths, he became part of the "hippie" generation, and, together with our oldest daughter, Claudia, who began to look like someone from the Haight-Ashbury section of San Francisco, represented our dubious contribution to the spirit of the times. Martin's room, on the third floor, occasionally emitted the unmistakably sweet, pungent aroma of "pot," until I told him if he wanted to indulge, he should get a room somewhere else. By and large, however, we were to survive this somewhat topsy-turvy time by gritting our teeth and trying to be as tolerant and understanding as possible. As things finally shook out, none of our children is the worse for wear for it, and all have made the metamorphosis to adult life, perhaps kicking and screaming along the way in the process.

Martin, now a student at UWM, would soon be joined by Claudia. Their developing lives were often a source of irritation and exasperation for their harried parents, but I figured if we could get them through their teenage years, we could start to relax a bit. In his first year or two, Martin did not do very well in school. He seemed more interested in playing guitar and partying, and Claudia, soon to be a student at UWM, worked as kitchen help in a downtown steakhouse. Doris, soon to graduate from Riverside High School, was a bit on the wild side, but would recover some equilibrium in subsequent years.

One thing which has always disappointed us was the lack of interest shown by our children in music, or in the arts in general. Although we had tried to introduce them to music, and Martin and Doris, had, in fact, studied violin for some years, none of them seemed the least bit interested in such things. I suspected the old saying about leading a horse to water may apply in their cases. As babies, the twins had been lulled to sleep during their afternoon naps by recordings of Mozart quartets, Martin and Claudia had both sat on the organ bench with me during recording or church services, assisting in registration, and the children heard me accompany Gudrun on a number of occasions when she played the recorder or cello, so it can't be said that they were not "exposed" to music. In addition, they regularly attended concerts with us, or when I performed.

I have hopes, however, that some of our grandchildren may become interested in the arts: Jaron, ten, is in his first year of cello study, and one of the girls' two girls, Danielle, eleven, and Bridgette, nine, are making excellent progress on piano. I didn't necessarily want my children to be musicians, I just had hoped that they might become interested in developing into sensitive listeners and supportive of artistic activities. I suspect that the explanation must have to do with what has been termed "peer pressure." Gudrun is of the opinion that German children have it easier in this respect: the arts and the life of the mind generally are not considered as "square" as it apparently is among young people here in the United States.

***

Having by now finished all the course work for the Ph.D. at Michigan State University, it became my duty to finish my dissertation on the keyboard music of Sorge. Before leaving St. Mary's I had been able to assemble all of Sorge's extant keyboard music, including some dubious attributions, by a lengthy series of inquiries at over two dozen libraries and other archives throughout Europe, and, in one case, here in the United States. Some of the information given in the standard reference works, such as *MGG* and *Grove V,* was either wrong or incomplete. Newman's *The Sonata in the Classic Era* also perpetuated some earlier errors, and added a few of its own, all of which had to be sorted out and corrected. I needed now to continue writing and finally finish the dissertation. I decided to fix up a room in the basement and transfer my library down there. I could work undisturbed, and as the children now had their own telephone line upstairs on the second and third floors, the constant ringing didn't bother me. In June of 1973 I was awarded tenure and promotion to associate professor, and the following year, at the "old" age of forty-eight, completed the requirements for the Ph.D. and finally had my union card.

***

In the summer of 1974, we decided to take the four girls to Europe to meet their cousins, and to visit some important sites. It was a fabulous trip, but I'm not sure they really appreciated some of the sights we showed them. We rented a large Volkswagen Minibus for the six of us, plus sixteen pieces of luggage, for a delightful, exciting trip through southern Germany, the Swiss Alps, central and northern Italy and western Austria.

Standing one day in Florence, Italy, waiting to enter the famous *Ufizzi galleria*, which contains much of the world's greatest art, Doris was heard to exclaim, "O, darn, I just realized, today is the opening day of Summerfest in Milwaukee." (For those unfamiliar with it, Summerfest is equal parts rock concert, circus and street fair.) I thought this a strange reaction indeed, to prefer that to such beautiful sights as the Pallazo Vechio, the Ponte Vechio over the Arno River, Giotto's Campenelle, Pisano and Ghiberti's baptistry doors at the Duomo, or Michelangelo's "David" in the Muncipal Gallery!

243

For Gudrun, one of the highlights of Italy was the visit we made to Ravenna, the seat of the Byzantine Empire from 585 to 751, and the site of glorious, multihued mosaics in the mausoleum of Empress Galla Placidia, and in the great churches of Sant' Apollinare Nuovo and Sant' Appollinare in Classe. Many years before, as a doctoral student in Göttingen, Gudrun had studied these monuments in an art history seminar. As the girls stood looking wonderingly at the sights Gudrun explained some of the symbolism of the mosaics. Later, we went to the tomb of Theodoric, an imposing, though not large stone building with a large, single-slab dome, somewhat like an upside down bathtub. As we climbed around on the monument, one of the girls said to me breathlessly: "Dad, I think there is actually a body lying in the tomb!" We walked over to the sarcophagus and looked in: Karin was lying in it, her arms crossed in front of her.

My brother-in-law, Ludwig Herrmann, was by now teaching in a German "Gymnasium" in Konstanz, and when the four Miller girls got together with the four Herrmann children, it was an exciting visit for all. They immediately understood each other, even when the words didn't always come easily. Ludwig's children were just about the same ages as our four girls: Gernot, the only boy, had three sisters, Almut and Otgild, and the youngest Ulrike, who was eleven. One afternoon we all went swimming at the Zellersee on the island of Reichenau. In the distance stood the Benedictine monastery where Hermannus (Contractus), the well-known music theorist of the Middle Ages, had lived.

***

Meanwhile, life was continuing on with ever more responsibilities and scholarly pursuits. In 1975, the president of the Midwest chapter of the American Musicological Society that year, J. Bunker Clark, of the University of Kansas, asked me to take over the job of editing the chapter Newsletter. The demanding work as editor of the annual publication was a source of great satisfaction to me, and I enjoyed coming to know an ever-expanding group of friends and colleagues in the society. In addition, I continued to serve on program committees, nomination committees, and in general, becoming ever more active in the Midwest chapter.

In the spring of 1976, Gudrun resigned from her position at the UWM library to seek another opportunity, and soon was hired by the Milwaukee Public Library, where she worked at the main library, specializing in serials and periodicals.

In the fall of 1977, Manny Rubin formed a small group to perform on period instruments. In addition to his musicological prowess, Manny was also a rather good horn player, and had recently begun serious study of the gamba. Locally, a group of players interested in performing on fretted stringed instruments had become active, led by Thallis Drake, a remarkable champion of early music, and herself a top-notch gambist. Joined by Ed Gogolak, the four of us formed an early music group which Manny dubbed "Musica Intima," and we performed regularly in the Milwaukee area for several years, often with changing personnel. Michael Babcock, another gambist, and theory faculty member, joined us for a few concerts as well. Occasionally Mary Kestell, a baroque flutist, played with the gorup. Some of my most satisfying musical experiences came from performing with them.

An undergraduate music history class around 1977 (no gray hair yet!) I believe I was discussing the Symphoniae Sacrae of Heinrich Schütz.

In October of 1978, a freshman student by the name of Timothy Noonan came to see me one day. He was, he said, interested in majoring in music history and literature, and perhaps going on to study musicology at the graduate and doctoral levels some day. He seemed rather quiet and a little shy, and I asked him about his previous study. He was born in Milwaukee, and had studied piano with Milton Peckarsky, a fine teacher in the public school system. Pekarsky had also studied musicology at Columbia University with Paul Henry Lang many years earlier. As a high school student, Tim had performed the Mozart Concerto no. 20 in

D minor (K. 466) in public on one occasion. Tim now studied with our own Armand Basile. I asked him about his general knowledge of the literature, and as we spoke further, it became obvious that he knew a good deal of music already, had attended concerts regularly and was acquainted with both symphonic and keyboard literature as well. In addition, he had absolute pitch which, though no proof of musical talent, was always an encouraging and positive sign. He became rather animated about some works as we spoke, and I couldn't help but see my younger self in him, and recall my first meeting, over thirty years earlier, with Hans Rosenwald at Chicago Musical College.

I asked him to play for me, and chose the Beethoven sonata, Opus 49, no. 1 for him to sight read. His playing was not only accurate, but also extremely musical. Here, I concluded, was a potentially excellent student. I encouraged him to continue his studies, and assured him I would function as his mentor as he worked through our undergraduate program. Suffice it to say that Tim fulfilled every possible wish I had for him. He was quite possibly the most gifted, intelligent student I had in forty-two years of teaching. He appeared to soak up knowledge with almost no effort; his reading command of languages was commendable, a skill which would be of great value to him as he eventually worked at the graduate level.

Tim graduated from UWM, and then began working on his master's here. On several occasions I took him with me to meetings of the Midwest chapter of the AMS and introduced him to a number of our members. He finished his master's with a thesis on the Beethoven Trios, and then began doing some

247

teaching for us. When I went on sabbatical in 1986, Tim was the unanimous choice of both Jane Bowers, my colleague, and myself, to replace me. Because one of Tim's interests was the music of the Classic Era, Haydn, Beethoven, Mozart and their contemporaries, I introduced him to James Webster of Cornell University, at the national convention of the AMS in Louisville, with the hope that he might pursue his Ph.D. there. Unfortunately, because of financial reasons, it was not possible for him to do so. He then decided to enroll at the University of Wisconsin-Madison, and recently finished his Ph.D. with a fine dissertation on some aspect of the symphonies of Boccherini. His "Doktor-Vater" was Professor Charles Dill.

Tim started teaching regularly at UWM over ten years ago, and has been a fine addition to the staff of the Music Department. He is now married, and the father of two boys. I trust he will able to find a good university position in the near future.

***

Meanwhile, my son Martin had met an interesting girl who, it turned out, was three-quarters Chippewa Indian, and one-quarter German, an interesting mixture. In June of 1977, Martin and this young woman, Rose Edwards, were married. He was now work- ing at a number of jobs, and becoming very knowledgeable about the recording industry, the various rock, blues and pop groups then active, and he was doing "gigs" as a guitarist. His schoolwork didn't seem to be going very well, but he appeared to be happily on his way as a clerk in various records stores on the east side of Milwaukee, and was a fount of information about every possible performer or group then active in the United States in the field of rock, blues, country and other popular music.

The girls were discovering the fellows as well, and began to assert their independence by moving to their own apartments or rooms. The time was not too far distant when Gudrun and I would finally become "empty nesters." For a few months Claudia and Doris roomed together at various apartments not far from the house. Claudia, now a UWM student, had become quite interested in librarianship and had determined that she wanted to become a librarian some day. She began to work as a library aide at the east side library on North Avenue.

***

The reader may recall that, at the time I first met my wife, she had been invited to our home in Sioux Falls, where she had met my parents, and had the opportunity to dance with my father, who was apparently a good waltzer. Over the years, Gudrun had often attempted to talk me into dancing as well, often commenting that she couldn't understand why I was so reluctant to get out on the dance floor, in view of my father's excellent dancing abilities. Every time she visited her mother in Germany, she would express the wish to dance at least one more time before she died. Unfortunately, the scholarly musicologist and academic in me simply could not envision himself engaging in such admittedly "popular" activities as dancing.

In November of 1978, the national convention of the American Musicological Society was to take place at the Leamington Hotel in Minneapolis, Minnesota, and when we received the official program for the conference, Gudrun immediately discovered that there was to be a "grand Viennese Ball" on the final night of the meeting, complete with a live orchestra of strings and winds performing Strauss waltzes. She said, "All right, I'm going to get you out on the ball floor again, and show you how delightful dancing can be. You're going to bring your tuxedo, and we'll dance some Viennese waltzes together." Little did I realize it, but this would be the beginning of a time, which, in future years, was to give me untold pleasure and satisfaction. Hilde Junkermann and I had driven up to Minneapolis together, and Gudrun flew in on Friday evening after she had gotten off work at the Milwaukee Public Library.

We came down to the large ballroom where the lilting strains of Strauss's "Wine, Women and Song," "The Blue Danube" and other works of the Viennese master were being heard. When this group took a break, a small combo played more modern swing tunes, as well as Latin dances. The floor was a bit crowded with enthusiastic dancers, but what really impressed me was watching some of my most esteemed, highly respected colleagues in musicology out on the dance floor seemingly enjoying themselves immensely. Claire and Barry Brook were a dynamite couple, dancing the jitterbug to a great swing tune; Alejandro Planchart's tango was an absolute sensation, and before I knew it I was also on the dance floor, attempting to put one foot in front of the other without tripping over myself.

I could see that Gudrun was in her element, especially when the prominent Slavic musicologist Miloš Velimirović invited her to be his partner in a Viennese waltz. As I watched the two of them dance, I finally began to understand Gudrun's love of dancing. At one point in the evening Gudrun even persuaded our dear friend Ed Kottick to join her out on the floor, where she attempted to teach him the elements of the Viennese waltz. My old CMC classmates Joe Leahy and Luise Eitel were also there enjoying themselves. I thought, *well, if all these serious, scholarly musicologists can have fun and enjoy themselves dancing, I guess it's not beneath me after all.* From then on, dancing was to become an important part of my life.

November, 1978, Minneapolis, Minnesota. Dancing a Viennese Waltz with Miloš Velimirović at the ball during the AMS convention.

There were other notable events which took place during that unforgettable evening. After the official ball was over, and the orchestra had already packed up and gone home around 1:00 a.m., many still wanted to hear some music, and continue dancing, whereupon a young pianist hopped up on the stage, and started to play some incredible ragtime tunes of Scott Joplin. A group of us stood around the piano as he played, marveling at his spirit and seemingly inexhaustible repertoire. The man's name: Joshua Rifkin, who had just recorded an LP of ragtime tunes for Nonesuch. He also was well on his way toward becoming an excellent Bach scholar.

This weekend also provided the unique opportunity to greet both President Jimmy Carter and Vice President Walter Mondale, in town to support the campaign of some Democratic candidate from the state. Headquarters for the event was on the top floor of the Leamington Hotel. As we all stood in the lobby of the hotel, the vice president got off an elevator and walked through, followed a few minutes later by President Carter, who stopped and greeted us all. For me it was an exciting few minutes.

***

In March of 1979, I began to suffer increasingly stressful attacks of indigestion, finally culminating in a hospital stay during which I had a gall bladder operation in June. Shortly before this, Gisela, one of the twins, was to get married to a young man by the name of Michael Smithers, from Coloma, Wisconsin. Between the middle of May and the middle of June, all sorts of exciting things happened: Gisela and Mike got married on May 19, I went into Columbia Hospital for a cholecystotomy on June 3, and while I was in the hospital Rose gave birth to our first grandchild, Ian, on June 7. Then, apparently inspired by Gisela, Doris decided to marry her boyfriend, Rustam Barbee. They were married on June 16 and that, too, is an interesting story.

Rustam Barbee had just graduated from UWM with a degree in Criminal Justice, and was soon to enter the University of Wisconsin-Madison to pursue a J.D. degree. He was the son of the prominent Milwaukee attorney Lloyd Barbee, a fascinating man for whom I have the utmost respect. Lloyd Barbee is an African-American, and at one time had been married to a white woman. Their son Rustam was a tall, handsome man of mixed race. Lloyd, I was told, had, at one time, seriously considered going into music; however, his interest in law finally took precedence, and he earned his J.D. from the University of Wisconsin. In the early 1960s he was a state representative from Milwaukee and, in addition, represented students and their families in a much publicized desegregation lawsuit brought against the city of Milwaukee school board, which he won for them. Lloyd's special musical interest is opera; his knowledge of the repertoire, fabled performers, recordings and other pertinent facts about the genre is phenomenal. He flies to New York each year for the Metropolitan Opera season, and he also sponsored a resolution in the State Assembly some years ago honoring the late Milwaukee-born composer Otto Luening.

In 1979 an event took place at UWM which was to have a significant impact on my life in later years. One of the ongoing problems in any music department is the constant struggle to fund scholarships for students. Unlike other students, serious, talented music students must spend large amounts of money just to purchase a fine instrument. In addition, the purchase of music and

The four daughters in the kitchen about December of 1979. (l-r): Karin, Claudia, Gisela, Doris, who is about to present us with another grandchild!

concert clothes to be worn in public appearances, adds to the expenses. An ongoing problem throughout the country is attempting to offer scholarships to worthy students to enable them to pursue their studies. Directors of performing organizations on college and university campuses are often desperately in need of gifted students. Good string players and double reed players (oboes, bassoons) are especially in chronic short supply.

In 1978, Professor Geoffrey Simon, the highly gifted director of the UWM Symphony Orchestra, casting about for ideas to generate scholarship monies, had a chance discussion with Professor Robert Thompson, bassoon instructor, who was a Yale University graduate. Thompson recalled that Yale had presented, at one time, a so-called "Viennese Ball," complete with an elegant four-course dinner, and used this occasion as a means to attract sponsors and generate music scholarship funds. The idea appealed to Simon, and plans were made for a Grand Viennese Ball, using members of the various performing organizations on campus to provide music for the evening. Two music students in the symphony, Desi Farley, violist, and Nancy Witte, a clarinetist, assisted by their mothers, Alice and Jean, respectively, took on the task of planning and coordinating the event, helping to design the program, gathering the money, decorating the ballroom and, in general, involving themselves in every aspect of the production.

The first annual Grand Viennese Ball was held at the Marc Plaza Hotel on Wisconsin Avenue in downtown Milwaukee in March of 1979. The ballroom was alive with the sounds of Strauss waltzes and polkas, and, when the members of the symphony took a break, the UWM Jazz Ensemble, under the direction of Frank Pazzullo, took the stage to play a set of "big band" tunes from the Glenn Miller era, appropriately dubbed by director Simon as "tender tunes." The wind ensemble, under the able direction of Professor Tom Dvorak, provided appropriate dinner music and the entire company enjoyed a beautifully prepared, four-course dinner, preceded by a delightful social hour.

Although my wife had introduced me to the pleasures of ballroom dancing the previous year at the national convention of the AMS, we did not attend the first year of the UWM Grand Viennese ball, as Gudrun was in Germany at the time; however, in 1980 we attended for the first time. It was to be the beginning of a long and satisfying association with the event. Gudrun was excited to be able to dance Viennese waltzes again, and was able to take a turn around the floor with the dance master himself, Bill Reilly. Bill, and his wife Shirley were a veteran Broadway dance team, and had come to Milwaukee a few years earlier to open a ballet school here. Simon had asked them to be dance masters for the evening, which they did, also providing patrons with a few lessons in the finer points of the Viennese waltz a few weeks before the event. Both were superb dancers, and made a beautiful couple on the dance floor.

A year later, in 1981, I was asked to take on the job of master of ceremonies for the Grand Viennese Ball, and thoroughly enjoyed the preparations and work involved in putting it on. Jean Witte and Alice Farley were indefatigable workers, doing everything on a volunteer basis. The second year, though the ball showed only a modest profit of approximately $2,000 in scholarship funds, the idea had now caught on.

We also heard that the University of Wisconsin-Eau Claire had started a Viennese Ball some years before ours, and, after inquiring about it, we began to attend regularly. The Eau Claire ball was the idea of a violinist in the school symphony who became an employee of the university. She suggested to the conductor of the orchestra that this could be a vehicle to assist in raising music scholarship funds, much in the same way as we were doing. Ada Bors was an incredibly able person, and her husband, Adam, a member of the German Department, spoke flawless German, and danced a beautiful Viennese Waltz.

Every year Gudrun and I drove up to Eau Claire to attend the ball on both nights; we always look forward to it with great anticipation. On a few occasions Adam and Ada Bors returned the favor, and attended our Grand Viennese Ball. (The photo of Gudrun and me dancing in the collage on the cover of this book, was taken at the 1994 Eau Claire Viennese Ball.)

***

Around 1980, I started to become increasingly involved with research on the history of music in Milwaukee. In doing preliminary study, it became clear to me that there was a treasure trove of primary source material just waiting to be worked on. The Milwaukee County Historical Society had complete records of such groups as the Milwaukee Musical Society, and, in addition, the public library had not only records, but also musical manuscripts of several Milwaukee composers. The arts and humanities librarian was June Edlhauser, who indicated to me that there were a number of large boxes containing uncatalogued materials which needed to be examined. There have been, of course, a few attempts at working on the materials. In 1974 a master's thesis by Tom Schleiss called *Opera in Milwaukee: 1850-1900* describes the importance of the genre in the developing city, though it suffered from some questionable scholarly procedures. It had been written at the University of Wisconsin, and in 1980 a doctoral dissertation from the same institution by A.B. Reagan entitled *Art Music in Milwaukee in the Late Nineteenth Century, 1850-1900* appeared as well. Since then there has been relatively little work done on the rich sources here.

As the result of my work on music in the city, I was asked to write the article on Milwaukee for the *New Grove Dictionary of*

American Music, and also contributed further articles on a Milwaukee music publisher, as well as writing the article on Milwaukee for the *New Grove Dictionary of Opera*. In November of 2000, the *New Grove Dictionary of Music and Musicians*, 2nd Edition, will include my new article on the history of music in Milwaukee.

***

In June of 1981, Emanuel Rubin, who had stepped down the year before as the department chair, announced his resignation to accept a position as dean at Ball State University in Indiana. The new chair of the department, Gerry McKenna, appointed me to head the search and screen committee for a new musicologist. Because it was already June before we knew of this opening, we had little time in which to conduct the search. Over fifty persons applied, at least four or five of whom appeared to be strong candidates. In the end, the search committee unanimously recommended that the position be offered to Dr. Jane Bowers of Portland, Oregon. Jane had significant teaching experience, a good publishing record, and was also a performer on early instruments: recorder, baroque flute and gamba. This was an important consideration, as we were also seeking a director of the *collegium musicum*. Almost as important as these qualities were her impressive credentials in the area of women in music, a field which was then beginning to have a good deal of relevance in musicological studies here and in Europe. I was convinced she was just what the department needed, as she could provide a good balance to the other musicologists. Jane has been a wonderful colleague these many years, and has been instrumental in making some needed changes and additions to the musicology offerings from which I have also benefited.

***

In the spring of 1982, Professor Geoffrey Simon, the founder of the Grand Viennese Ball, announced his resignation to take a position on the faculty of North Texas University in Denton. The chairman of our music department, Gerry McKenna, called me in to his office to ask if Gudrun and I could take on the responsibility of running the event in the future, as it was now beginning to be successful in raising scholarship money. I was flattered and also excited at the prospect, but accepted only on the condition that Alice Farley and Jean Witte stay on as my lieutenants in the endeavor. Thus began a wonderful, though demanding association with the Grand Viennese Ball, which has been a source of great joy and satisfaction for Gudrun and me. Even to this day many remember with much pleasure those early days of the ball, when I did almost single-handedly what is now being handled by a committee of approximately twenty people. The ball has, by now, become one of the prominent occasions of the winter social season, attracting the movers and shakers of the city of Milwaukee, including Mayor John Norquist, who appeared with the UWM jazz ensemble a few years ago as featured vocal soloist. Most important of all, it has become the primary source of scholarship monies for the Music Department, raising over $40,000 each year from the sale of auction items and drawings whose first prize is a round-trip ticket for two to Vienna for the Emperor's Ball on New Year's Eve.

Without question, the most thrilling experience we have had, was the opportunity to actually go to Vienna ourselves to attend the world-famous "Kaiser-Ball," held each year in the Hofburg, the Imperial apartments in the center of Vienna. It was to be the visit of a lifetime. Attired in our finest formal clothes, we walked the two blocks to the Hofburg on New Year's Eve from our *pension* in the city center and entered the elegant setting for a delicious, five-course Viennese dinner. International guests from Turkey, France, Switzerland and the United States sat at our table for dinner, and after the meal was over we danced in the enormous ballroom until 5:00 a.m.

After a short sleep, we attended a delicious brunch at 11:00 a.m. at the Hotel Intercontinental, and afterward heard the traditional New Year's Day concert by the Vienna Philharmonic played in the Musikverein down the street. As it is almost impossible to get tickets for the event, we watched it in a large banquet room in the hotel on huge, closed-circuit TV screens. As Gudrun and I sat down, I happened to glance to my right. Sitting not six seats away from me was the beautiful and famous Italian actress Sophia Loren. I figured if she could put up with hearing the concert at a distance from the hall itself, I guessed I could, too. By the time the concert was almost over, Gudrun and I could no longer restrain ourselves, and getting up from our seats, we managed to get out into the hall and began dancing the last few Strauss waltzes.

In subsequent days we visited Mozart's apartment in Domgasse 5, at the rear of St. Stephen's Cathedral, took a tour of the wine-making area of Grinzing, where we saw the building in which Beethoven is said to have penned the famous "Heiligenstadt Testament," and attended performances of Strauss' *Die Fledermaus* and Mozart's *Magic Flute* at the Vienna State Opera. We also visited the Kunsthistorisches Museum, where I was able to play pianos owned by Brahms, Hugo Wolf and Schubert. We enjoyed ourselves more than we ever had in any place, and it is our fond wish, before we die or get too old to travel, to be able to visit Vienna again.

***

My family was beginning to grow. In 1980 Doris and Rustam had their first child, a boy, Aaron, and they moved from Milwaukee to student housing on the campus of the University of Wisconsin in Madison when Rustam entered law school there. In April of 1983, they had their second child, a lovely baby girl whom they named Leah. She would become, for me, my favorite grandchild, perhaps because she was the first girl. Martin and Rose also had another boy in January of 1986, and named him Kyle. So we were quickly adding to the family with four grandchildren in six years.

The Grand Viennese Ball of UWM was becoming ever more successful, providing us with a great deal of pleasure and raising more scholarship funds for the department. Meantime, a group of Milwaukeens, inspired by the model of our Grand Viennese Ball,

July 4, 1982. "Max and Moritz," or the "Katzenjammer Kids!" Ian Miller, 3 years old, and Aaron Barbee, 2-1/2 years old. These are the first two grandchildren.

A picture by a photographer standing outside the room. Graduate seminar examining 14th century isorhythmic motets. I am standing at the far right of the picture.

began an organization known as "A Night in Old Vienna," which employed UWM students to provide music for dancing, in addition to an elegant dinner.

***

Upon the retirement of Hilde Junkermann from the UWM faculty, I was appointed director of graduate studies in the Music Department, a post I held for four years. I also was elected to a prestigious office in the American Musicological Society when I won election as president of the Midwest chapter at the 1982 spring meeting at the University of Kansas in Lawrence. On this occasion we met together with the Sonneck Society, and I presented a paper dealing with the results of some of my research into the history of music in Milwaukee. The opportunity to serve as president of our chapter was a great honor, and I was proud to serve in this capacity for a two-year term.

At the spring meeting of 1983, held at the University of Wisconsin, Madison, Gudrun and I had driven down from Eau Claire, where we had attended the Viennese Ball the night before, in order for me to conduct the annual business meeting of the chapter after the Saturday afternoon sessions. A musicologist from Mainz University, Germany, had presented a paper that morning, and I introduced myself to him. Friedrich Riedel was a name known to me, particularly in the field of German keyboard music. We chatted during a social hour, and at the conclusion of the meeting on Sunday. I told him of my studies in Heidelberg, and inquired about the possibility of perhaps doing some lecturing for him at Mainz sometime. He appeared very interested, and we pursued the matter a bit further. I discovered that he was also the president of the newly organized International Joseph Martin Kraus Society, dedicated to research on the composer's music and times. Because of my interest in the composer, I joined the society on the spot.

In the latter part of October I received the official invitation from Professor Riedel to teach at Mainz the following summer. I was asked to present public lectures and conduct a concentrated seminar on "Music in den USA seit 1900" ("Music in the USA since 1900"). Because of my interest in the music of Joseph Martin Kraus, I was also invited to present a lecture at the annual meeting of the Kraus Society in June of 1984 at Buchen. By the time I had gotten around to working on the music of Kraus, however, another scholar had already carved out a niche for himself in this area. Bertil van Boer was in the process of finishing an excellent dissertation on Kraus, and had already been contracted to do a volume of his symphonies for Garland Publishing Company's series: *The Symphony, 1720- 1840*, edited by Barry Brook. This has often been my fate in doing research: about the time I had become deeply involved with some composer's music, subject or specific field, though had not yet published anything, another scholar had seized upon it and brought out the fruits of his research. These, of course, are the perils in any scholarly endeavor and I have no regrets or hard feelings toward anyone intending to do such work. Our field is still large enough, and with enough opportunities for solid scholarship that one may still be challenged in a variety of ventures. As a matter of fact, I have had a number of interesting and fruitful contacts with Professor van Boer, during which he has kindly shared much of his research with me. I am also grateful to him for making available to me materials which he encouraged me to investigate, dealing with Kraus's chamber music.

***

Just before we left for Mainz for my summer teaching appointment in 1984, another family milestone was reached. Claudia, our oldest daughter, had by now graduated with a master's degree in Library Science from UWM and was working for a local law firm as a legal librarian. For several years she had been dating David Butschli, a wonderful young man, also a UWM graduate, and now an electrical engineer employed by the Wisconsin Electric Power Company. On June 2, David and Claudia were married in a beautiful ceremony at St. Mark's Episcopal Church, just down the street from our house, and the same church where both Martin and Gisela had been married a few years earlier. The occasion marked a joyous reunion for many of my family as well. Martha and her husband Jim, with their younger son Sam; Libby and her new husband, Bob Clark, as well as our dear, wonderful aunt Elinor, now eighty-two, were all present, as were my children and their spouses. In addition, Gudrun's two cousins from Evanston, Erich Lenz and Irene Anderson, with their spouses, were also in attendance. Two days after the wedding Gudrun and I left for Mainz.

June 2, 1984, Claudia's wedding. Four year old Aaron Barbee is helping her open the wedding gifts. David Butschli, the groom, is standing behind her.

Upon our return from Mainz, I began a regular habit of swimming in the pool at UWM. This regimen has been of great value to my health, both physically and mentally. The lower back pains I had suffered from for so many year as the result of having worked in a carpet firm in Wilmette, Illinois in 1953, have almost completely disappeared, which is not to say that I had no other medical problems. I will save that for a later chapter.

In the fall of 1984, I applied for a sabbatical leave, in order to do research on the chamber music of Joseph Martin Kraus. I also applied for a Fulbright grant, to lecture at a German university for one semester. In the early part of 1985 I was informed that I had been awarded a sabbatical for the academic year 1985-86, and in

266

June I was notified that I was the recipient of a one-semester award under the Fulbright Scholar Program to teach at Heidelberg University during the summer semester of 1986. (Because the award was for one semester only, rather than a full year, those of us receiving such grants sometimes referred to ourselves as "Half-brighters," rather than "Fulbrighters.")

For some years Karin, one of the twins, had dated a young man by the name of Kevin Hayes, the son of a Milwaukee attorney. Both of them had attended the same grade school and the same high school, and on July 6, 1985, we finally got our youngest daughter married off. Kevin's family has an interesting parallel to our own: He was the first child, followed by four girls, the last two of whom were twins, precisely the order of our family. Kevin is an extremely bright, motivated young man who is a vice president of W.H. Brady, a Milwaukee corporation with branches all over the world. He is always flying off to France, Florida, or a number of other locations worldwide. The wedding was unique, just as they wanted it and was held at Villa Terrace, a beautiful Italian residence on the east side. The wedding dinner, held in a large building overlooking Lake Michigan in Lake Park, was delightful for everyone on both sides of the family, with Erich and Hedi Lenz the only persons present who had also attended our own wedding, some thirty-two years earlier. (They had also attended Claudia's wedding a year earlier.)

July 5, 1985, Karin's wedding. The Miller and Hayes children pose for the camera. (l-r): Karin, the bride, her twin sister Gisela, Doris, Claudia, Martin, Kevin Hayes with his sisters, Connie and Kara. (Unfortunately, I cut off Liz and Eileen, the Hayes twins, on the far right).

CHAPTER 10

A SABBATICAL AND A HALFBRIGHT;
THE PAROLE PETITION IS DENIED,
AGAIN AND AGAIN
(1986-1993)

As I began to plan my teaching in Heidelberg, it became clear that it would make little sense for an American musicologist to come to Germany and lecture on some aspect of German music, Bach, Beethoven, or others. Ludwig Finscher my host at Heidelberg, suggested I lecture on developments in American music in the last fifty or so years. Though this area is not my field of specialization, I had taught a number of courses which dealt with 20th-century American music, and was conversant enough about the subject that I decided to begin preparing a series of seminars and lectures to be entitled "Musik in den USA seit 1900" ("Music in the USA since 1900"). The reader will recall that I had lectured on the same subject two years earlier in Mainz.

My son, Martin, his wife and their two children, Ian, 7, and baby Kyle, who had just been born in January, were to live in our house during the time we would be in Germany, and I left for

Frankfurt the first week of March 1986. Immediately upon my arrival I went to the university housing office, where I had applied for an apartment in the guest professor quarters in Schlierbach, just outside Heidelberg, and almost directly across the Neckar River from my first living quarters in Ziegelhausen, back in 1952. If I walked around outside, I could almost see, across the river, in the distance, the small chapel in which we were married over thirty-three years earlier.

Gudrun arrived in a few days, and later that week I reported to the Musicology Institute of the University, where I met Heidi Löffler, the departmental secretary, and was introduced to Bärbel Pelker, who was to be my teaching associate. I was given an office for my private use and for student conferences, with a typewriter, cabinets and bookcases. My office looked out on the plaza in front of the Jesuit church, where, as a young student, thirty-three years earlier, I had heard a magnificent performance of the Beethoven *"Missa Solemnis,"* actually sung as a part of the Sunday Mass. That had been an extraordinary experience.

From March 13-21, Gudrun and I took part in a week-long Fulbright seminar in Berlin, consisting of orientation, workshops, formal receptions and lectures by the officials of the Fulbright organization and others. The train trip through East Germany was a sobering reminder of the oppression and terrible living conditions under which the populace lived. In addition, I couldn't get over the ever-present pall of industrial smog hanging over cities. The use of soft coal, and the inefficient motors of the Trabant, one of the few makes of cars, all contributed to this depressing scene. As the train passed through Bach's birthplace of

Eisenach, it was interesting to note that the main street of the city was only a dirt road. It was also chilling to observe police dogs sniffing the undercarriages of the railroad cars in each town where the train came to a stop. Anyone who has not experienced this type of atmosphere, cannot appreciate the freedoms that are enjoyed in the western sector of Germany, and in other parts of the world.

Dr. Ulrich Littmann, the executive director of the Fulbright Commission in Bonn; Richard E. Burt, the United States Ambassador to Germany and Dr. Richard von Weizsäcker, the German Federal President, were featured speakers at a number of formal gatherings which took place during the week. Awardees were also given the opportunity to visit some of the great sites in and around Berlin, and Gudrun and I visited the Museum Dahlem, the National Gallery, and the Egyptian Museum (which contains the original bust of Nefertiti). For Gudrun, as a doctoral student in archeology, by far the most impressive visit was to the famous Pergamon Altar in East Berlin, which she had studied in a seminar at Göttingen.

There were also a number of visits to other, more depressing locations, such as the Berlin Wall, the Reichstag, jails where dissidents were executed during the Nazi regime, and the site of several attempts by people to scale the infamous wall, resulting in their deaths.

In Heidelberg, the semester began on April 1, and I held my seminars and presented my first lectures the following week. It was indeed a stimulating, exciting time, and I occasionally had to pinch myself to make sure I wasn't dreaming it all. With the

271

March, 1986, at the Berlin Wall

assistance of Bärbel Pelker, I purchased a small, cream-colored, two-door Mitsubishi automatic which was to serve us well for the next half year. 1986 also marked the 600th anniversary of the founding of Heidelberg University in 1386, Germany's oldest university, and there were a number of extra events to celebrate the occasion. I was assigned an official parking spot just a few meters from the Musicology Institute, which was extremely convenient, as parking is at a premium around the university.

My weekly schedule included an intensive two-hour seminar each Friday morning conducted for doctoral candidates and other advanced graduate students and formal lectures to students of the university on Wednesday afternoon from 4:00 to 6:00 p.m. In addition, I maintained office hours almost every day for private conferences with students. Each student was required to choose a seminar topic, normally a specific piece of music, or works of a specific composer, and prepare a class presentation of his/her seminar topic. I had arranged with the music library at UWM to ship a large number of books and scores to be used in the seminar. In addition, all the scores were represented by cassette tapes, for which I had received permission from the record companies to copy for our use in the classes and lectures.

Lecture presented in the renowned "Alte Aula" of Heidelburg University. I spoke on string quartets of Schnittke and Peter Schickele, to be performed by the Audubon String Quartet, Virginia Polytechnical Institute, Blacksburg, Virginia. Professor Herbert Schneider and Professor Ludwig Finscher can be seen at the far right.

Some of the most satisfying and exciting experiences during my guest professorship in Heidelberg, was being invited to lecture at other universities throughout the country. Several of my old classmates from thirty-three years earlier now held important professorships in German universities, and they asked me to come to their school for a lecture on some aspect of American music. In Würzburg, Wolfgang Osthoff and Martin Just invited me to speak on Ives and his music, and in Tübingen, I was invited by Ullrich Siegele and Arnold Feil to speak about the use of folk songs and popular music in the works of Copland and Thomson. I was also invited to lecture at Wuppertal by Werner Breig, and in Munich I lectured in Theodor Göllner's musicology seminar. That was an interesting visit, incidentally. The day after my lecture, I spent my time in the Bavarian State Library working on Kraus and other research topics. Göllner had invited Gudrun and me to join him and his wife, Marie Louise, for lunch at a pizza restaurant. Theo said rather mysteriously that someone would be joining us for lunch whom I'd enjoy meeting. It turned out to be my old friend Chuck Atkinson, from Ohio State, a faithful member of our Midwest AMS chapter, in Germany for several weeks to do some research.

Partly as a result of my guest professorship in Heidelberg, I was asked by Professor Finscher to come back to the university in the fall to present a formal address to a meeting of doctoral students in musicology from the German-speaking countries of western Europe, Switzerland, Germany and Austria, in which I was to contrast the study of musicology in American and German universities. Finscher thought that, since I had studied and taught under both systems, I could bring some special insights to the conference.

Following this meeting, the regular national conference of the Gesellschaft für Musikforschung (Society for Musical Research) met, and I was invited to partake in a panel discussion as a part of a symposium panel which would address the question of "Musik in der Universität." The panel comprised some of the best known musicologists in Europe: Wolfgang Rehm, from the Mozarteum in Salzburg represented Austria; Pietro Petrobelli presented the Italian perspective; France was represented by Nicole Sevestre, Paris, and England by B. Smallman. The United States was represented by Alexander Ringer from Illinois, and me.

For almost a week, I had the opportunity to be in the presence of some of the most outstanding musicologists from all of Germay, such as the late Carl Dahlhaus, Silke Leopold and Rudolph Stephan from Berlin, Lothar Hoffmann-Erbrecht and Albert Riethmüller from Frankfurt, Martin Just and Wolfgang Osthoff from Würzburg and Christoph Helmut Mahling and Friedrich Riedel from Mainz. It was a heady atmosphere in which to be, and I shall always be grateful to Professor Finscher for his gracious invitation. I was partly able to attend these meetings because of a stipend from the dean of the School of Fine Arts, Robert Hickok, and also from the graduate dean of the university, George Keulks, for which I was especially grateful.

The entire experience, first as a Fulbright visiting professor, then as guest lecturer at a number of different German universities, and finally the opportunity to address a gathering of European musicologists, represented the high point of my academic career to that point. However, there was to be one more series of experiences which would provide what I considered a capstone to the achievements of my life.

October, 1986, Gesellschaft für Musikforschung conference at Heidelburg University. Participating in a symposium on "Music in the University." (l-r): Professor Ludwing Finscher, Director, Musicology Institute, Heidelburg University; Professor Alexander Ringer, University of Illinois; Pierlugi Petrobelli, Italy; the author.

The years between the fall of 1986 and the spring of 1989 were busy ones, with lots of satisfying teaching, additional research, and, of course, lots of dancing at a number of Viennese balls from one end of the country to the other. Gudrun and I regularly attended the Eau Claire Viennese Ball for both nights, and, in addition, drove to Chicago for the American Friends of Austria Ball at the Ambassador West Hotel on State Parkway on the near north side. At these events, Gudrun especially enjoyed dancing with Paul Jennewein, the Austrian vice consul in Chicago, whom she considered the best Viennese waltzer she had danced with. We also flew to Detroit on a number of occasions to attend the Detroit Viennese Ball, often with our good friends and dancing partners Gary and Judy Runk, who were competitive dancers at one time. I was now hooked on the Viennese waltz and dancing in general. (I'd even become an expert on how one starches those attachable collars, and the formal vest, which goes with them.)

***

Around 1987, Gudrun and I began to give some consideration to possible locations where we might eventually like to relocate upon my retirement from UWM. Our first trip was to my hometown of Sioux Falls, South Dakota, where we enjoyed seeing my former teacher and mentor, J. Earl Lee, now retired, but still active in various projects, including an annual piano competition which had been established at Augustana College in his name.

South Dakota has no state income tax. Property taxes in Sioux Falls are relatively moderate, living expenses are modest, there is a minimum of congestion, the city is clean, basically crime free, with a wealth of educational and cultural opportunities. We were impressed with the friendliness of the people as well. It was certainly high on our list of locations we wished to consider. And, after all, it was the place where I had first met and got to know my dear wife. The only thing which caused some hesitation, aside from the distance from family and friends, was the long and bitterly cold winters. For some reason, the older I have become, the more I object to the cold weather, and the less hot weather bothers me. Maybe it has something to do with our poor blood circulation as we get older.

While we were in Sioux Falls, I also had an opportunity to examine the work of a local organ builder by the name of John Nordlie. For the most part using mechanical action, the instruments were not only visually striking in appearance, but also exhibited a beautiful sound, reminding me of some of the glorious ensembles of the Schnitgers of north Germany. Nordlie had built instruments mainly in the immediate area, including a large, three-manual installation at First Methodist Church in Sioux Falls, and smaller instruments in Brandon Lutheran Church, and Hope Lutheran Church in town. Each time I have made subsequent visits there, I have seen John to find out about his latest installation. His workmanship is without equal, the cabinetry alone of the highest quality.

In August of 1988 Gudrun, and I undertook another exploratory trip, this time to North Carolina and the area around Asheville, as a possible retirement option. We contacted realtors to inquire about buying a house in the area, but in the end, we abandoned plans to retire there. Apart from the long distance to our family and friends in Milwaukee, we were disappointed to again sense a subtle resentment against us "Yankees," and a kind of insular, parochial attitude which I simply have never been able to fully comprehend or accept.

On our way back from North Carolina, we stopped in New Buffalo, Michigan, for a long-overdue visit with our dear friends Walt and Midge Wade, who have a summer home just a few hundred feet from the eastern shore of Lake Michigan. This visit was to be the beginning of a tradition of spending a long weekend with them each summer, which has continued to this day. The area around New Buffalo is famous for its fruit orchards: strawberries, blueberries and cherries in the summer, apples in the fall, and we always stock up for the entire year while we're there.

In October, we were off once more to a possible retirement destination, when I was able to combine attendance at the national convention of the Fulbright Association in Albuquerque, New Mexico, with the annual meeting of the College Music Society in Santa Fe. After two days in Albuquerque, during which I had the opportunity to visit with Dr. Ulrich Littmann, the executive director of the German Fulbright Commission, whom we had last seen in Berlin in 1986, we drove up to Santa Fe, where I immediately fell in love with the city, with its charming ambiance of Native American culture, the "adobe" style of architecture, the mountainous terrain and the warmth of the southern sun. We took a guided tour through northern New Mexico to Taos, and visited the Pueblo Indian reservation there, and one Sunday afternoon, drove over to Las Vegas, New Mexico, a quiet small town near the eastern slopes of the Sangre de Cristo range, which also had a university (New Mexico Highlands University). An added bonus on the trip to Santa Fe was a visit from my sister Martha, who had been on a hiking expedition near Gallup. She drove over to Santa Fe to spend the weekend with us.

Although we found much to like about the area, with its mild, dry climate, real estate prices were generally too high for us, and again, the problem of being so far from family and friends tended to dampen our enthusiasm and cause us some hesitation as to the feasibility of settling there. In addition, something was to occur the following spring which would place any plans for retirement on "hold" for several years.

***

In the spring of 1989, a number of events occurred in the Music Department which were to provide me with opportunities which I could never have envisioned in my entire academic career. The chair of the Music Department, Gerard McKenna, was an extremely able administrator, but it was clear that he was sometimes frustrated by conditions over which he had little control. We were often faced with critical issues dealing, for the most part, with funding questions. Central administration, in Madison, continually demanded that we return certain sums of money each year, in a process known euphemistically as "salary savings." On April 4, 1989, Professor McKenna made a surprise announcement at a departmental Executive Committee meeting, that he intended to resign as the chair of the department, and that an election would have to be held to elect a new chair for the following year.

The election for a new chair was scheduled for Tuesday, April 25, but on the day of the election, Dr. McKenna announced to the Executive Committee that not a single name had been deposited in a box signifying that a likely candidate would be willing to serve as the new chair of the department. At this point, a motion was taken asking the dean of the School of Fine Arts to appoint an "interim" or "caretaker" chairman for the following year, and we would meanwhile go forward with a plan to eventually find a permanent, external chair after one year. Some faculty members objected to what may have been perceived as an abrogation of our duties and obligations as a legally constituted governing body, and the meeting began to take on a more and more contentious atmosphere. At this point Professor Paul Kramer asked: "Is there anyone here who would be willing to be the chair of the department for a year?" For a minute there was no reaction of any kind, until I raised my hand, and said I might be willing to try it for one year only. There was a collective sigh of relief, and the meeting adjourned amid condolences for the apparent sole candidate for the "honor."

I was informed of my election as chair by Gerry McKenna and began an almost daily round of meetings and conferences with him, during which I was thoroughly grounded in the procedures and regulations governing the conduct of the department. I also met regularly with Professor Corliss Phillabaum, who had been name acting dean of the School of Fine Arts by Chancllor John Schroeder after Robert Hickok had left. I met Corliss when we first moved to Milwaukee almost twenty years earlier, and considered him one of the most brilliant minds in the School of Fine Arts.

On Tuesday, May 16, I addressed the Executive Committee of the department, thanking them for their confidence. I also asked "only that [hey] as patient as possible with my first months on the job, and as tolerant as possible of any shortcomings...in my conduct as the chief executive officer of the Music Department." The following week the other shoe dropped: Gerry McKenna announced that he had accepted the deanship of the School of Fine Arts and Communications at the University of Wisconsin-Stevens Point.

On July 1, at the age of sixty-three, I officially took office as chair of the Music Department for what I thought was to be only a one-year assignment. It was not, however, to be, for at the end of the year my election was confirmed for a second year. Again and again what I came to refer to as my "parole petition" kept being denied by my faculty, until finally, after four years, in 1993, I announced that I would definitely retire on July 1, despite repeated entreaties on the part of faculty members that I continue for a fifth year.

In many ways, the years I spent as chairperson were some of the most exciting and productive of my life. Although there were often insurmountable problems, most, but not all of a financial nature, I began to find the challenge of running an organization of over forty full and part-time faculty members, some 300 undergraduate and graduate students, and a departmental budget of over $2,500,000 to be the source of great stimulation to me, as well as a tremendous test of my intellectual capabilities, my mental facilities and my emotional stability. I often said that I was confronted at every turn with raging paranoia, and chronic egomania.

I would never have been able to handle it, had I not been able to call on the assistance of several incredibly helpful and supportive people. My associate chairs were two men for whom I had the utmost respect: Wayne Cook, an easygoing Texan of boundless good spirits; and Bill Duvall, a singing actor of great talent and unquestionable ethical standards. (Bill's brother, incidentally, is the movie actor Robert Duvall.) Another person for whom I have undying respect and admiration was the assistant dean of the School of Fine Arts, Robert Scudder, who controlled the purse strings of all the departments in the school, and who regularly assisted me in finding enough money to cover a number of projects and activities. Bob could be a tough and uncompromising taskmaster, but I always knew his counsel was wise. I also am indebted to my secretary, Mary Eichstaedt, whose steady and even hand was evident in many ways as I tried to administer the department.

Shortly after I had begun my tenure as department chair, Professor James Sappenfield was named interim dean of the School of the Fine Arts by Chancellor John Schroeder. Sappenfield was a professor of English in the School of Arts and Letters, whose field of expertise were the works of James Fennimore Cooper. I was pleased that a humanist of his standing was now heading the school, and my three years with him were indeed exciting and fruitful.

One of the things I was finally able to accomplish was the repair and renovation of a number of physical spaces: the recital hall, new acoustic treatment of the band and orchestra rehearsal spaces, repair and purchase of new instruments, secure storage areas for the jazz instruments, and, finally, creating a small, but important source of money in order to make it possible for faculty members to attend scholarly and professional meetings in order to upgrade and improve their skills. We were also able to fund a number of visiting scholars and performers to come to campus for presentations, lectures and workshops. Among them were Richard Crawford, an American music specialist, and Nancy Reich, who has done much work on women composers and musicians, especially Clara Schumann and Fanny Mendelssohn.

In August of 1989, Gudrun, who had not worked for a number of years, noticed an advertisement in the Milwaukee Journal for a librarian and receptionist at the Goethe House of Milwaukee, a branch of the better know Goethe Institute of the German government, which serves as a source of information about German culture and history. She applied for the position, which was only part-time, and was immediately hired by Dr. Ernst Edlhauser, the director of the Goethe House. For the next eight years, she enjoyed challenging activities and opportunities in a field close to her abilities and interest, and when Dr. Edlhauser retired, she was named administrator of the facility, a position she retained for a few years until retiring herself in January of 1997.

In the third week of August, 1989, our family had a wonderful reunion at a comfortable retreat center south of Sioux Falls, in honor of our dear aunt Elinor, now eighty-seven years old, and as spry as ever. It was good to see many whom I'd not seen in years, including my ninety-two-year-old uncle Ashley, together with his new "bride" Betty, aunt Esther having died a few years earlier. Unfortunately the only members of my family who were able to be present were Martin and Claudia, with David and her baby boy, Alex. It was great to be with them all, if only briefly.

Family reunion, August 20, 1989, Sioux Falls, SD.
With my two sisters, Martha and Libby.

I had particularly hoped that Doris, Rustam and their family, with handsome Aaron, and pretty little Leah, could have been present, but Rustam had recently accepted a new position and they were in the process of moving at the time. Since he had graduated from the University of Wisconsin Law School, Rustam had worked in the offices of State Attorney General Donald Hanaway, being involved as a prosecutor in a number of high-profile fraud and embezzlement cases. In the summer of 1989, a position in the federal court system of Hawaii had become available, and Rustam, having grown up in the islands, had applied. He was hired as a public defender there, and they moved to Hawaii at the end of August. I sometimes kidded Rustam, saying that it seemed unusual for him to be now, as it were, on the other side of the "aisle', from a prosecutor to a public defender, but he pointed out that he now knew both sides of the field.

At the end of December, Gudrun and I flew to California to spend New Year's with my sister Libby, in Danville, before flying on to Hawaii to visit Doris and her family, arriving there on January 2. This was the first time I had been in Hawaii since 1945, while I was in the navy. We were impressed by the beauty of the scenery, the rugged Ko'olau mountains, and the subtropical climate. We also enjoyed the easygoing ways of the people, the comfortable intermingling of numerous cultures, the generally accepting, nonjudgmental way of life, and the friendliness and cordiality of everyone.

However, we immediately saw that there were drawbacks to this paradise. First and foremost was the high price of everything. One must always consider that almost everything, from breakfast cereal to automobiles, must be imported from the mainland, some 2,400 miles distant. Practically the only local products are sugar cane, pineapples and coffee. The number-one revenue producer in Hawaii is tourism. With no industry to speak of, the skies are incredibly clear, especially at night. However, living costs are sky high: A simple lunch for two in a modest restaurant can cost over $25, and an evening meal in a fine restaurant, with wine, often comes to $80 for two. The simplest one-bedroom apartment, without utilities, rents for over $800 a month. Most families work two or even three jobs in order to survive in this paradise.

The first year we were in Hawaii, we stayed with Doris and her family, but in subsequent years we found a delightful little bed-

and-breakfast to which we return each year. Owned by Irene Hedemann, a wonderful, tennis-playing widow, the property overlooks Kaneohe Bay, and is just across the water from the Kaneohe Marine Corps Air Base. (Often, in the morning, I hear reveille wafting across the water.) Incidentally, this air base was the first installation to be bombed by the Japanese during the attack on Pearl Harbor December 7, 1941.

***

In 1990, through the Vilas Fund grants, which are administered through central administration in Madison, we were able to present an outstanding Mozart festival, one year before everyone else began to celebrate the composer's bicentennial. Jane Bowers, Margery Deutsch, Judit Jaimes and others put together a terrific series of programs which brought the international Mozart scholar Neal Zaslav to campus, along with Malcom Bilson, the superb performer on the forte-piano. Robert Porter conducted the most exciting, moving performance of the *Requiem* (K. 626) I have ever heard, to a standing-room-only house at St. John's Catholic Cathedral downtown, and Jeffry Peterson performed the F minor Fantasie (K. 608) on the magnificent Noehren organ of the cathedral during the same concert. On one other evening during the festival, Judit Jaimes was heard in a beautiful, sensitive performance of the C minor piano concerto (K. 491) with the UWM Symphony Orchestra, conducted by Margery Deutsch. Voice faculty were also heard in vocal selections during this concert. Zaslav spoke to students in lectures during the week, and also visited music history classes and other classes as well.

We also began to attract some rather good students, especially to our double graduate program in music history and library science. UWM was one of the few graduate schools in the nation to offer this degree, and it is significant that, with few exceptions, every one of our graduates were placed in positions at music libraries of colleges and universities. One of the first was Kathy Lutz, who went to the College of St. Catharine in St. Paul, Minnesota. She was actually offered the position before she had finished her thesis. She wrote, under my direction, on a subject which was then just becoming important, but which is today very much alive: the music of Hildegard von Bingen. Another was Ralph Gola, who wrote a thesis with me on some of the cantatas of Hans Eisler, something that no one had worked on. For a few years Ralph was music librarian at Western Kentucky University. Another very gifted student is Dina Kaye, who is music librarian at the University of Wisconsin-Parkside. Dina has a beautiful voice well suited to early music and reminds one of Emma Kirkby, the British singer known for her superb recordings of this repertoire.

***

In October of 1990, Gudrun, ever interested in furthering our dancing skills, asked me to accompany her to the Fred Astaire Dance Studio in the Brown-Port shopping center. She hoped we could learn the foxtrot, rhumba and tango. In addition, she was particularly interested in learning swing, which she did not know, having grown up in Germany. For a month we learned the basics of some new dances, and I had to admit it was great fun. Now, in addition to the Viennese waltz, I could add other dances to my repertoire. It was the beginning of a whole new way of life for me, one that would come to give us untold pleasure, a sense of accomplishment, and best of all, a chance to meet many wonderful new friends.

We began to derive lots of satisfaction out of attending a number of informal dances, discovering in the process, that Claudia's parents-in-law, Joe and Audrey Butschli, were avid ballroom dancers as well. On several occasions we went with them to afternoon dances which took place at small halls around town. The bands were three or four-piece groups led by Vern Meisner, Don Fleury and Roman Haines.

"A Night in Old Vienna" had by now become a fine occasion to exhibit our Viennese waltz skills. It had grown each year in size and elegance to include a Viennese meal, with a live orchestra, the Concord Chamber Orchestra, playing Viennese waltzes and polkas. It was good to see that others were becoming excited about the wonderful ambiance which such occasions provide. There were only a few really top-flight dancers at these events, but one couple who caught Gudrun's eye, seemed to not only dance beautifully, but were also handsome and elegant looking. We assumed they were professional dancers. At one point during the evening the man asked Gudrun to join him in a Viennese waltz. She thought he was extremely musical, moving beautifully to the music. Meeting this couple was to be the beginning of a cherished friendship for us.

***

Meanwhile, some rather momentous changes were taking place in our family circle. In 1987, Martin and Rose parted ways; she was given custody of the two boys, moved to the Chicago area, and soon remarried. Martin finally completed the requirements for his bachelor's degree in electrical engineering and computer science at UWM and was soon working on campus as a computer consultant to various professors. One of his most extensive projects was writing the software program for a computer-generated Hebrew/English dictionary with Professor Alan Corré.

About this time, Martin met a wonderfully bright woman, a professor of political science at the university. Rebecca Hendrick was, like me, a Michigan State University Ph.D. graduate, and had just been granted tenure and promotion at UWM. She would soon be named director of the master's program in public administration. "Becca" is among a group of brilliant, young academics helping to transform a number of elements in administration and planning of governmental bodies. Her work is at the cutting edge of new technologies in the area of budgeting and management of municipal and state governments.

***

In May of 1991, Gudrun and I undertook a trip to Germany again, this time in order for me to finally visit Lobenstein, which was now, since the reunification of the two Germanies, open again. Lobenstein was the city in which Georg Andreas Sorge, the composer whose keyboard music was the subject of my dissertation, had lived and worked. I had always wondered about a large number of works, mostly sacred vocal music: cantatas, motets and oratorios, which Sorge had listed as having been composed by him, though there was no indication in the sources which I had consulted that the music still existed. As music for the church services was considered expendable, and did not enjoy the kind of commercial success which keyboard and later chamber music enjoyed, this music was seldom published. (It might be recalled that of the several hundred cantatas which Bach wrote, only one [BWV 71, "Gott ist mein König] was ever published during his lifetime, and this was because it was written in celebration of the town council election in Mühlhausen in 1708.)

Keyboard music, on the other hand, found a ready market with the music buying public; amateurs often performing in the privacy of the home. Sorge's keyboard music is available, often in multiple editions. On the other hand, the vocal and choral music was unknown anywhere, though I knew, from Sorge's own published lists, that he had written a good deal of this kind of music. I was hoping, therefore, to be able to discover manuscripts of Sorge's vocal music in the church or city archives of Lobenstein, and we spent several days in the city attempting to locate manuscripts, unfortunately, with no success.

***

Meanwhile, back at the ranch, that is, back at the university, my days were filled with many crises of various kinds. We had been operating without a dean in the School of Fine Arts for almost three years. Jim Sappenfield was doing an outstanding job, but apparently the higher echelons of the university needed to seek an outside candidate, although many of us made it known that we were in favor of Dr. Sappenfield's being named the permanent dean.

Finally, the search and screen committee, after a number of exhaustive national searches, chose Dr. Will Rockett of the University of New York-Fredonia as their choice. I thought Rockett, who had done a lot of work in film and theater, to be an outstanding choice, and felt comfortable with him. He was an author of plays, and, in general, was a strong and forceful man who would support the school, and make our voices heard effectively. He officially took office on July 1, 1992, with a desire to shake up the school and try out some exciting, provocative ideas and projects. However, it was not to be.

Within six months, tragedy struck: in February of 1993, Dean Rockett was diagnosed with an inoperable brain tumor. Going through a series of debilitating sessions of radiation and chemotherapy, he survived until the following September, two months after I had retired. His death was a devastating blow to me personally, and to the school and the department, which I had come to love and respect.

***

In October of 1991, we attended another "Night in Old Vienna," now under the able direction of Bob and Eileen Kalupa, and finally had the opportunity to formally meet the fine dancing couple we had seen the previous year. As Gudrun and I waited to enter the spacious ballroom of the Grand Hotel on Milwaukee's far south side, she noticed the man who had asked her to dance a Viennese waltz with him the year before, standing nearby and smiling at her, perhaps remembering his waltz with her. We decided to introduce ourselves.

Henry and Irene Ratenski turned out to be an utterly charming couple, with whom we began a friendship which would turn into one of our most enduring associations in years to come. Although I always thought Henry, with his dark hair and swarthy good looks, resembled a Mafia "hit" man, both he and Irene were, of course, not Italian at all, but pure Polish. Henry was an investment counselor with a number of Milwaukee firms, as well as an accountant by training.

In addition to his professional work, Henry, in recent years, had been developing a lively sideline as a disc jockey for area dance clubs, providing music for them as well as presenting dance programs of his own for the public. He invited Gudrun and me to be his guest at their next dance party, which was scheduled for Saturday night, November 27, at a facility called "Marchese's Danceland," at the intersection of county route "J" and Silver Spring Drive in the town of Sussex, about 25 miles northwest of Milwaukee. This venue would become, in future years, the scene of some of our most delightful dancing experiences. We attended the function, and were impressed by the wonderful dancing, the great music, and most of all, the friendliness and warmth of all who were in attendance.

In return, Gudrun and I invited Henry and Irene to join us the following February for dinner at the Marc Plaza Hotel, where the Grand Viennese Ball is held. After dinner, I had proposed that they accompany us to the final dress rehearsal for the ball that evening in the Crystal Ballroom on the fifth floor.

293

As we began to chat during dinner on Friday evening, February 28, 1992, we discovered some amazing coincidences in our lives. The Ratenskis and their three children had lived in South Bend, barely a mile from us, for several years before leaving for Milwaukee in 1968, just two years before we did. In addition, Henry was a Notre Dame graduate, both came from Michigan City, Indiana, and we had many mutual friends at St. Mary's College in South Bend. Henry had gone to high school with Sister Miriam Patrick, a mathematics professor and colleague of mine at St. Mary's; he also knew Sister Madeleva, a former president of the school and one of its guiding lights.

After dinner, we went up to the rehearsal, where Margery Deutsch, our orchestra conductor, was leading the students through Strauss waltzes and polkas. Although Irene had recently had foot surgery, we did manage a little waltzing around the ballroom floor. This was to be the beginning of one of the most delightful and warm friendships I've known. I also learned much about the entire world of ballroom dancing from Henry, and continue to this day to be grateful to him for introducing us to this splendid and healthful hobby. At the Grand Viennese Ball in 1993, Henry and Irene presented a smashing cha-cha routine during the jazz ensemble's set, dancing to the popular "Patricia." They were a sensation, and the guests enjoyed the show.

***

When it became known that I was planning to retire at the end of June 1993, a number of faculty members were kind enough to ask me to consider staying on for at least another year. One commented to me, "...several of us are very sorry you are retiring. You have grown into a top-notch executive in these four years. You're at the top of your form...." As I now began to prepare for my eventual retirement from the faculty of the university, it became necessary to seek my successor and I appointed Jane Bowers to be chair of the Search and Screen Committee. Other members of the committee were Greg Suchy, Wayne Cook and Mary Pautz. A national search began in the early months of the year.

After examining the credentials of some excellent candidates, the Search and Screen Committee recommended Dr. Mitchell Brauner. Dr. Brauner was already doing some part-time teaching for us, and had made a very good impression on the committee. His special area of expertise is the early Renaissance, which I thought made for an excellent balance on the faculty. As a matter of fact, we'd not had a Renaissance specialist, and I thought the choice was excellent. Brauner was a highly-qualified scholar with a Ph.D. from Brandeis University, and was a popular classroom teacher with a sharp mind. His wife, Marna, was a professor in the Art Department of the School of Fine Arts.

As I began to prepare to step down as chair of the department, and retire from the faculty, I began to create a detailed "Department Chair Manual," in which I attempted to distill what I had learned about administering the department over the past four years into a modest, sixteen-page document which I would present to the new department chair for whatever use he or she might be able to make of it. An election for chair of the Music Department was held in March, and I was pleased to see that my personal

295

preference as the new chair was elected by an overwhelming majority of the faculty. It was Professor Wayne Cook, my own associate chair for the past four years. He was eminently qualified for the position, and I was grateful that the faculty had chosen him.

In May, Jane Bowers hosted a lovely retirement party for me and Dan Nelson, who also retired that year, and on Wednesday, June 30, 1993, I officially handed over to Wayne Cook the famous "Grand Master" key to the department, gave my faithful secretary, Mary Eichstaedt, a farewell hug, and walked out of the office for the last time.

***

As a postscript to my years on the faculty of the University of Wisconsin-Milwaukee, I would like to make a few observations about the department, the School of Fine Arts and the university itself, based on my twenty-three years of experience. A number of concerns about the role of this university in the community, and its relation to the larger campus at Madison, has made me sensitive to a number of issues which have been faced in the past, but which still need to be addressed.

My perception of the entire problem was that, at the time of the change-over from a state teacher's college to the University of Wisconsin-Milwaukee, the funding formulas had not been sufficient enough to enable the campus to grow as expeditiously as it should have. The basic issue, it seemed to me, was that, inasmuch as the capital in Madison was but a stone's throw from the campus there, and it was easy for the school to obtain funding from the legislature, and, in turn, legislators could always proudly point out the new School of Agriculture, or the new School of Medicine for which they had been instrumental in obtaining funds, in the case of the Milwaukee campus, there has always been an identity problem, compounded by the fact that legislators in this community were more involved with furthering the agendas of the industrial giants, Harnischfeger, Briggs and Stratton, Harley Davidson or Allen Bradley, than in furthering the goals of a new, urban university.

To this very day, UWM is perceived by many in Milwaukee as "just" a branch of the Madison campus, not as an individual entity with as much vitality and sense of purpose as its more venerable institution on the shores of Lake Mendota. I have often had to patiently explain to outsiders that I was at the University of Wisconsin *AT* Milwaukee. Some were even unaware that there was such an institution.

As a result of this identity problem, such departments as Music have suffered thrice: First, funding levels of the entire campus have traditionally been less than at Madison; second, the School of Fine Arts has suffered in comparison with such high profile schools as Business, Architecture and the hard sciences, which can depend, as a matter of course, on the industrial institutions of the city of Milwaukee, aptly called the "machine shop" of America, for their continued support. And then, finally, the Music Department, within the School of Fine Arts, suffered because of a perceived idea that music (and the arts) was not really a necessary part of the kind of instruction going on in such fields as business and the hard sciences.

This became crystal clear to me at the time that a new School of Business was being planned. The original plans for the new structure, to be erected on the site of the old Baker Fieldhouse, called for a large, desperately needed performing space for the Music, and Theater/Dance departments to be provided for on the first two floors of the new building. No theatrical or dance productions or Music Department activities requiring ensembles such as an orchestra, band, wind ensemble or choral group had any place to perform, and were always forced to rent space in venues at a distance from the campus.

My understanding was that pressure had been brought to bear on the university back in the 1960's by downtown interests not to build any kind of performing arts center on campus, for fear of reducing needed revenue generated by audiences attending musical events downtown and patronizing restaurants and parking facilities in the area. As a result, nothing was ever built on campus. In my travels to other campuses around the state, I was always singularly impressed by the excellent performing facilities, although our faculty as well as student ensembles, were, in many instances, superior to those of the other schools.

As department chair, I was acutely aware that the ever-increasing costs of renting the Pabst Theater and Vogel Hall in the Performing Arts Center downtown, paying for truck rentals to transport large instruments, and other attendant expenses, were draining inordinate amounts of budgeted funds, so that our music groups had little or no extra money for the purchase of music or any kind of special instruments. More recently the directors of the ensembles have come up with some ingenious solutions to the problems: Many concerts now take place in large neighborhood churches, such as St. Robert's Catholic Church in Shorewood, or in other churches in the area. In addition to savings realized by lower rental fees, most of the churches also have excellent acoustics, better than either the Pabst Theater or Vogel Hall in the Performing Arts Center downtown.

Therefore, when plans for the new School of Business were unveiled, members of the Music, and Theater/Dance departments were understandably enthusiastic about the prospect of finally having a fine new performing venue on campus. However, due to a number of unfortunate turns of events, mostly of a political nature, the entire plan was eventually scrapped and the facility was never built. However, the New School of Business, with obvious encouragement and support from the Milwaukee business community, has a gorgeous new four-story building. The Music and Theater/Dance departments were once more shut out of any consideration, and are still scrounging around trying to find suitable spaces in which to present our highly-talented faculty, and bright, motivated students.

Although it may seem self-serving, I am convinced that, the Music Department of UWM has been, and continues to be, an extremely strong department, in some ways superior to Madison. We have had the Fine Arts Quartet, internationally acclaimed composers John Downey, Yehuda Yannay and Greg Suchy, a superbly equipped electronic studio directed by Jon Welstead; we have a piano faculty headed by the outstanding, internationally acclaimed Venezuelan pianist Judit Jaimes; we have an orchestra program headed by the superb conductor Margery Deutsch, and a wind band program headed by Tom Dvorak, surely one of the finest and most imaginative persons in the field today. Added to this are musicologists Jane Bowers and Mitchell Brauner, both of whom enjoy international reputations, and Will Schmid, who, until he became the department chair in 1999, had been immediate past president of the Music Educators National Conference. In addition, the UWM Music Department, in cooperation with the School of Library and Information Science, is one of twelve schools in the nation offering the double degree of master of music, and master of library science. The department also offers a master's degree in accompanying, both vocal and instrumental, one of only a few in the United States.

The appointment, in 1999, of Nancy Zimpher as the chancellor of UWM, seems to indicate that a new era of proactive community leadership and greater visibility for the school is to be expected. Each year since about 1990, I have sensed continual progress and increased influence of the university of which I have been proud to be a member, and my fond wish and hope is that, in the 21st century, it will take its place as the premier urban university in the United States.

(Names and Things, silhouettes by Kathy. Used with permission.)

CHAPTER 11

RETIREMENT; ELDERHOSTEL INSTRUCTOR; THE DANCING FOOL (JULY 1, 1993-2000)

When I retired as chair of the Music department, I reflected on my years as the chief executive officer of the department, and wondered what I could possibly find to do which would be as engaging, often as exciting and challenging as those highly complex duties: trying to balance the expenditures of the department with available funds, gingerly attempting to sooth ruffled feathers, refereeing faculty squabbles, placating bruised egos and, in general, trying to keep a sense of sanity. I would soon find out.

One of the most satisfying activities which had already begun to take up some of my time was the opportunity to teach in Elderhostel, an international organization for people over fifty-five. Founded back in the 1960s by a university professor in New Hampshire, Elderhostel has since expanded to include hundreds of

301

where adults study, for a week, such diverse topics as presidents of the United States, American and British authors, both past and present, scientific, political and cultural "hot-button" issues, the arts (including hands-on experience in painting, sculpting and photography), lectures on music of all kinds, and local history, architecture and cultures. One of the great advantages of teaching in Elderhostel is that the "students" take no examinations; the participants are simply interested in learning for the sheer pleasure of expanding their knowledge. It is a wonderfully satisfying way to teach, and I very much enjoy the opportunities.

In 1991, I taught in an Elderhostel on the UWM campus, and in subsequent years started teaching at both Cardinal Stritch University, and more frequently at Geneva Bay Centre, a charming, ideal location in the small town of Lake Geneva, about forty miles southwest of Milwaukee. For the past seven years I have taught courses on the music of Bach, Mozart, Beethoven, Brahms, 20th century American music, aspect of German music of the 17th and 18th centuries, and presented lectures on the history of Milwaukee's music, based on my research in this area.

The reader may have noticed my increasing addiction to the art of ballroom dancing, an activity I could never have imagined having the slightest interest in fifteen years ago. I found myself totally immersed in this newfound pastime, only one of my *other pastimes.* My friendship with Henry Ratenski had made me gradually aware of important aspects of the musical portion of dancing, and of the critical role which proper tempos play. I learned about the concept of "strict tempo," though it is more properly termed "correct tempo."

Teaching at a course on Bach at Elderhostel, 1996, Geneva Bay Centre, Lake Geneva, Wisconsin.

Henry Ratenski, who has had much success as a DJ providing music for numerous dance clubs throughout the Milwaukee area, probably taught me everything I now know about proper tempos, appropriate orchestral sonorities and various dances, which one encounters at a typical ballroom event. Although Henry has no training as a musician, and, as a matter of fact, I don't believe can even read music, he has an infallible sense of tempos, and a rhythmic sensitivity which can tell him almost exactly what the speed of a certain piece of music is. He is a fine dancer, who invariably moves to the music at all times. He explained to me that changing the speed of a dance by no more than two or three measures per minute would alter the music so as to make it difficult, if not impossible, to dance to. I have found that this is, in fact, often the case, when we have attempted to dance, especially to live bands, who didn't have a clue as to the proper speed at which dance music must be performed.

I had to learn to discard the musician's way of looking at tempo as the number of beats per minute, or which value an eighth, quarter or half-note received, and think in terms of measures per minute: A typical fox trot, for example, has a speed of 30 *measures* per minute. (The musician would say that the value of the quarter note is 120; that is 120 divided by 4 = 30.)

Although I knew comparatively little about the finer points of ballroom dancing, I began to understand the entire subject of dance, and to appreciate the subtlety and beauty of dance in its myriad forms and styles. Gudrun had already had good training in social ballroom dancing while a teenager in Germany, and although I had had some lessons in my younger years, I'd probably forgotten all that I had learned in the meantime. When we attended Viennese balls, I found that the lessons we had received at the Fred Astaire studio in Milwaukee stood me in good stead, but I wanted to learn more, to catch up with Gudrun's skills, as it were.

The more intrigued I became with the whole world of ballroom dancing, the more convinced I became that I needed to study seriously. Gudrun's dancing skill and knowledge of the various steps far exceeded mine. Now that I had free time in which to pursue this newly discovered activity, I needed to somehow reach her level of accomplishment. As we attended various ballroom dance parties, we became acquainted with a large number of men and women who had already taken instruction, either in classes or privately. I had heard about a young, independent teacher who had recently moved to Milwaukee from California, and was teaching at the studios of Bill and Shirley Reilly, who operated a ballet school on the south side. I had been at their studio on several occasions during the time that they had served as dance masters for the UWM Grand Viennese ball.

In the fall of 1993 I began to study with Gary Allen, and can honestly say that, in the course of almost five years, I have never enjoyed anything quite so much as those Thursday afternoon sessions. Although I am a slow learner, and Gary was a demanding teacher, I finally learned a number of new dances, as well as adding new steps to dances I already knew. The sense of accomplishment, combined with the increasing knowledge of the various types of music appropriate to each ballroom dance, provided me an entirely new and exciting facet of life.

I also began collecting CDs and tapes of some of the top dance orchestras in the world, many of which were German. This was music that I wouldn't ever have imagined appealing to me fifteen years earlier. Pop artists such as Stevie Wonder, John Lennon and Paul McCartney, Ray Orbison, Lionel Richie, Nicholas Ashford, Neal Sedaka, the late Tito Puente and Perez Prado, even some of the older Broadway writers, such as Richard Rodgers and George Gershwin, have all written tunes which make excellent dance music.

I also purchased special dancing shoes, with suede soles and heels which male dancers wear to provide traction and control while dancing and became acquainted with the arcane terms employed, such as "forward basic," "twinkle," "promenade position," "underarm turn," "rock steps," "lock step," "cuddle position," as well as many others.

Gudrun also noticed how much better I was getting and occasionally we would study together. She was still working at Goethe House, eventually being appointed administrator of the facility, when Dr. Edlhauser, the director, retired in 1996.

***

In October of 1993, Gudrun and I flew to Germany so that I could attend a musicological conference in Freiburg, where Ludwig and Karl Otto, my two brothers-in-law lived. The yearly meeting of the Gesellschaft für Musikforschung was an opportunity to see some of my German musicological colleagues again.

At one point during the conference, Gudrun and I stood one afternoon conversing with James Webster of Cornell: All three of us were speaking German. *Strange, I reflected, two Americans and a German.* Jim had just given a splendid lecture, in beautiful German, which was received with much respect by our German counterparts.

One day during the conference a group of us took a bus trip to Colmar, in France, to see the wonderful Grünewald Altar, which I'd not seen since 1964. The Hindemith opera on the life of Matthais Grünewald includes music which the composer later made into a symphony, *Mathis der Maler*, depicting three of the paintings in the polyptych. I invited Ludwig, my brother-in-law, and his wife, Gisela, to be our guests on this brief excursion,

306

which also included a visit to a vineyard in the Kaiserstuhl area north of Freiburg. A number of our American colleagues who were attending the conference went on this delightful outing, including Karol Berger of Stanford University, his charming wife Anna Maria, as well as Anthony Newcomb of the University of California-Berkeley.

In addition to the conference in Freiburg, we also attended the wedding of Karl-Otto's daughter Sabine. We enjoyed ourselves immensely at a beautiful wedding dinner, complete with waltzing to Strauss. Sabina herself danced with her dance instructor. We also spent some time in the Heidelberg area, visiting Aunt Gertrud, and I attended a small conference there devoted to papers on the rich archives of the Capella Sistina in Rome. My successor at UWM, Mitchell Brauner, was one of the presenters at the conference.

I look forward to every visit I make to Germay, and enjoy being with my in-laws as much as Gudrun enjoys being with her family. In the Heidelberg area we stayed at the home of our dear friends Elizabeth and Gustav Jung, who live in the village of Neunkirchen. They have a beautiful home: large, modern and well appointed. We had the entire first floor, complete with two baths, to ourselves. Two bedrooms look out on a back yard and garden with all kinds of homegrown fruits and vegetables. Elizabeth really has a green thumb, it seems. She is very health conscious and cooks only naturally raised things from her garden. Neunkirchen is strategically located less than fifteen miles from Mosbach, Gudrun's hometown, and Heidelberg, which in thirty miles the other direction. Gustav was an amazing man: At the age of ninety-two, he was still actively interested in astronomy (he had a telescope set up in his study with an unobstructed view of the sky) and he was a master chess player as well. Well read in a number of disciplines, he was a fascinating man.

***

In 1984, while teaching at Mainz, Gudrun and I had met a charming couple. Elmar Seidel was professor of music theory at Mainz University. His wife, Magdalena, is the daughter of the German musicoloigst Franz Arnold Schmitz, who taught first at Dortmund and Bonn, later at Mainz, where he founded the Musicology Institute at the university after World War II. We had continued to stay in touch with the two of them in the intervening years and try to visit them each time we go to Germany. They met us one rainy Saturday afternoon in Heidelberg, during our 1993 trip, and we later had a superb meal in the five-star restaurant at the Kurphälzisches Museum in the Hauptstrasse. Professor Seidel is now retired from the university, and has recently published a new theory book dealing with the harmonic language of chorale settings by Bach.

For a few days Gudrun and I took a "Fahrt ins Blau" ("Trip into the blue"), and visited some areas I'd never seen: Miltenberg on the Main River, then southeast to Tauber-Bischofsheim, Bad Mergentheim, and the tiny village of Stuppach, were we saw a well-known Grünewald madonna in a church there. As we had just seen the Isenheim altar in Colmar, it was interesting to see another painting by the same man in a totally different location. We then wound our way through the picturesque Jagst River

Valley to the imposing cloister church in Schöntal, eventually returning to Neunkirchen by way of Mosbach.

For me it is always wonderful to return to Mosbach, the scene of my first meeting with Gudrun's family. What memories we have of these exciting times, now more than forty years ago. Mosbach, in many ways, has retained its quaint, medieval charm. The old section of the town, with its famous "Fachwerkhäuser" ("fieldwork houses," or "half-timbered houses"}, has changed very little since the Middle Ages. The city hall itself is an ancient Benedictine monastery from the ninth century. For Americans, it is difficult to grasp the fact that inhabitants of these cities and towns in Germany, as well as most of Europe, live surrounded by a thousand years of history. One day we had a nice visit with Herta Stecher, a childhood friend of Gudrun's, together with Frau Heinrich, the mother of Karl Otto's wife. These visits are always interesting for me, as I get to hear all sorts of reminiscences of Gudrun's childhood and youth in Mosbach.

Our last sightseeing jaunt during our trip to Germany was to the unique city of Wimpfen on the Neckar, a few miles beyond Mosbach. Elizabeth and Gustav Jung were our guests on this trip. I had last visited Wimpfen in 1964. It is almost like stepping back into the Middle Ages in places, with an ancient city wall, and charming back streets and alleys.

***

After spending Christmas of 1993 with Martha and Libby, my sisters, in California, Gudrun and I left for Hawaii on December 28 to see our daughter Doris Barbee, and her family. We engaged in all sorts of new and exciting adventures while there. On New Year's Eve, I went to the north shore with Doris, Rustam and the children, to a party. It was interesting to hear, for the first time, authentic Hawaiian music, played by natives. It is mostly soft, and they sing in an easy, relaxed manner. New Year's Eve is celebrated with all sorts of fireworks. There is such an over-abundance of firecrackers that the smoke makes it almost impossible to drive on the roads and streets. The next morning everything is covered with the remains of the firecrackers.

On New Year's Day, Rustam had arranged for us all to fly to the "Big Island," which is the island of "Hawaii" itself, to stay at a luxurious resort for two days, and visit the great Kilauea volcano. Wisconsin, it may be recalled, was playing in the Rose Bowl in 1994, so Rustam and Aaron opted to stay at the resort and watch the game, while the rest of us drove up to the volcano. I was given the job of driving the rented van, the four-hour trip, on a two-lane mountain road, taking until almost 3:00 p.m.. We enjoyed wandering around the lava fields that were still smoldering from frequent eruptions in the 1980s, but saw immediately, that we'd never make it to the volcano itself, another hour away, toward Hilo. We decided, instead, to take a rest at a small restaurant looking out on some smoking lava fields. As we sat drinking coffee and having something to eat, a cry went up from the people in the restaurant, Wisconsin had just won the Rose Bowl, in the last two or three minutes!

The next day was a delight. We spent it on a large boat swimming, scuba diving, snorkeling and watching for whales out in the ocean. The owner of the boat had apparently been successfully represented by Rustam in some court action, and we were all his guests for the day. Arriving at nine in the morning, we were treated to a bountiful breakfast, complete with Bloody Marys. Then it was out to the ocean, where Rustam and Aaron, but not me, thank you, received instructions in scuba diving. Lashing on their oxygen tanks, the two of them, along with eight or ten others, and two instructors, soon sank into the depths off the boat and were gone in two minutes. Thirty minutes passed; Doris was becoming a bit anxious for their return. After about forty minutes, they all reappeared, none the worse for the experience. I tried a little snorkeling, but I'm afraid I'm not that much of a "water person," and found I couldn't master the technique. The colorful saltwater fish under me were striking looking, however. Incidentally, we didn't see any whales all day. We returned that night, after a delightful meal, to the island of Oahu. This was one of the most refreshing and interesting of our trips to Hawaii. We returned to Milwaukee on January 9, 1994.

***

Lots of dancing events filled out the spring and summer calendar of 1994: At the end of January the American Friends of Austria Ball was held again at the elegant Ambassador West Hotel in Chicago, with Franz Bentler and his orchestra providing fine music for dancing; the UWM Grand Viennese Ball, for which I was still master of ceremonies, was on February 26, and in the middle of April we attended the Eau Claire Viennese Ball. Our dance calendars were certainly full. We also joined the Latin Dance club of Milwaukee, and I was promptly asked to become

311

the publicity director, responsible for sending out all notices of dances to a membership of over 150. I was glad I'd invested in a personal computer by then. This made the job of typing up address labels, and sending out notices easier.

After another trip, this time to Las Cruces, New Mexico, to explore a possible retirement location, we finally decided to stay in Milwaukee, and not consider a move somewhere far away. We had investigated, in the past eight years, a large number of possible retirement options: North Carolina, Arkansas, Sioux Falls, California, Hawaii, and now New Mexico, but finally came to the conclusion that, everything considered, the best thing we could do was to remain in the house, near the university, with our large circle of friends in the music and dancing community, as well as our family. We may soon give some thought to moving to a smaller house, though still in the Milwaukee area. Brookfield, Menomonee Falls, or West Bend are possibilities.

In the fall of 1994, I took on a new musical assignment: I began to work as an accompanist for the String Academy of Wisconsin, a preparatory institution which rented space in the music building at UWM to give instruction to a large number of grade school and high school children. I received a small salary for the work, and enjoyed observing the youngsters learning to play string instruments. Many of them were genuinely talented, and it was a pleasure to watch their progress month after month. I worked with them every Wednesday afternoon for over a year. It was very satisfying.

***

In August of 1995, I was pleased to hear from my sister Martha, that she and her new boyfriend, Steve, were flying to Lake Geneva to attend my Mozart Elderhostel. Martha's husband, Jim, had died tragically five years previous, and she had sold the house in Piedmont and bought a new condo in Moraga. (Steve had recently moved in with her.) He was a retired gynecologist who had his own plane, and Martha and he did a lot of flying together. It was a pleasure to see her again, and to meet Steve. After the Elderhostel sessions, I drove them to the airport and saw them off. They were flying to Independence, Missouri, where Steve wanted to visit the Truman library there.

Saturday noon, August 26, the telephone rang at my house. It was Martha. "Franklin," she began, "the plane has crashed, and Steve is critically injured and in intensive care at a hospital in Kansas City." I was practically speechless. The following week, I flew to Kansas City. The weather was ghastly hot, in the mid-90s and humid. Luckily, Martha suffered only some bruises and a black eye, but Steve was in a coma, with many broken bones in his face where he had smashed against the "yolk," the steering wheel of the plane. He also had a broken arm.

I stayed at a small facility at the hospital, with Martha in the next room. Steve looked like death warmed over as Martha, a registered nurse who knew her way around hospitals, attempted to bring him out of his unconscious state. She was extremely dedicated, and I marveled at her composure in the face of some daunting responsibilities: talking with the insurance people, the FAA, sending log books and other details of the airplane and its condition to the proper authorities. We visited them in January of

1996, and I am happy to report that Steve was almost completely recovered from the near-fatal accident; however he had, by then, decided his flying days were over.

Martha and Steve knew Gudrun and I were very much "into" the ballroom dancing scene, and thought we'd enjoy seeing a new stage production in San Francisco called "Forever Tango." It was to be the beginning of a great fascination with the Argentine tango, its music, and especially this wonderful, colorful production, which continues to this day. "Forever Tango" uses native Argentinians, with six or seven couples presenting a kind of history of the Argentine tango. The small orchestra includes four "bandoneons," a kind of finger accordion, with enormous expressive possibilities, especially when played by an artist such as Lisandro Adrover, the musical director of the show. The orchestra also includes a gifted pianist, violins, viola, cello and double bass, plus an electronic keyboard and percussion. It was undoubtedly the most exciting, intoxicating music I had ever heard, and I fell in love with the dancing, the atmosphere, and the music. Since that time, we have attended four more performances of "Forever Tango," three in Chicago, and one, in the fall of 1988 at the University of Wisconsin-Green Bay. Anyone who wishes to be wonderfully entertained, and also have a real thrill seeing superb dancing of the Argentine tango, should take the opportunity to see "Forever Tango." You will never forget it.

***

In March of 1996, we undertook yet another trip to Germany, this time to help my brother-in-law Ludwig Herrmann celebrate his seventieth birthday. A party was held at a lovely hotel in Weilersbach, a small town just outside of Freiburg. There were over fifty people in attendance, and all sorts of delightful skits were presented, including one in which I dressed up in a grotesque beard and delivered a pompous lecture about "Ambrosius von Mailand," the subject of Ludwig's doctoral dissertation at Heidelberg. Reminiscences of Mosbach were recalled; balloons floated through the air, and a wonderfully festive time was had by all.

***

A number of unfortunate family problems began to develop in 1995. Gisela, one of the twins, went through a nasty divorce from Mike, and was given custody of Jaron, her six-year-old son. Soon after this occurred, Doris called to tell us that she had moved out of their house in Hawaii, was filing for divorce from Rustam, and would be making plans to return to Milwaukee with Leah in the summer of 1996. These sorts of things tear us apart and it is sad to see them happening to our children. I suppose one must be patient, because, as the saying goes, "time heals all wounds," except in these cases, I wondered if perhaps "time wounds all heels" would be a more appropriate observation.

In June of 1996, Doris and Leah returned to Milwaukee, and Doris was able to stay with her company, Service Corporation International, which operated funeral homes and cemeteries throughout the country. She went to work at Borkwardt Funeral Home in West Allis, and they found a nice two-bedroom apartment in Greendale. We could tell that Leah was unhappy to

315

be away from her friends in Hawaii, and she did not look forward to entering school in the fall, although the school was less than 500 feet away from the apartment, through a pleasant wooded area. In addition, Henry Ratenski's daughter Kay, an attractive woman who was a staff member at the school, volunteered to assist Leah in adjusting to her new environment. Sadly, Leah was desperately lonely and depressed, unable to fit in and make friends, and after only three weeks of school in Greendale, in September, her father sent her the money to return to Hawaii. Doris lost her child support payments thereby, and took in a girlfriend as a roommate.

***

Tuesday, July 23, was Doris's birthday, and we had made arrangements to meet her and Leah for dinner that night. About 3:45 p.m. our rather impatient cat, "Kieto," started bothering me for some supper. Stepping out of my study, I headed for the steps leading to the kitchen. Suddenly I found myself falling down the stairs, finally coming to rest on the first landing! I lay there for a moment, while Gudrun, shocked to see me displaying such an ashen-gray appearance, offered to call 911. Attempting to regain some composure, I looked at my left arm, which was giving me intense pain. My wrist and hand looked somewhat like the letter "S": I had obviously fractured my wrist!

Driving with my right arm, I immediately got over to Columbia Hospital Emergency Department, was sent to X-ray, and returned to a bed, where Dr. Donald Middleton, an extremely young, boyish-looking orthopedic surgeon examined me, confirmed that the wrist was fractured, and placed it in a temporary cast. I called Doris and explained what had happened, and about an hour later she and Leah showed up. Throwing her arms around me, Doris exclaimed: "Well, Dad, you sure know how to upstage me on my birthday!"

After an additional visit to surgery the following Saturday to reset the bones, I was fitted with a permanent cast, and spent the following six weeks learning how to write with my right hand. (It is instructive to observe how much we use *both* hands to do something: Have you ever tried to tie your shoes or cut meat with one hand only?)

I should also mention that, at the time, I was teaching an Elderhostel at Cardinal Stritch University, and was due to discuss some of the music of Brahms the next day. Appearing at the lecture hall, I mounted the stage, keeping my left arm covered until I had reached the podium, at which point I dramatically showed my left arm, saying: "We have a little problem, ladies and gentlemen: Yesterday I fractured my left wrist, and today I shall play for you the music which Brahms wrote for the right hand only."

Gudrun was a real trooper, and assisted me with all kinds of daily chores. The first week of September the cast came off, and I spent the next six weeks in painful therapy trying to increase the range of motion in the wrist. I was convinced that my physical therapist, Sue Austin, was a real sadist. I complained to her that I was certain she was going to break it again, but she reassured me that would not happen. After about two months, it was almost as good as new, thanks to her persistence and constant encouragement. She was a real professional.

***

Because of my total involvement in ballroom dancing, and because of my conviction that everyone should learn to dance, I gave my five children and their spouses a Christmas gift of four dance lessons with my superb teacher, Gary Allen, in preparation for a gala party to be hosted by Gudrun and me at Marchese's on January 17, 1997, my forty-fourth birthday, and our seventy-first wedding anniversary, or is it the other way around?

On four Sunday afternoons preceding the party, we all met at Gary's studio in order for him to teach them some fundamentals of dancing. They made excellent progress, and by the night of the party, had become fairly proficient. Although the temperature was hovering around four degrees below zero, there were over eighty of our dearest friends in the dancing community present for an evening of great music hosted by Henry Ratenski. He and I together chose everything which was played that night, and I gave a brief speech thanking all those who had been so helpful in assisting me in my newfound hobby.

I invited Suzana Madsen, the owner of North Town Ballrooms, and had the great honor and thrill of dancing a quickstep and a bolero with her, while Gudrun swept around the floor to a Viennese waltz with Jeff Kurth, another instructor at Northtown. By the way, I must report that, unfortunately, my five children have never appeared on the dance floor again after that night. You know the old saying, "You can lead a horse to water..."

January 17, 1997, Marchese's danceland, Sussex, Wisconsin. Ready to lead off the first waltz at our 44th wedding anniversary celebration. It is my 71st birthday. On the stage is my dear friend Henry Ratenski, the DJ for the evening, ready to start the music.

In April of 1997, our Midwest AMS chapter held their spring meeting at the University of South Dakota in Vermillion. I had never been to the campus, and wanted very much to visit the stunning museum there known as the "Shrine to Music Museum," established many years ago by Arne Larson, a music faculty member, who had slowly built up an impressive collection of instruments from all over the world. I decided to combine a visit to Mary and Milt Husby with attendance at the conference. The "Shrine to Music Museum" must be seen to be believed! It houses an absolutely incredible collection of all kinds of instruments, and, in many ways, is as fine a collection as some of the more famous museums in Europe. It compares favorably with the Kunsthistorisches Museum in Vienna, and, in some ways, is even superior to it.

The president of the Midwest chapter that year was my good friend Ted Albrecht of Kent State University, and he prevailed upon me to serve as a member of the program committee for the following year. As the spring chapter meeting was to be in Madison, it seemed only natural. Larry Earp of the Madison campus of the University of Wisconsin, and Mike Campbell, from Western Illinois University in Macomb, were the other members of the committee. During the summer our program committee examined a large number of proposals, and came up with excellent papers for the fall meeting in Chicago, and eventually the spring meeting in Madison. For me, it was a most rewarding exercise and I was grateful to have been able to be of service to the chapter.

After the 1998 AMS Midwest chapter meeting in Madison, I drove out to Sioux Falls to see my dear aunt Elinor, now ninety-six years old. In making plans for the trip, I happened to hear of an all Brahms concert to be played by the South Dakota Symphony, consisting of the second symphony, the double concerto for violin and cello, and the *Academic Festival Overture.* I knew nothing of the group, only that it was an outgrowth of the old Augustana Symphony Orchestra in which I played tympani for two years, and in which Gudrun had played cello during her stay as an exchange student at the college in 1951-52. I thought the program extremely ambitious for a regional orchestra, and wanted to hear it with my own ears. I was to be in for the treat of a lifetime! Not only did the orchestra play exceptionally well, the conductor himself was superb. Henry Charles Smith knew the score, there was no wasted motion, no unnecessary lectures, yet with a light touch, and a warm, generous presence, he conducted a remarkably fine performance. I was bowled over! They played as well as many of our best, large-city symphonies.

While I was in Sioux Falls, I had a delightful visit with our old friends Roland and Marie Arlton, Stan and Dean's brother and sister-in-law. We have always tried to stay in touch with the two remaining Arlton brothers, Stan and Roland. Tragically, Dean had drowned during a boating accident on the Hudson River in the early 1970s.

My visit with Aunt Elinor was rather sad. I could see that she was beginning to fail, and was not in very good health. She had, a few years earlier, been in an automobile accident, and had not made a complete recovery. She appeared to be getting more frail, and she was also somewhat forgetful and occasionally irrational as well. I was glad to have been able to visit her with Martha, who was in town as well. On October 24, about eight in the morning, with Mary Eloise at her side, she died.

***

On a happier note, we had the great pleasure of welcoming Gudrun's sister Gisela for a visit in September. She had never been to America, and it was a delightful visit for both of us. Gisela had the chance to meet most of the children and many of the grandchildren as well. We showed her a good deal of the Midwest in a number of trips, including one to South Bend and Howe to visit places where we had lived many years ago. Finally, we took a trip across Lake Michigan in a large car ferry from Ludington, Michigan, to Manitowoc, Wisconsin.

***

In December of 1998, I began to suffer from pain in my jaw and upper arms as I swam at Klotsche physical education center. I had been swimming regularly there since 1984, and had had no problems. I mentioned it to my doctor, who immediately recommended that I stop swimming, and made an appointment for me to be examined by Dr. James Botticelli, a cardiologist, for a stress test and other appropriate examinations. On January 12, 1999, I went through the entire procedure and was told that, while the tests did not show any serious problems, I might care to take it a little easy before starting to swim again. I also noticed that cold air made it more difficult for me to breathe, and caused pain as well. I was given a small bottle of nitroglycerine to carry with me at all times, being instructed to take one of the small pills immediately if I began to have any symptoms of an angina attack.

***

Grandson number two, Aaron Barbee, had graduated from high school, and was on the mainland visiting friends and family. He would occasionally show up totally unannounced, to spend a few hours with us as he did that day after Christmas in 1998. A good-looking, rather laid-back fellow, he decided in January of 1999 to join the army, and looked forward to training as a paratrooper eventually. Out of basic training in April, he went on to get advanced work as a ranger, until it was discovered that he was diabetic. At this point, he doesn't know what his future will be, but assumes he will receive a medical discharge, possibly before his "hitch" in the army is to end.

At the end of the second week in April, 1999, Gudrun and I attended the spring meeting of the Midwest chapter of AMS Kent State University in Ohio. I always enjoy these wonderful get-togethers, now that I am perceived as one of the "elders of the clan," as they say. It seems only yesterday that the "elders of the clan" were people such as Bob Warner and Gwynn McPeek from Michigan, Carol McClintock from Indiana, or Andy Minor from Missouri, and now I'm among the "elders!" At a party at Ted Albrecht's house after an evening's concert, I heard, for the first time in my life, a duet for two Alphorns, performed by Ted and Ed Kottick. It will probably also be the last time.

***

Two weeks after we returned from our trip to Kent State, I again began to suffer from pain in my jaw and upper arms. I was scheduled to begin a new series of Elderhostel lectures on Beethoven's music, starting Sunday evening, April 25. On Friday, speaking with Patrick Roe, my doctor, I mentioned that I was not feeling too well. He advised me to come in at four-thirty that afternoon. Parking the car, I ran up the stairs to his office, borrowed a quarter from Wendy, his receptionist, ran down to the car and plugged it in the meter, and ran up the stairs again. By the time I had gotten back into the office, I was having a full-fledged angina attack, crushing chest pains in addition to the other complaints I'd had earlier. I took two nitroglycerine tablets, and lay down on Dr. Roe's examining table while he called my cardiologist, Dr. Botticelli. Botticelli said for me to schedule another stress test for Monday. "But, Dr. Roe," I answered impatiently, "I'm doing an Elderhostel which starts Sunday night; I can't get out of that at this late date." "Dr. Miller," Dr. Roe emphasized, "you are *grounded*, now go home and take it easy this weekend."

I said, "Okay, if I can't do the Elderhostel, then you better call Toni Jooss down at Geneva Bay Centre to inform her of your decision in this matter." He assured me he would do it, and I went home.

The next morning about 2:30 a.m., I had another bout of crushing chest pain and broke out in a sweat. I took two nitro pills and tried to sleep. At 4:30 a.m. I had another attack, and was now rather frightened. As soon as I had had some breakfast I called Dr. Roe's answering service. He returned the call, and said to get in touch with Dr. Botticelli immediately. I did, and Botticelli said he wanted me in Columbia Hospital by noon that day. Even while I was in the hospital, I suffered two more severe angina attacks, with the typical tightness and crushing sensation across my chest. An oxygen tube was placed in my nose, and I gradually came out of both attacks.

On Monday morning, April 26, I was wheeled into the cardiac intensive care unit, and a balloon angioplasty was performed, in which a tube was inserted into the femoral artery in my groin and threaded up into the heart, after which a dye was introduced to show the circulatory system of the heart. I was awake during the entire procedure, and the doctor asked if I wanted to watch on the TV monitor. I looked, and was reminded of a large mass of small snakes. "Good," I said, "I'll take a dozen 8' x 10' glossies!"

After Dr. Botticelli found that my coronary artery was almost 90% occluded, he then performed a stent placement in the area of the occlusion. This involved threading a piece of very fine wire mesh up through the tubing into my heart and placing it against the blocked portion of the coronary artery, where it then was made to press into the sides of the artery, thus opening it up. I was out of surgery in less than an hour, stayed overnight, and was discharged at noon the next day. I have the greatest respect for cardiologists, who do these procedures regularly. After an initial period of recuperation, I started to swim again in May.

In the years since I've begun to swim regularly at our athletic facility, the Klotsche Center (named for the first chancellor of the university, J. Martin Klotsche), I've derived a great deal of satisfaction from the sense of accomplishment which physical exercise gives me. I have already noted the salutary effects it produces; even more important, I think, are the mental and emotional benefits gained by a regular program of conditioning. I feel better in the last five years, both physically and mentally, than I have in my entire life. The migraine headaches, which I had suffered for several years, are almost completely gone, and the back problems are a thing of the past.

***

In July of 1999, the family held a beautiful family reunion at Spearfish, in the Black Hills of South Dakota, to celebrate the life of Aunt Elinor, who had died the previous October. She had loved the "Hills" and we thought this would be an appropriate place to get together. Leah and Katie, Deede's daughter, got to know each other, and now write emails back and forth almost weekly; Tom Brown, my first cousin, whom none of us had seen for many years, turned out to be an utterly charming man, and we all were grateful to be able to renew our family connections with him, as well as all the other members of the Brown family.

All of our five children were there, and six of the ten grandchildren. There were two, large family dinners for the forty-two participants, and a lovely memorial service in the local Episcopal church, where Aunt Elinor was remembered. At theconclusion of the service, my cousin Mary Eloise, an Episcopal clergy, who was leading us, asked if anyone had anything further they wished to share, reminiscences of Aunt Elinor, other memories. Eight-year-old Bridgette Hayes, without a word, got up and walked to the lectern, where she spoke into the microphone:

326

July 23, 1999, family reunion at Spearfish, South Dakota. Almost the entire family is present. (four grandchildren missing). First row (l-r): Andrew Butschli, 6; Jaron Smithers, 9; Bridgette Hayes, 8; Adam Butschli, 9; Alex Butschli, 10; Second row: Karin Hayes, twin, the author, Gudrun, Doris Barbee, Claudia Butschli, David Butschli, Gisela Smithers, twin; Third row: Kevin Hayes, Leah Barbee, Martin Miller, Becca Hendrick.

"Well, I didn't know this lady, but I know my Opa [that's me] loved her very much; I'm very glad to be here tonight-and-praise the Lord!" Memories of Aunt Elinor continue to be recalled; we are already hoping for another reunion, possibly in three years.

In September I began to volunteer as a "docent" for the youth concerts of the Milwaukee Symphony. This involves preparing school students for their attendance at the regular youth concerts by the orchestra at the Performing Arts Center downtown by talking to the students about the music to be heard, the composers, and other information which will enhance their enjoyment of the programs. It has been a richly rewarding experience for me, and I have learned how to connect with young students and get them excited about music.

***

Gudrun and I began to plan another trip to Germany for October of 1999, at which time there was to be a reunion of her grade school class of sixty years ago in Mosbach. One day Gudrun received a letter from a "Hildegard Schmitt" in California. Did she know who it was? She wasn't certain, until she opened the letter and read it. The woman turned out to be a childhood friend of Gudrun's from Mosbach, Hildegard Nerbel, who had emigrated to America shortly after Gudrun, in the early 1950s. As Gudrun read the letter I saw she was crying.

The family of Hildegard Nerbel ran a small dry goods store in Mosbach, and in the immediate post-war period from 1946 to 1949, during a time of great hardship and shortages, Gudrun's father, dean of the Evangelical church in Mosbach, and one of the outstanding citizens of the town, had been helpful in providing the Nerbel family with funds to sustain themselves. Gudrun recalled that her father would send her and Gisela, her sister, to the store to buy whatever they could in order to give the store some business.

Hildegard Nerbel, whose married name was Schmitt, was so touched at Gudrun's father's generosity and concern for her family so many years ago, that she now wished to do something special in memory of Gudrun's father: she presented Gudrun with a round-trip ticket on Lufthansa Airlines to attend the class reunion in

Mosbach. (Her brother Willi Nerbel, a classmate of Gudrun's, still lived in Mosbach, and had apparently written her that Gudrun was planning to attend the class reunion.) Gudrun was touched by this generous offer, and accepted it, as a tribute to her father.

I don't know when I've enjoyed myself so much as this visit. Gisela had found us a lovely, small hotel in Nüstenbach, just outside of Mosbach, where our room looked out on the countryside, often bathed in fog early in the morning. Next to the hotel was a small church where the bells rang softly every fifteen minutes. Gudrun recalled how often she had walked the two miles or so from Mosbach, through the woods with her father to this small church, where he would conduct services on Sunday morning, often after having already conducted two services in Mosbach. (Due to a wartime shortage of Lutheran ministers, her father had to serve several parishes.)

The class reunion was something very special for me. What I particularly enjoyed was being accepted by Gudrun's classmates and included in all the wonderful festivities. An official school photo was taken on the steps of the City Hall in Mosbach. Of course, I thought that Gudrun was still the youngest and prettiest looking of all in her class. There were dinners, bus excursions during which the growth of the city was shown, and a festive final evening in Mudau, where Gudrun and I were part of a hilarious skit. I could even joke in German. I don't know when I have enjoyed myself so much. We also visited our dear friend Elisabeth Jung in Neunkirchen. Unfortunately, Gustav had died in 1996 (only three days after we had last visited them.) We also spent a day in Heidelberg with Aunt Gertrud before driving on to Freiburg

329

for another family gathering with Ludwig, Karl-Otto and their respective families. Also present were the wonderful Wodlis from Pfaffenhoffen in France, friends of the family who are always included in our family celebrations. We stayed at our favorite hotel in Weilersbach, the Hotel Schützen, where we had stayed before when Ludwig had celebrated his seventieth birthday in 1996. A great time was had by all; I did some shopping in downtown Freiburg, picking up some new dance CDs, we saw lots of the beautiful countryside in the nearby Black Forest, and Gudrun finally had a fond wish of many years fulfilled.

A beautiful, antique sewing table over 150 years old had stood in her bedroom as a youngster, and when her mother died in 1985 it had been placed in storage, first at Gisela's in Mosbach, and more recently with Ludwig in Freiburg. Gudrun was finally able to arrange, with the help of Gisela and Ludwig, to have this precious furniture piece shipped to us in Milwaukee. It is the only piece of "home" she has ever had in America, and she was thrilled when it arrived at the end of November. It stands today in our guest bedroom.

In December, I flew to California to visit Martha and Libby, and had the opportunity to visit someone I'd not seen for fifty years: "Muffy" (Ellen Kindt McKenzie), whom I'd met while still in the navy. We went together for a time, and after we broke up, in the fall of 1948, she had eventually married my very good friend Art McKenzie. With three children, they later divorced, and she now lived about fifty miles from Martha in Los Altos, California. I'd known she was writing children's books, and wrote her saying I'd be in the area, and would enjoy coming for a visit.

Art still lived in the vicinity, and the four of us had dinner and a lovely visit at Muffy's home, high up in the Santa Cruz Mountains. It was wonderful to see her and Art again, and to reminisce about our student days at Chicago Musical College almost fifty years ago. "Muffy," or as she now prefers to be called "Ellen," has received awards for her books, and she gave me two of them as presents.

In February of 2000, we made our annual visit to Doris and Leah in Hawaii, and Gudrun celebrated her seventieth birthday while we were there. We invited John and Stephanie Doughty, with their daughter Caitlin, to be our guests for a stupendous brunch at the Turtle Bay Hilton on the north shore of Oahu. The Doughtys had been very helpful to Doris during some difficult times, and we wanted them to know how grateful we were. The view from the hotel dining room of the awesome surf there is quite impressive. We enjoyed every minute of our stay in the sunny, warm climate.

In April of 2000, we took another one of our delightful road trips to Sioux Falls, to hear the Beethoven Ninth Symphony performed by the South Dakota Symphony. It was a riveting performance; I simply could not believe that, way out here on the South Dakota prairie, I would hear a performance of such musical excellence. Henry Charles Smith, now in his last year as conductor of the orchestra, tells me that, according to all accounts, this was the first performance of the Beethoven Ninth Symphony in the state of South Dakota. I can believe it. The performance took place in the glorious new concert hall, which had built from the ground up from the old auditorium of Washington High

School, which I had attended. We invited our dear friends Marie and Roland Arlton to be our guests for the concert. I was stunned by the performance, the high-caliber playing of the orchestra, the fine singing of the chorus, the excellence of the soloists. As I sat and listened, tears welled up in my eyes as I heard those words of Schiller: "Alle Menschen werden Brüder!" ("All humans shall become brothers!")

We are already planning our next road trip. We will drive to Toronto, Canada, for a convention of fifteen scholarly societies, which will take place from November 1 to 6, 2000. This "mega-convention" will bring together the American Musicological Society, College Music Society, Society for Music Theory, Society for Ethnomusicology, Society for American Music (formerly the Sonneck Society), Canadian University Music Society, American Musical Instrument Society, and several other scholarly and professional organizations, all meeting together, to my knowledge, for the first time. With an expected attendance of over 3,000, it promises to be one of the most exciting and stimulating meetings I will have attended. There will be an opportunity to hear Lully's 1682 opera *Persée* for the first time, with the superb Canadian early music ensemble "Tafelmusik," in the pit for the performances.

CHAPTER 12

"PUT IT IN THE ANHANG."
"Anhang" is German for "appendix" or "supplement."

I would ask the reader's indulgence to allow me a number of observations about music in general, and the history of music more particularly. These are matters which I often cite in a number of contexts and to different groups of students, both young and old, old being my Elderhostel students. It is probable that much of what I have to discuss has already occurred to the majority of my readers; to others, however, these matters may not have been considered in much detail.

First, let me observe that the idea of listening to and performing music of the distant past is less than 200 years old. While it is true that there are some exceptions to this rule-- Beethoven discovered Bach -- as did Mozart, the basic premise is nevertheless valid. The music which Beethoven played was "modern music;" that is, music which he had recently composed. The same holds true with Mozart, Haydn and even earlier composers. True, Johann Sebastian Bach was acquainted with some early music, particularly by Palestrina, for whose *Missa sine nomine* he put together an instrumental doubling of the vocal parts, providing the whole with a new *basso continuo*. As a part of his library he also owned three copies of Nicolaus Ammerbach's *Orgel oder Instrument Tabulatur*, from 1571 and, as a young man had made a copy of Frescobaldi's *Fiori Musicali*. (It no longer exists.) However, aside from Ammerbach, one must remember that Palestrina had died probably less than a hundred years before Bach became acquainted with his music, and that Frescobaldi was only two generations removed from him, having died just forty-two years before Bach was born. (That would be the equivalent to our having no knowledge of any music earlier than Gustav Mahler, Max Reger, Rimsky-Korsakov or Giacomo Puccini!) Basically about the only music that audiences heard in the 17th and 18th centuries, whether in the opera house or the church, was contemporary music; that is, what we would call "modern music." It is a phenomenon we often lose sight of, when we grumble about "that awful modern music."

We continually marvel at the copious amounts of music turned out by a Vivaldi (453 concertos alone, or in the words of one 20th century Italian composer, "one concerto, 453 times") or a Telemann (over 3,000 sacred cantatas or motets) or a Haydn (over 104 symphonies). However, what we sometimes fail to consider is that audiences of the nobility, even church congregations wanted "up-to-date" music, and to them there was nothing so old-fashioned as last months opera, last week's symphony, or last year's Mass. Someone once observed that the loss of the manuscript of a Haydn symphony may provide a great opportunity for some musicologist to rediscover it, but for Haydn it was nothing but an excuse to write another symphony.

The idea of preserving music from a long-past era was apparently something that did not, in large measure, occur to the people of the 15th through the 18th centuries. Almost every piece of music which was heard was "modern music," that is, it had been composed no longer ago than six months or a year, at the most.

The idea of establishing a "canon" of "great" classics, of pieces of music which were to be somehow preserved for future generations, is largely a development of the 19th century. Unfortunately, however, the music of today, of a comparable repertoire of "modern music", is heard to a far lesser degree than did the music of eras prior to about 1820. It is strange that what was considered "modern music," "up to date" or "contemporary" in the 17th and 18th centuries is now considered "THE classics." We should bear this in mind when we look at the relatively little "modern music" which is performed by major symphony orchestras, chamber ensembles and solo instrumentalists. This situation has improved in the past few years, mostly because of the pioneering efforts of a few conductors and performers, but the percentage of "modern music" is still small, when compared to "THE CLASSICS."

I hasten to add, of course, that I do not, in any way, advocate doing away with these so-called "classics." I would only hope that we recognize the irony of enshrining the music of earlier centuries as the only "real" music, while not recognizing that this music was also, at one time, "contemporary," and "modern." Would that our contemporary composers, from Schönberg to Glass and beyond, could have the same status as legitimate composers of "modern music" in the same way that a Mozart, Beethoven, Chopin, Bach or Brahms were considered writers of "modern music."

Another observation I would make is that the concept of music as simply something which one group of people "do", (the performers), while another group of people simply sit and hear (the audience), it is not only a rather new idea, but, in many parts of the world, is not even recognized as a legitimate precept. The idea of a group of musicians sitting on a stage and doing nothing but playing instruments, while another group of people, sit and watch them, or, we hope listen to them, can only be traced back to about the second decade of the 18th century. Prior to this, music was a part of other activities: dance, theatrical productions, church services; in other words, it had, for the most part, and for the largest number of listeners, a function which was to embellish, to add to the enjoyment of other activities.

This philosophy of art as functional is still a large part of non-Western civilizations. In Africa, for example, music is performed by large numbers of persons, who participate equally. Although, of course, there are certain rather elite groups of musicians, and there are even instruments which are played only by men, most music making is considered a function of the lives of everyone. There is music to accompany every conceivable type of activity, for example, there is one kind of song or instrumental piece when paddling a canoe downstream, another when paddling upstream!

In other words, music is, by and large, functional. It is a concept with which we in the West are less familiar. Though, to be sure, we may find examples of functional music in such tunes as

"I've been workin' on the railroad," which may have arisen among laborers driving the spikes and putting down the ties for the tracks. Many additional examples, especially from the 19th century, could be cited as well.

I also have a bit of a pet peeve to express. I have often been struck by the attitude of many performers toward learning, not only the repertoire for their own instrument, but, particularly music for another instrument or medium. How often have I found myself asking piano students, as an example, whether they KNOW a certain piano sonata by Beethoven. Invariably the answer tends to be something such as: "No, I don't PLAY that piece." Or one might ask an oboist or a clarinetist if they knew a Bach cantata. Instrumentalists, and singers, too, so often consider that if they have not performed a piece, that they are somehow prevented from coming to know the piece! I didn't ask whether a person PLAYED something, I asked whether they KNEW a piece, which is not necessarily the same process.

If the only music I knew was limited to the music I could actually perform, I would have missed a lifetime of knowledge of the Beethoven string quartets and symphonies, Mozart operas, Debussy piano preludes, Renaissance polyphony, or the madrigals of Monteverdi, even the majority of modern music. The truly literate musician cannot simply limit his musical horizons to the end of the bell of his instrument, so to speak.

With the rich plethora of music spanning over 1,500 years easily available on CDs, from chant and Hildegard von Bingen, down to Glass and beyond, no one claiming to be musically literate has any excuse for not knowing a good deal of the literature, and not just for his or her own instrument. My advice to anyone wishing to become a literate musician is to hear as much music, in a variety of genres, as possible, study intensively scores, attend concerts, particularly of new or unusual repertoire, read as much about the music and its genesis as possible, and be receptive to all kinds of musical stimuli.

In recent years we have become aware, through the work of our colleagues in ethnomusicology, of the richness of non-Western musics. One must remember that there is nothing sacrosanct about the major and minor modes and scales, or rhythms of 2/4, 3/4 or 4/4. Many cultures, those of Africa, large portions of Asia, and the Pacific use not only different scalic constructions, but also generally more complex rhythmic subdivisions. To maintain that the tonal configurations of so-called "Western music" is somehow "superior" or "better" than any others, is to confuse the issue. No music is "better" or "worse" than any other. (Do we mean it is "better FOR you" perhaps?) The musics of the world represent different modes of expression, in the same way as clothes or artistic expression in the plastic arts is different in other cultures and civilizations.

An interesting recent experiment in performing Beethoven string quartets for natives of an African tribe, was said to have produced gradual boredom on the part of the listeners, and after a few minutes, they simply began to talk with one another, completely ignoring what we would consider a "beautiful," "profound," or "complex" piece of music! So much for the old canard about music being the "universal language."

***

For several years, I had been toying with the idea of purchasing a used upright piano so that I could begin to practice a little and perhaps learn some repertoire. Although I owned a beautiful harpsichord, based on the Yale University Taskin, it was obvious that it was no good for the Beethoven "Appassionata," the Chopin "Revolutionary" Etude, Opus 10, no. 12, or anything later, not that I could ever learn to play these works. Gudrun read the for-sale ads in the paper, and I looked at a number of old instruments. Either they were real "dogs," or were spinets, which I did not want. Finally, in the summer of 1999 I found an instrument which I liked well enough to purchase. The action was about right, not too heavy, the tone was excellent, and the instrument seemed to be in generally good condition. It was an Ivers and Pond, one of the better Boston manufacturers, and I estimated that it was approximately eighty years old. I bought the piano for $300, spent $115 to have it delivered to the house, and then invested another $750 to have our very fine piano technician at UWM, Jonathan Moberg, do a thorough cleaning and regulating of the action, replacing a string, and tuning it to a modified well-temperament.

I had begun to tackle the Beethoven Sonata, Opus 31, no. 1 even before I purchased the instrument; now I began in earnest to learn the first movement. Quickly, I learned how truly rusty my pianistic technique was, but I also found out something even more revealing. The more I practiced, and the more I repeated, over and over again, the scale patterns and hand positions, the better I could play. The sheer physical energy required to practice intensely for three or four hours (I can never do it for more than an hour) is just as demanding as any other physical activity, be it long-distance running, championship ice skating, or high-level ballroom dancing. As Ferrucio Busoni said: "One must practice!"

Learning to perform just a portion of this Beethoven sonata has been one of the greatest challenges I have had in many years. I've not yet learned it, and probably never will; but I have the satisfaction of proving to myself that, if I had the physical energy, the patience and the determination to do it, could probably accomplish something. I have also found that my memory has improved as I have worked on this music. Of course, I would never dare to perform in public; I do admit to stage fright. Nevertheless, it is good to have a piano in the house again, and I enjoy "working out," as it were, from time to time.

***

I also have a few musicological projects in mind. For some years I have wanted to do an edition of the most significant keyboard works of my dissertation subject, Georg Andreas Sorge, and it may be that the time is ripe to do this. In William S. Newman's *The Sonata in the Classic Era,* he speaks in laudatory terms of Sorge's music. Speaking of the sonatas in one of Sorge's extensive collection of keyboard music, Newman has the following to say:

These sonatas would, in fact, provide material
of considerably more appeal and artistic value for
today's young students, were they to be reintroduced
in a modern edition, than many another
piece from the same period that has been disinterred
apparently for no better reason than the notion
that it must be good because it is old. Sorge's writing
has the advantage of achieving unusual melodic,
expressive, and textural interest for so few notes.*

AR Editions in Madison is waiting for a proposal from me, and I suppose I should get to work on it. After all, it was something Ralph Kirkpatrick encouraged me to undertake over thirty years ago.

Another project which seems to be germinating in my mind is a survey of the 20th-century string quartet, since Béla Bartók. This study would, by definition, also include an examination of new and unusual string techniques, the use of improvisation, fractional tonal usage, chance operations and other late-20th-century devices. Some composers whose work I would discuss are: Hans Werner Henze, several of whose six quartets are superb works, Morton Feldman, Elliott Carter, Ligeti, John Cage, the Russian composer Alfred Schnittke, as well as the late Otto Luening, also the two quartets of my dear friend and colleague John Downey, of the

---

*William S. Newman, *The Sonata in the Classic Era* (Chapel Hill: University of North Carolina Press, 1963, p. 390.

UWM faculty. His second quartet, especially, I consider one of the masterpieces of 20th century chamber music. Whether this ambitious project will ever come to fruition is another question. Perhaps this will be something for another musicologist to tackle. In any case, it is a worthwhile project for someone to consider.

Over the past several years, I have derived great pleasure from investing in a superior sound system, with a CD player and twin tape decks with dubbing capabilities. I have built up an increasingly eclectic collection of CDs, including everything from chant and Hildegard von Bingen, to Philip Glass. At present, I am learning the 2nd and 3rd string quartets of Elliott Carter, very tough nuts to crack, incidentally, and follow the scores intensely for the most part. I belong to a good CD club and add to my collection unusual or interesting new CDs regularly. I try to always have access to the score of a work, either by buying it through one of the normal sources, or by checking the score out of our UWM music library, which becomes more richly endowed with each passing year, due first, to my insistence, and Gudrun's assistance, in continually adding to the musical holdings many years ago. A line position for a music librarian was one of the first additions to the library budget over twenty-five years ago. Music librarians such as Richard Jones and Dr. Linda Hartig did much to further augment the holdings, and Rebecca Littman, the present music librarian, together with her assistant, Elizabeth Walloch, continues this work, serving students and faculty with efficiency and graciousness.

***

Coming now to the end of this necessarily fragmented, highly personal tale of my life, I wonder if anyone will be interested in what I have had to say. I think my children and a few close friends might enjoy reading about the boy from Sioux Falls, South Dakota, whose passionate love of music, determination to learn as much about it as possible, and desire to teach what he loved, has brought me to this point in time. For Gudrun and me, it has been a joyous journey, fraught with many hazards, but containing moments of great beauty and supreme satisfaction.

I have done just about everything I have hoped to accomplish these past seventy-four years: taught music history, musicology, theory and organ at several colleges or universities; engaged in research; published some articles and monographs; performed as a conductor, organist and harpsichordist, albeit in a rather modest way; assisted my wife in raising five children who have made us very proud; taken many wonderful trips to various countries in Europe; stayed solvent and in reasonably good health; and retained most of my faculties and senses. And now, I have finally published a book. Best of all, I have made it to the twenty-first century, a goal which seemed so far in the future that I seldom gave it any thought. What more can one ask of life?

INDEX OF NAMES AND PLACES